BLOOD MEMORY

BLOOD MEMORY

THE TRAGIC DECLINE
AND IMPROBABLE RESURRECTION
OF THE AMERICAN BUFFALO

DAYTON DUNCAN

BASED ON A DOCUMENTARY FILM BY KEN BURNS,
WRITTEN BY DAYTON DUNCAN

WITH AN INTRODUCTION BY KEN BURNS

PICTURE RESEARCH BY EMILY MOSHER AND SUSAN SHUMAKER
DESIGN BY MAGGIE HINDERS

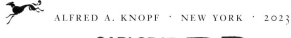

ALFRED A. KNOPF · NEW YORK · 2023

THIS IS A BORZOI BOOK
PUBLISHED BY ALFRED A. KNOPF

Copyright © 2023 by The Buffalo Film Project, LLC

All rights reserved. Published in the United States by Alfred A. Knopf,
a division of Penguin Random House LLC, New York, and distributed in Canada
by Penguin Random House Canada Limited, Toronto.

www.aaknopf.com

Knopf, Borzoi Books, and the colophon
are registered trademarks of Penguin Random House LLC.

ISBN: 978-0-593-53734-3 (hardcover)
ISBN: 978-0-593-53735-0 (eBook)

Jacket photograph by Valerie Shaff
Jacket design by John Gall

Manufactured in Germany
First Edition

DECEMBER 2023

This book is dedicated to N. Scott Momaday,
who for a quarter century has generously shared with us
his wisdom, wit, and words—but most of all his friendship.

Contents

Introduction:
The Things We Love

Gentlemen, why in heaven's name this haste? You have time
enough. Why sacrifice the present to the future, fancying that you
will be happier when your fields teem with wealth and your cities
with people. In Europe we have cities wealthier and more popu-
lous than yours and we are not happy.

You dream of your posterity; but your posterity will look back
to yours as the golden age, and envy those who first burst into this
silent, splendid Nature, who first lifted up their axes upon these
tall trees and lined these waters with busy wharves.

Why, then, seek to complete in a few decades what took the
other nations of the world thousands of years? Why, in your hurry
to subdue and utilize Nature, squander her splendid gifts? You
have opportunities such as mankind has never had before, and
may never have again.

LORD JAMES BRYCE

THE AUTHOR of that heartbreaking, melancholy, and remarkable
quote was a Belfast-born, Scottish-educated British diplomat who
would go on to be the ambassador to the United States from 1907 to
1913. Back in 1888, Bryce had published *The American Commonwealth*, an
attempt to understand the political and social experiment that was
the United States nearly half a century after Alexis de Tocqueville
wrote his celebrated treatise *Democracy in America*. In the 1830s, de
Tocqueville had traveled throughout the country and then shared

with the world what he saw as our unique egalitarian spirit and our relentless pursuit of perfection: "The greatness of America," he said, "lies not in being more enlightened than any other nation, but rather in her ability to repair her faults." But he also noted that "I know of no country, indeed, where the love of money has taken a stronger hold on the affections of men." By the time Bryce had completed his third trip through America, and had written his magnum opus, focusing mostly on the mechanics of the American political system, he had reached a different set of conclusions about the people he had so meticulously studied, expressing disappointment in the inequality he found almost everywhere in the country. The relentlessness that de Tocqueville found so profoundly optimistic Bryce now saw as evidence of the "haste" and missed opportunities of those who had "first burst into this silent, splendid Nature."

For several decades, as documentary filmmakers and writers, we have been engaged in trying to understand and tell complex stories about the great failings as well as the great promise of our Republic. Like de Tocqueville and Bryce, we see impressive strengths and pro-found weaknesses in our collective past, and we have striven to rep-resent and evoke the many instances of pride, poignancy, and pain in honest measure. During our nearly fifty years of exploration, we have embraced neither blind exceptionalism nor unforgiving revisionism, preferring a clear-eyed recounting of our history—and its histori-cal characters—warts and all. The contradictions and undertow that continually derail a simplistic binary view of the past provide for us a fuller understanding of *who we are*—our animating inquiry—if not making our efforts that much harder to do. Indeed, our main editing room has a small, discreet neon sign in it, a not-too-subtle reminder for all of us of the pitfalls of a superficial, facile view of things. In lowercase cursive, the sign reads simply: "it's complicated." When a scene is working, there isn't a filmmaker on Earth who willingly wants to change it, even as new and sometimes conflicting and confounding information inevitably comes to light. But we have learned (and are still learning) to embrace that perpetual disruption and chaos, and to refashion our narratives into something more representative of what actually took place, even if that sacrifices what was supposedly "working." We think that discipline makes for better films, and our most recent two-part, four-hour documentary, *The American Buffalo*, from which this book by Dayton Duncan was written, is no exception to the quandary of trying to reconcile so many diverse perspectives.

Over the past half century, we have been compelled to leave the beautiful but relatively limited vistas and horizons of our homes in New England for the seemingly limitless ones of the American West, particularly the American prairie, whose distances seem at times to us almost stupefying, even oppressive—and yet, in the next moment, both exhilarating and liberating. Some of us have gone there seeking adventure and some solace from grief—"Black Care," as Theodore Roosevelt called it. All of us feel that somehow a unified sense of our identity, in all its myriad manifestations, might be found out there. In the process, over the many years spent visiting the West, we have begun to feel, as Roosevelt also said, that we are "at heart as much a Westerner as I am an Easterner." There, in what is called the "American Serengeti," we have had our molecules rearranged, our worldviews challenged, our lives enriched by trying to see things as others see them. And what has been abundantly clear, with no disrespect to Lord Bryce's poetic "silent, splendid Nature," is that that part of the country is not silent. Nor is it—or has it ever been—empty.

The psalm of Manifest Destiny has been for most Americans a comforting tune that we have sung to ourselves for generations. But it's really like whistling by the graveyard, an attempt to paper over with distracting myths the anxieties over identity and happiness that Bryce so beautifully expressed. Those myths have reinforced our collective belief that this majestic land was somehow meant to be ours, that the radical experiment of American democracy required, according to the influential newspaperman John O'Sullivan in 1845, that we "overspread the continent allotted by Providence for the free development of our yearly multiplying millions." That unquestioned gospel would never fully acknowledge the natural, animal, and human casualties wrought by its implementation. George Horse Capture Jr., a member of the Aaniiih tribe, told us in an interview for our film, "Everything had to get out of the way. When Europeans came, everything that's natural has got to get out of the way. It's just a matter of fact."

Let it be said: We *love* the buffalo, our national mammal, the largest land animals on the continent. We love their shagginess. We love the way they move, the way our hearts beat a bit quicker when they are near. We love the *fact* of them. And we love that they are ours, "the symbol of America with a capital 'A,'" the historian Clay Jenkinson said in an interview for our film. We struggle to comprehend that tens of millions of them roamed the Great Plains less than two hundred years ago, and, as Jenkinson lamented, that "our Indian policy and our greed and our industrialization would just blink this thing out and we would say, 'Well, that was then and this is now.' That seems like a repudiation, somehow, of the very idea of America."

But the heedless killing of the bison was as American as apple pie, and it was our intention to produce a "biography" of that animal that would attempt to obliterate some of the pernicious mythology that distracts us still, and to try to provide a new dimension to a story too many of us think we already know. That story is essentially about the long, beautiful relationship between Native peoples and the buffalo, punctuated dramatically by the arrival of Europeans and the carnage they inflicted on both. By telling a complex narrative, we hope in the spirit of de Tocqueville to be able to help this country to confront and to "repair her faults," and not continue to, as Bryce suggested, "sacrifice the present to the future." Marcia Pablo, a member of the Pend d'Oreille/Kootenai tribes of Montana, said it best: "We're supposed to make decisions that go seven generations beyond you. But we aren't looking to the future. We're looking at right now. And that's not far enough. She's all we have, this Earth. We destroy that, we're destroying ourselves."

We've been incubating this story of the buffalo—and their interrelationship with the original inhabitants of this country—in our minds and in our hearts for nearly forty years, and perhaps we've needed that amount of time to be able to understand most of the contours of this epic American calamity: "There is no story anywhere in world history," the historian Dan Flores told us, "that involves as large a destruction of wild animals as happened in North America in the western United States."

"The first time I met a buffalo, I looked into his eyes, and it was like looking into the past and the future at the same time," the writer Dan O'Brien said in an interview for our film. "They have seen the whole tragedy of what has played out on the Great Plains. I think that one of the ways they survive is they turn into the wind. They move through the storm, rather than being chased by it."

We've touched on the story of the bison before in previous films, but never as in depth as we were able to pursue here. In *The West* (1996), we dealt with the impact of the coming of the railroad and the slaughter of millions of buffalo by the hide hunters. In that series, we met many characters who would return again in this story: the rancher and Indian fighter Charles Goodnight; Theodore Roosevelt, of course; and the Lakota leader Sitting Bull, to name a few. We also got to know the Kiowa poet N. Scott Momaday and grew to love his gigantic heart and exquisite eloquence. He gave us, for this current film, the idea of the interconnection—over thousands of years and hundreds of generations—between Native peoples and their "brothers," the buffalo. He called that kinship "blood memory," a "capacity for remembering things," he later wrote, "beyond our own corporeal existence." Scott allowed us to begin to question our own inherited mindset, one diametrically opposite to that of Indigenous cultures, who for centuries had coexisted with and sustainably used every part of the buffalo—from its tail to its snort.

Shooting for our film *Lewis & Clark: The Journey of the Corps of Discovery* (1997), we encountered in the Dakotas some herds of buffalo just like the earlier expedition had (though ours were much smaller), and I met Gerard Baker, a Mandan-Hidatsa Indian, whose ancestors had kindly helped Lewis and Clark through their incredibly cold and harsh first winter. Later, Gerard would sing a Hidatsa blessing to my newborn third daughter, Olivia, his immense frame seeming to fill our cramped New Hampshire farmhouse bedroom, this gentle giant towering solicitously over my tiny baby. In our new film,

Gerard starts to break down, struggling to express how devastating the destruction of the bison was to Indian people. "I couldn't imagine it. I couldn't imagine what the people went through, especially a father, saying, 'I've got to take care of my children. I've got to take care of my clan. I've got to take care of my society and I can't do it.'"

In *The National Parks: America's Best Idea* (2009), we went west again with Theodore Roosevelt and met his friend the naturalist and early conservationist George Bird Grinnell, who would grimly predict the buffalo's demise and with it the catastrophic effect that destruction would have on Native peoples, and then tried to protect the remnant buffalo herd in Yellowstone National Park. We spent time back then with a National Park ranger named Shelton Johnson, who vividly brought to life the story of the Black Buffalo soldiers of the U.S. Cavalry—and like Momaday and Baker gave us a glimpse of the continent before the acquisitive greed and waste of Europeans were unleashed upon it. After each of these past productions, we vowed to ourselves that we would try to tell a much fuller story of the buffalo, the peoples so closely intertwined with that magnificent animal, and the collision of two different views of the natural world that played out on our continent in the nineteenth century.

Just as every schoolkid knows that Lewis and Clark made it back from their long journey safely, so too do we know that the buffalo did survive and did not disappear forever. And yet both of these (interrelated) stories—the near extinction of the species and then its revival—retain their drama and their power to surprise. We try to create and structure narratives where we hope the viewer (and now the reader) begins to wonder if things *will* turn out the way they know it will. That's the key to telling good history. At first glance, this epic could be seen as an uplifting parable of de-extinction, where we got the chance to correct our mistakes—and it is, and we did. But like Dante's *Inferno* and then his *Paradiso*, this devastating chronicle of reckless destruction and greed lingers and continues to trouble us, eroding the knee-jerk faith in the myths and fables we have constructed to comfort ourselves. Now, a truer West comes into sharper and more painful focus.

Those new perspectives we've been compelled to consider and

absorb—including the enthralling cosmologies of Native peoples—begin to diminish the old bankrupt narratives we've inherited, suggesting an alternative universe, one where notions of commonwealth, as manifested in our national parks idea, begin to take root: *we* own these buffalo in Yellowstone; *we* need them saved from the poachers determined to kill every last one. At one point, George Horse Capture Jr. incredulously asks us to rethink every assumption about property, and the crimes that have hemorrhaged from it, urging us to see things from another's vantage point, to indeed rearrange our molecules. He mocks the conventional:

> Let's get rid of the buffalo so my cows can run here. *My* cows. Not this, what's free for the taking for all of us. But "my," so I can make money. And it's odd to get rid of something that everybody could enjoy just for the "my," the ownership of livestock. I can't even comprehend that. I don't know if there is an Indian alive, or was alive, that could comprehend that. It seemed like a lack of ability to enjoy what the Creator made.

All of this suggests that the story of the buffalo is still being written, that saving them means saving their habitats as well, a daunting task that flies in the face of those stubborn prerogatives of property—and, as George Horse Capture Jr. would rightfully scold, "my." But there are individuals and groups in this century, working in concert with dozens of Native tribes, who are committed to doing just that, insisting that bison must be able to roam wild and free. Still, we are forced back to the immensity of the wanton slaughter of these magnificent beasts and the inexcusable collateral damage consciously done to the people so dependent on that animal for their physical and spiritual survival. That both were eventually fetishized—in popular culture and even on the nickel—by the very people indifferent to their annihilation just adds to the layers of tragedy that attend this still heartbreaking story. As George Horse Capture Jr. said,

> You look at that old nickel, there's a buffalo. At one time, they almost wiped them to extinction. Why did the European put that

buffalo on that nickel? Was it just a curiosity, or was it something that kind of meant something to them in an odd way? So, in my confusion, and my need to understand, is: Do you have to destroy the things you love?

Ken Burns
Walpole, New Hampshire

Throughout this book, the words *buffalo* and *bison* are used interchangeably. While the American buffalo's scientific name is *Bison bison* (as explained on page 10), for centuries it has more commonly been called buffalo, and both terms are generally accepted as referring to the same animal. Likewise, to avoid repetition and enhance readability, the text uses the terms "Native people," "Indigenous people," "Native Americans," "American Indians," and "Indians" interchangeably.

In making our PBS documentary, we conducted eighteen extended on-camera interviews, totaling more than thirty hours, only portions of which could be fit into our four-hour film. This book draws extensively from the fuller transcripts of what was said in those interviews. Short biographical descriptions of the interviewees appear on pages 297–9.

In quoting from the interviews we conducted, some minor edits were made for purposes of space and clarity. Likewise, in quoting from historical texts, some word spellings have been standardized and some minor edits have been employed for clarity.

Blood Memory

Prologue

In the late spring of 1805, the Lewis and Clark expedition reached what is now Montana, moving farther west than any white Americans had ever gone on the Missouri River. Wildlife seemed to be everywhere, and in astonishing numbers—particularly the buffalo. "I think that we saw at one view nearly one thousand animals," Sergeant John Ordway of New Hampshire wrote:

> They are not today very wild for we could go within a 100 yards of them in open view … before they would run off; and then they would go but a short distance before they would stop and feed again.
>
> Saw a buffalo calf which had fell down the bank and could not get up again. We helped it up the bank and it followed us a short distance.

A few days later, Meriwether Lewis noted in his journal, "The [buffalo] are now so gentle, the men frequently throw sticks and stones at them in order to drive them away."

Less than a century later, in 1887, another expedition would explore the same region, where the Yellowstone River meets the Missouri. They hoped to find some buffalo to kill—and then preserve—for an exhibit at the American Museum of Natural History in New York City.

They searched for three months without seeing a single one.

·   ·   ·

They are the largest land animals in the Western Hemisphere, survivors of a massive extinction that erased ancient species that were even larger. Nourished by one of the world's greatest grasslands, they proliferated into herds of uncountable numbers—and in turn, by their grazing, nurtured the prairie that sustained them.

For more than ten thousand years, they evolved alongside Native people who relied on them for food and shelter—and in exchange for killing them, revered them. "So much of my blood memory has to do with buffaloes," the Kiowa poet N. Scott Momaday said in an interview. "We have regard for each other, and we are friends. We are brothers. We are related. I think of them in a particular way, and it's always with reverence." A century earlier, a Kiowa woman named Old Lady Horse, talking to an ethnologist, elaborated on the bison's centrality to her people:

> Everything the Kiowas had, came from the buffalo. Their tepees were made of buffalo hides, so were their clothes and moccasins. They ate buffalo meat.
>
> Most of all, the buffalo was part of the Kiowa religion.... The priests used parts of the buffalo to make their prayers when they healed people or when they sang to the powers above.
>
> The buffalo were the life of the Kiowas.

Newcomers to the continent would find them fascinating at first, but in time come to consider them a hindrance to a growing nation's continental expansion. And when buffalo hides became useful in running the machines of a new industrial age, they would be slaughtered by the millions, with their carcasses left to rot on the prairies. Then, teetering on the brink of disappearing from the face of the Earth forever, they would be rescued by a motley collection of Americans, each of them driven by different—and sometimes competing—impulses.

The American buffalo is a shaggy, unlikely beast that nonetheless found itself at the center of many of the nation's most thrilling, most mythic, and most heartbreaking tales. It has inspired some of our most popular songs and our greatest art; attached itself to our coins and currency, the names of our cities, and some of our most memorable characters; and somehow survived to become the official mammal of the United States. Along the way, it emerged as an embodiment of the nation's contradictory relationship with the natural world: venerated and mercilessly destroyed, a symbol of both a romanticized frontier and the callous conquest of a continent.

"They occupy the set piece in America's historical relationship with nature," said the historian Dan Flores. "No other relationship we have with any other species quite summarizes our own interaction with wildlife over the last five hundred years in North America the way what happened to the buffalo does."

Their story "is a cautionary tale," according to the historian Sarah Dant. "It shows us what happens when we don't understand the complicated interconnectedness of all things, of nature and people. It tells us that we need to pay attention, not to just one thing, but to the interconnectedness of all things."

PART ONE

THE TRAIL
TO EXTINCTION

ONE

The Buffalo
and the People

I'm not sure we can say just what the core appeal of the American bison is to us. Part of it is simply the size of the thing. You know, nobody ever looked at a bison and said, "Gee, I always thought it was larger."

They're these big, slightly strange looking but, in a way, magnificent animals. And they're ours. Right? They're *our* animal.

ELLIOTT WEST, historian

FULLY GROWN, an American buffalo can weigh more than a ton; stand taller than six feet at the shoulder; and stretch more than ten feet long, not including the tail. But they are deceptively agile, capable of running thirty-five miles per hour—nearly the speed of a top racehorse, yet with the endurance to maintain that pace for more than ten miles. "If you see one out grazing, it looks so slow," said the writer Steven Rinella. "It's like a parked car sitting there. But they're fast. They can clear six-foot fences. They can jump, a horizontal jump, of seven feet. And you're talking about something that's eighteen hundred pounds. It's like a souped-up hot rod of an animal, hiding in a minivan shell."

Huge as they are, they are puny in comparison with some of the prehistoric animals that once roamed the continent: mastodons and woolly mammoths, giant ground sloths and camels, and a series of bison species, one of which, *Bison latifrons*, had gigantic horns that measured nine feet from tip to tip. *Bison antiquus*, considered a separate species, was only somewhat smaller. Humans arrived in North America more than twenty thousand years ago, and sometime after the last Ice Age (roughly twelve thousand years ago) all of the biggest animals—along with nearly fifty other species, including horses—went extinct on the continent, from either hunting, changing climate, or perhaps a combination of the two.

In their place, the modern American buffalo—a "dwarfed" species called *Bison bison* by scientists—evolved and thrived. (Technically, in taxonomy, what we call the American buffalo are a different species from the Cape buffalo and water buffalo of Africa and Asia, although they are all from the same family, *Bovidae.* The genus *Bison* includes the European species *Bison bonasus*, or wisent, and the North American species *Bison bison*, itself separated into two subspecies: *Bison bison athabascae*, or wood bison, from the boreal forests of the North, and, on the plains, *Bison bison bison*, a repetition that thankfully makes it easier to remember.)

The American buffalo were "essentially a wild species [that] survived this die off because they were smaller," according to historian Andrew Isenberg. "They required less forage; they could outrun those human hunters much more capably than these larger mammals could."

The disappearance of *Bison latifrons* and *Bison antiquus*—as well as other ungulates like mammoths, mastodons, camels, and horses—left a huge vacancy of grazers on the North American grasslands, particularly the Great Plains. Without such competitors—and with the extinction of large predators like the fearsome saber-toothed tiger and dire wolf—the American bison population exploded, multiplying into the tens of millions. They were roughly half the size of their Pleistocene predecessors, faster both on the ground and at reproducing (a natural annual increase of 18 percent), according to Dan Flores. "No amount of predation from either gray wolves or humans seemed to diminish them," he said. "That made the modern bison one of the most perfectly adapted American species ever fashioned by natural selection for a continent where humans were present."

During late spring, they begin to shed their thick coat as summer temperatures on the Plains rise into the 100s. In fall, they grow it all back to survive brutal winters that reach 40 degrees or more below zero; they have ten times more hair per square inch than domestic cattle. Both males and females have solid, pointed horns and massive heads, which prove useful in winter to clear crusted snow off the ground and reach the grass underneath. Bulls also use their horns to compete with other bulls for dominance in the summer mating season, called the rut. If wolves try to attack a herd of cows and calves, the mothers form a protective circle around their vulnerable young ones and fight the predators off. Most wolf predation occurs when a pack can isolate a calf or an aged or injured buffalo.

The bison's other principal defense is its speed. (Newborn calves can stand for the first time within minutes—and run within a few minutes more.) When a lead buffalo senses danger and takes off, the entire herd bolts. They have good hearing and a heightened sense of smell to detect threats; their eyesight is their weakest sense.

Over the centuries, their grazing habits on the yawning expanses of the Great Plains proved crucial to its ecology—the types of grasses that grew there, and the other species that flourished alongside the buffalo. Bison dung not only fertilized the soil but also fed insects, which in turn fed small birds. Buffalo carcasses provided food to a host of scavengers like coyotes, eagles, crows, and vultures. Scientists consider bison the "keystone" species of the Plains.

"Their movement across the prairie stimulated the growth of grass and kept down woody plants that would otherwise have taken over," said the writer Michelle Nijhuis. "So they make the prairie what it is." Dan O'Brien, a writer and bison rancher, compared the buffalo's grazing habits to a "manicure" of the prairie: "They eat a little and move on. That's the secret. What happens is that grass gets a rest so it can build root structure. It builds the soil. If you eat it all the way, it doesn't get any rest."

Even when they stop and sometimes dig through the grass with their horns, and then roll in the dirt to help shed their coats and dust off pesky insects—creating so-called buffalo wallows—the bison's habits help support other forms of life. Millions of buffalo created millions of circular buffalo wallows, indentations in the semi-arid and flat Plains landscape that became shallow pools of water after it rained, which benefited other animals and plant life. A plant called lamb's-quarters—an edible, nutritious green related to quinoa—sometimes sprouted in these disturbed patches of bare earth; Native people harvested it and added it to their diet.

"When the buffalo are here, the land is good. When the land is good, the buffalo are healthy," said Germaine White, an educator on the Flathead reservation of the Confederated Salish and Kootenai tribes in northwestern Montana. To help describe how long her people and the bison have interacted in the history of North America, White conjured a clock:

> We have lived here for six hundred generations. We have been here, conservatively, twelve thousand years. Imagine that on a timeline and wrap it around a twenty-four-hour clock. What that means is that Columbus arrived at about 11:28 p.m., and Lewis and Clark, at about fifteen minutes before midnight. So, the time that we have had in relationship with buffalo is huge.

Native Americans seamlessly wove the animals into every aspect of their daily lives and religious beliefs. "It became a relationship so immediate and personal, I think, that they had to formulate an idea of the buffalo being equal to them in many ways," said N. Scott Momaday. "The buffalo was iconic and sacred, and became so deeply ingrained in the life of the tribe that they could not imagine existence without the buffalo. They were indivisible."

In the ancient origin stories of many tribes, the bison were among the earliest animals created, often emerging before human beings from underground crevices or caves in what became sacred sites—like Wind Cave in the Black Hills of what is now South Dakota, or Oklahoma's Wichita Mountains.

These buffalo, it was said, had their own families and clans, their own societies and customs, and were capable of changing forms to communicate directly with humans. In some stories, bulls married women, or men mated with buffalo cows. Gerard Baker, a Mandan-Hidatsa whose long career with the National Park Service included being the first Native American superintendent of Mount Rushmore National Memorial, remembers hearing his elders tell how "some of our old people could even talk to the buffalo and get advice from the buffalo, about how the buffalo came to being, and how they could change, about people who changed themselves into the buffalo:

> And the first thing I was told about buffalo was the spirituality part of it.
>
> About how they were created by our Creator; how they were put on this Earth to help us survive, not only with clothing, with warmth, with food, with tools, but then they start talking about the essential, which was the spirituality of the buffalo and how the spirit was part of us and we were part of them.

According to the Blackfeet, in the beginning, humans were killed and eaten by the buffalo—until *Napi*, their culture hero, also called Old Man, made bows and arrows for his people and taught them how to shoot the bison and how to make fires to cook the meat. But he also told them to pay close attention if the animals appeared in their dreams. "Be guided by them," he said. "Whatever these animals tell you to do, you must obey them." The Cheyenne and Lakota Sioux each have stories about a contest between people and bison to determine which one would have mastery over the other. In a long and arduous race circling the Black Hills, some of the animals died and stained the soil red forever with their blood; but in the end, thanks to the last-minute help of a magpie, the people won. John Stands in Timber, a Cheyenne, once recounted the tale to the historian Margot Liberty:

> That race gave mankind the right to use animal flesh for food . . . If the animals had won, they would have lived on his flesh instead.
>
> The old buffalo [bulls] called the young man to come to them. "Well, you have won," they said. . . . "You are on top now. All we animals can do is supply the things you will use from us—our meat and skins and bones. And we will teach you the Sun Dance."

Man was thankful that he won. The Cheyennes have offered
the Sun Dance every year since that time, remembering the Great
Race.... The path where the race was run is still there also, going
right around the [Black] Hills.

And the Cheyennes are thankful to the magpie for her part in
winning the race, so they do not kill her.

Every tribe on the Plains held spiritual ceremonies related to
the buffalo. The Mandan, in what is now North Dakota, had the
White Buffalo Cow Society—respected older women whose leader
wrapped herself in the robe of a sacred white buffalo as they danced
all night to call the bison herds closer in winter. In a different ceremony, experienced hunters costumed themselves as buffalo bulls,
whose power—called "medicine"—could be shared with others in
the tribe.

Each summer, the Lakota—like many tribes—gathered for a Sun
Dance, their most important ceremony, which renewed their relationship with *Wakan Tanka*, the "great spirit" or "great incompre-
hensibility" of the universe that permeated everything. Buffalo were
considered the animal with the most direct connection to that life
force. Ceremonies lasted for days, usually just before a communal
bison hunt, and included fasting, long periods of staring at the sun,
and rituals in which young men had their chests pierced by buffalo
bones and attached by thongs to a central pole. They were expected
to pull back until the flesh was torn from their bodies—a symbolic
self-sacrifice for the sake of the people.

Over the course of many generations, the Kiowas moved from the
mountains near the headwaters of the Yellowstone River, down to
the northern Plains; then to the Black Hills; and eventually farther
south to the Wichita Mountains. Along the way, they learned their
Sun Dance from the Crows. "During the migration down upon the
Plains, the people were following the sun," N. Scott Momaday said:

They encountered the buffalo, and it was as if the earth was giving
them something that they needed—spiritually needed, as well as

materially needed—and they identified it with the sun. It was part of their pilgrimage. It was proof that they were coming close to the sun's house. That's the way they regarded that whole Wichita Mountain region. That was where the sun lived, as far as they could see.

The Sun Dance was an indispensable part of the Kiowa life. And the buffalo was the sacrificial victim of the Sun Dance. You could not have a Sun Dance without killing a buffalo bull and displaying its head in the Sun Dance lodge.

What more valuable a sacrifice could you make, than to kill a buffalo and offer it to the sun? The buffalo was recognized as sacred—the representation of the sun.

The sun made the grass grow. The bison ate the grass. Native people ate the bison—and understood the larger interconnection of it all.

The horses of North America were one of the species that had become extinct. For hundreds of generations, Native people ventured onto the Plains by foot, relying on dogs to pull their belongings.

Hunting buffalo was difficult—and often dangerous. To get close enough for a kill with a bow and arrow or a lance, some hunters covered themselves with buffalo hides or wolf skins and crept up within striking distance. Others attacked when the herds were crossing rivers, sometimes climbing onto the back of a swimming buffalo and stabbing it with a knife. In winter, hunters chased the heavy beasts onto frozen rivers, hoping they would get trapped by thin ice, or pursued them into deep snow drifts, assisted by shoes webbed with buffalo sinew. "It's an adversarial style of hunting; you're mixing it up with that animal," Steven Rinella said. "This isn't shooting with a gun, two hundred yards away. You're breathing its air." "They knew how to watch the tail," Gerard Baker added. "When you watch a buffalo's body language, and that tail goes up, it means one of two things. It means it's going to dispatch some waste, or it's mad and it's going to come after you. It's going to discharge or it's going to charge, either one."

Tribes occasionally set the prairie grasses on fire to drive herds toward a particular ambush—and more often regularly burned grasslands to encourage a fresh growth that would attract the grazing animals. According to Rosalyn LaPier, a Blackfeet-Métis ethnobotanist and historian, "Indigenous people used what we call 'anthropogenic fire,' which means fire that was created by humans, to make grass grow much more abundantly and healthy in certain areas. If they can make the grass grow in certain areas, that means they don't have to go looking for the bison. The bison are going to be right where they are growing the grass." There were other advantages, she said. A springtime grass called needle and thread has a curlicue seed head that sometimes attached itself to grazing bison, who then distributed the seeds as they moved across the Plains. On the eastern portion of the Plains, Indigenous use of seasonal fires on the tallgrass prairies prevented vast areas from becoming forests, creating peninsulas of prime grazing land that stretched across modern-day Iowa and beyond the Mississippi River into what is now Illinois.

The biggest summer hunts involved the entire village: slowly hazing herds into coulees or log-and-stone corrals, where they were met by a hailstorm of arrows; or stampeding them over cliffs. The "buffalo jump" method comprised a complicated choreography that required advanced planning and strict coordination. First, a site had to be found with a gradual slope that ended with a steep drop— one not easily discernible from ground level until the last moment. "Drive lanes" needed to be established that acted like a funnel leading to the precipice; people hid behind rocks or crouched in a small depression, ready to spring up and shout or wave blankets at the appropriate time.

Then began what LaPier called a "push and pull" maneuver. Indians wearing wolf skins slowly began pushing the herd toward the drive lanes. The "pull" began when a decoy out in front of the herd, cloaked in calf skins, would imitate the cries of a calf in distress and start heading toward the edge of the cliff. "Many of the leaders of bison herds are cows; they're female," LaPier explained, "and so, because they're listening to this baby calf crying, they're just like, 'Oh, calf in distress. Let's go save it.'"

Sara Dant continued describing the scene:

> When it sort of goes into motion, what a thrilling thing this must have been, because the bison would begin to move into the drive lanes. The Indians, who are on the sides, would rise up in unison to get the herd moving in one direction. And here come these stampeding bison. Your job, if you're the decoy, is to do some quick head fake and get out of the way, or maybe jump into a crevice. And then, the bison go over the edge.

"And when they start going over," Gerard Baker added, "if the front ones would see the cliff, of course, they'd try to stop. But the others [behind them] would hit into them, and they'd all go down."

Some of the bison might survive the fall, but they would be severely injured. Members of the tribe, waiting at the bottom, would finish them off. Then everyone would gather to process the carcasses. Some tribes believed that if any survived and escaped, those buffalo would tell other herds about what happened and where, and ruin any chances for the location to be used again. One buffalo jump in Montana was used for so many centuries that skeletal remains of bison accumulated fifteen feet thick. The Blackfeet referred to this type of location as a *pishkun*, meaning "deep blood kettle." George Horse Capture Jr., an Aaniiih from the Fort Belknap reservation in Montana, described how much a successful hunt like this meant to the people:

> Sometimes, you can go to buffalo jumps when the wind is just right and when people ain't talking like a bunch of magpies. You get a little quiet time.
>
> You could almost hear the joy of the humans, because, for a week, a month, six months, into the winter, we're going to eat. And that makes people happy, knowing that they're going to eat.

Stripped of its hide, each carcass provided hundreds of pounds of meat—which could be roasted or boiled; cut into strips and dried on racks; or mixed with tallow and berries to make pemmican, a dehydrated concoction that was easier to transport, preserved the meat longer, and provided five times the food value per pound. Some of the freshly killed bison was eaten raw. "A delicacy would be eating raw liver and raw kidneys," Gerard Baker said, "and that's candy. Plus, it gives you some of the spirit of the buffalo. It gives you strength. It gives you knowledge, we believe."

From the moment a Plains Indian child was born—and wrapped in a soft layer of buffalo hair and a tanned calf skin—to the time his or her corpse was shrouded in a bison robe, every day of life was connected with the buffalo. Most estimates figure that Native people needed six bison per person each year for subsistence purposes.

In winter, when the coat was the thickest, the bison's hide would be tanned and turned into a warm robe. In the summer, when hides had less hair, they could be sewn together into coverings for tepees. Stretched over a frame of curved willow branches, a hide was transformed into a bowl-like boat for crossing rivers. A sweat lodge was covered by a buffalo hide; inside, people used the fluffy end of a buffalo tail to sprinkle water onto the hot rocks to create the steam needed for physical and spiritual cleansing.

A buffalo's bladder became a water container; its shoulder blade a digging tool; its horn a spoon or a cup. Some women wore buffalo teeth as ornaments; others painted their faces with buffalo grease to protect their complexions from the sun and used the rough side of a buffalo tongue to brush their hair. Splinters of bones were transformed into paintbrushes or into awls for sewing (with dried sinew as thread).

Buffalo ribs could occasionally be turned into bows, tendons into bow strings, and a sharpened horn fragment into an arrowhead—for warfare against enemies, or for hunting more buffalo. Ribs were also used for children's snow sleds, horn tips for spinning tops; a small piece of buffalo skin, wrapped around a handful of fur, became a ball to throw around. Dew claws (from above the buffalo hoof) made good rattles for babies. The Hidatsas hung a cluster of them at the entrance of their earth lodges, for visitors to shake to announce their presence and be invited in.

Dried buffalo droppings made excellent fuel for fires—an essential commodity on the essentially treeless Plains. "Even the waste wasn't wasted," Gerard Baker said. "Everything was used except the grunting—and even then, they were used in some ceremonies to imitate the buffalo. So even the sounds were used."

Over the centuries, every tribe encountered seasons when the buffalo seemingly disappeared and the people suffered. It was believed that the herds had returned where they came from, usually underground. Special ceremonies—and often the intervention of a culture hero—were required to call back the buffalo. "It gives itself to the people as a sacrifice," N. Scott Momaday said:

> "Here I am; you can make use of me. I can help you. We can be related on a spiritual plane." And, so, when the people did something wrong, if that trust, if that bond were broken, the buffalo might well react and withhold their affection. "No, I will not make myself available to you for hunting; I will hide. You will have to find me, and it will not be easy."

The Kiowas believed that the buffalo's hiding place was in the Wichita Mountains, inside what is now called Mount Scott, from which the animals had first emerged. The tribe's most sacred medicine bundle contained special stones and a small figure representing *Taíme*, who had saved them from starvation in the distant past. The bundle was unwrapped only during the annual Kiowa Sun Dance to assure that the buffalo would return to be hunted. The Mandans said that Speckled Eagle had been angered and in retaliation took the bison with him beneath Dog Den Butte—until Lone Man was able to get them released. The Cheyennes told of a time when the buffalo were gone for four years and the people began to starve—until Sweet Medicine brought the herds back and taught them respectful rituals to keep the animals from disappearing again.

According to an ancient Lakota story, a woman appeared during a time of famine and presented the tribe with a sacred pipe, which she said was a gift from the Great Spirit; its smoke would reestablish the sacred bond between humans and bison. "I represent the buffalo tribe," she told them. "When you are in need of buffalo meat, smoke this pipe and ask for what you need and it shall be granted you." As she left, she turned herself into a white buffalo calf and vanished.

"The stories almost always convey a sense that it's been human hubris that's caused the animals to withdraw," said Dan Flores:

> And the only way to get them back is to perform some kind of really profound ceremony, some act, that convinces the animals, and the animal masters who are in charge of them, that humans are, once again, willing to be fellow travelers in the world. Not exceptional. Not standing apart. But part of the ecology of all living things.

Joseph Campbell, the renowned authority on comparative mythology and religion, first became interested in the topic through his fascination with American Indian culture as a young boy in New York City; he considered such ceremonies an "invocation . . . representing a mystic covenant between the animal world and the human." The songs and dances, he wrote, were "the vehicles of the magical force of such ceremonies."

No one knows exactly how many bison once existed on the continent, but it was in the tens of millions. And though the greatest numbers were found on the grasslands of the Great Plains, their range extended from Florida to Lake Erie, from northern Mexico into Canada, and west of the Rocky Mountains into parts of what are now Idaho, Oregon, and Washington.

The Cheyenne had followed them so closely and for so many years, they had twenty-seven different words for a buffalo, depending on its sex, age, or condition. "As I now think upon those days," a Cheyenne named Wooden Leg remembered, "it seems that no people in the world ever were any richer than we were." But according to their stories, the prophet Sweet Medicine had given their ancestors more than sacred ceremonies when he returned the buffalo. He also delivered a warning:

> There is a time coming … when many things will change. Strangers … will appear among you. Their skins are light-colored, and their ways are powerful.
>
> These people do not follow the way of our great-grandfather. They follow another way.

TWO

Strangers

I N 1492, seeking a water route to the Indies on behalf of the Spanish monarchy, Christopher Columbus stumbled upon a world that
Europeans had not known existed. Nothing would ever be the same
for people on either side of the Atlantic Ocean.

For the Indigenous populations of both North and South America, it would prove catastrophic. In the wake of the first contacts with
Europeans, wave after wave of epidemics swept across the hemisphere, carrying deadly diseases for which the inhabitants had little
immunity. Modern studies estimate that 90 percent of the Native
people—perhaps as many as 56 million, one-tenth of the world's
population—perished in this "Great Dying" during the century following Columbus's arrival. Some projections contend that such a
dramatic decline in human beings—who relied on fires for cooking
and heat—reduced the airborne carbon in the atmosphere enough
to contribute to the Little Ice Age, when the Earth's climate cooled
and moistened for roughly three centuries.

In North America, the number of Native people is believed to
have collapsed from nearly 5 million to about 900,000 during the
hundred years after first contact. With the sharp decline in human
predators and the increase in wet years from the changing climate,
wildlife experienced a resurgence. At the same time, especially in
the East, previously cleared and cultivated landscapes seemed to
be emptying of the people who had done that work. For the early
European explorers—and then colonists—this "New World," or
"Virgin America," as some called it, appeared to possess bountiful

resources and countless natural wonders waiting to be taken and exploited.

One of the most fascinating wonders was the bison.

In the 1530s, wandering across what is now Texas, Álvar Núñez Cabeza de Vaca and three other survivors of a disastrous Spanish expedition became the first Europeans to encounter American buffalo, when a tribe they met fed the starving strangers with the animal's meat. It was, he reported, "finer and fatter than that of [Spain]."

A decade later, in 1541, a conquistador named Francisco Vásquez de Coronado led his mounted soldiers from Mexico across the Texas Panhandle onto the plains of what is now Kansas, pursuing rumors of cities filled with silver and gold. Instead, he found villages of Wichita Indians living in huts. But he and his men were astounded by the endless, horizontal landscape and the huge herds of buffalo—which they called "cows"—roaming across it. "There was not a day I lost sight of them," an amazed Coronado wrote; the only way to describe their numbers was to compare them to the fishes of the sea. His army killed and ate five hundred bison on their futile quest, and stacked piles of bison dung to mark their route for the return trip across the trackless *Llano Estacado* (Staked Plains). Coronado informed the king of Spain that a fortune could be made in turning buffalo hides into leather—and with that message in effect announced the arrival of a new and very different perspective about the continent's natural world. The buffalo—and everything else—were to be considered commodities for commerce.

"They saw this animal in incredible profusion, and they thought, 'You know, what's in it for us?' That was their first thought: 'How can we profit from this?'" said the historian Elliott West. "The idea was that we might tame these animals, or, perhaps, interbreed them with our own cattle to make a new breed or new species." Pedro de Castañeda, chronicler of Coronado's expedition, struggled to describe the beasts for his countrymen back in Spain, relying on references to animals more familiar to them:

Their beard is like that of goats . . . [and] on the [front] portion of the body a frizzled hair like sheep's wool . . . sleek like a lion's mane.

They always change their hair in May … as the adders do their skin.

Their tail is very short, and terminates in a great tuft. When they run they carry it in the air like scorpions.

Exploring the upper Mississippi River on behalf of the king of France in the 1600s, Father Louis Hennepin and his men saw Indigenous hunters pursue a small herd of buffalo into the water in order to kill them, and witnessed the use of grass fires to force them through a passage "where they take post with their bows and arrows." The Frenchmen managed to shoot an old bull on the riverbank in what is now Illinois—and then spent hours trying to retrieve its massive carcass from the mud. (Hennepin's description of the animal resulted in a line engraving, created in France by an artist who had never seen one in person. It makes the buffalo look as if it has just had its fur shampooed and curled. Other early drawings of bison gave them human-like facial expressions.)

In 1613, sailing up the Potomac River to what is now Washington, D.C., one of the early Jamestown colonists came across a herd of buffalo. "We found [the meat] very good and wholesome," he reported, and the animals "very easy to be killed in regard [that] they are … not so wild as other beasts of the wilderness."

The newcomers gave the strange animals different names. Some Spanish explorers called them *vacas jorobadas*, "humped-back cows." The French referred to them as *Le Boeuf sauvage*, *Le Bison*, sometimes *buffle* or *buffelo*. To some, the animals looked like a curly-haired and humpbacked version of the Cape buffalo. English colonists adopted the name *buffalo*—and it stuck.

Regardless of their name and numbers, the buffalo east of the Mississippi River (perhaps 3 million or more) steadily dwindled almost from the moment British colonies were established along the Atlantic Coast.

Georgia was a case in point. In 1733, shortly after landing at what is now Savannah, the colony's founder, James Oglethorpe, held his first treaty meeting with Chief Tomochichi of the Yamacraw, who gave him a buffalo skin decorated with a painting of an eagle. "He desired me to accept it," Oglethorpe wrote, because "the English were as swift as the bird and as strong as the beast, since, like the first, they flew from the utmost parts of the earth over the vast seas; and, like the second, nothing could withstand them." Two years later, a different chief presented Oglethorpe with another buffalo hide, on which the Creek migration legend had been depicted. (Oglethorpe sent it to London, where it was exhibited at Westminster.) In 1759, Georgia's Commons House of Assembly found it necessary to make hunting buffalo illegal in some parts of the colony. No one apparently enforced the law, and by 1763, the Indians were complaining that the bison and other game were being driven off their land by settlers and the domestic livestock. Multiple places named Buffalo Creek and Buffalo Swamp dotted maps of Georgia, and the Treaty of Augusta in 1773 designated Great Buffalo Lick as a key boundary point between the colony and Native nations. Yet by the time the naturalist William Bartram returned from his extensive tour of the South in the mid-1770s, he reported that he hadn't seen any living buffalo, despite having been told how plentiful they once were.

Farther north, when Daniel Boone opened the Wilderness Trail over the Appalachian Mountains into Kentucky for pioneers eager to settle new lands, the route he followed through the Cumberland Gap was called a "buffalo trace," which the animals had been using for centuries. West of the mountains, he wrote, "the buffaloes were more frequent than I have seen cattle in the settlements. Sometimes we saw hundreds in a drove, and the numbers about the salt springs were amazing." Like the colonial assembly in Georgia, Boone soon introduced a law to stop the "wanton destruction of game," but the American frontiersmen regarded it as a restriction on their freedom, and within a few years the area around Boonesborough was devoid of buffalo.

As a young surveyor and soldier, George Washington had once hunted buffalo near the Ohio River. In 1775, just before he left for the Second Continental Congress, he hired a man to capture some calves so he could raise them on his Mount Vernon plantation in Virginia. "Try and buy me all the buffalo calves you can get and make them as gentle as possible," he instructed. "I would not stick at any reasonable price for them, especially the cow calves, but I should like at least two bull calves [because] I am very anxious to raise a breed of them."

In what is now West Virginia, settlers called twenty-three different streams Buffalo Creek or Buffalo Run; there were six different Buffalo Forks and Buffalo Licks on their maps. In western Pennsylvania, according to some accounts, an unsuspecting settler built his log cabin near a salt lick. Bison enjoy rubbing up against trees, rocks, and other solid vertical surfaces nearly as much as they love wallowing in prairie dirt. When a herd of buffalo showed up at the settler's new cabin near the salt lick, so many of them scratched their sides against it, the building collapsed. Over the next two years, he and his neighbors killed seven thousand of them merely for their hides, which they sold at two shillings each.

By the early 1800s, nearly all the bison east of the Mississippi were gone. But in the Great Plains, an estimated 30 million buffalo still roamed—along with 120,000 Native people. Life there—for both the Indians and the buffalo—had already been transformed by something else the Europeans had brought to the New World. The Cheyenne prophet Sweet Medicine had told his people about it:

> There will be [an] animal you must learn to use. It has a shaggy neck and a tail almost touching the ground. Its hoofs are round. This animal will carry you on his back and help you in many ways.
>
> Those far hills that seem only a blue vision in the distance take many days to reach now; but with this animal you can get there in a short time, so fear him not. Remember what I have said.

Spanish conquistadors had brought horses with them into the Southwest—and used them to great effect in battles with Native people, who had never seen such animals before. But in 1680 the Pueblo tribes rose up in revolt and drove the Spanish out of New Mexico. Their horse herds remained—and multiplied. In less than a century, the horse had spread from one tribe to another throughout the West. By 1800, the horse population on the Great Plains was nearing an estimated 2 million and growing rapidly.

After an absence of nearly a hundred centuries, which included an evolutionary migration across all of Asia to Europe, the horse, which had originated in North America, had finally come back home. Its impact was revolutionary.

For Native Americans, "the coming of the horse was magic and changed their lives completely," N. Scott Momaday said. "Suddenly, the Indian hunter, elevated to a height on the back of a horse, could see farther than he had ever seen before, could go faster and farther than he'd ever seen." A mounted hunter could now kill enough buffalo in one day to feed and clothe his family for months. And with horses—not dogs—pulling their tepees and belongings on a travois, families could bring more with them and travel deeper into the daunting vastness of the Plains. In recognition of the dramatic change, the Pawnee name for "horse" roughly translates as "superdog"; to the Comanche they were the "magic dog."

Some tribes abandoned their fields and permanent villages altogether and moved from the margins, deeper into the Great Plains to live year-round, becoming semi-nomadic hunters—and among the greatest equestrians in the world. Pretty Shield, a Crow woman, remembered the time fondly:

> The great herds of buffalo were constantly moving, and of course we moved when they did.
>
> All that was changed by the horse. Even the old people could ride.
>
> Ahh, I came into a happy world. There was always fat meat, glad singing, and much dancing in our villages. Our people's hearts were then as light as breath-feathers.

"Think of a human being on the back of a horse as a kind of new species, a single animal, a 'horse-man'; not a 'horseman,' but a 'horse-man,'" said Elliott West:

This is an animal that has the strength and the power of a horse, drawn from the sunlight and those grasses, and the grace of a horse. But it has the intelligence—and the imagination, the ambition, and the arrogance—of a human being. That's a new animal. And it becomes a very powerful animal, people fused with this horse, with this new sort of mythic power, this sense of dreaming possibilities. This gave them the power to move and to hunt far more effectively; but for the bison, this was, in effect, a grass-eating predator. They had never seen that before. That was trouble.

The historian Andrew Isenberg considers the horse "not just as an exotic animal that's moved into the Great Plains, but as a new technology. It's a way for Native people to get on horseback and a new way to hunt the bison. The return of the horse to the Great Plains was nothing short of a social revolution for some Native groups." "Horses really were the first precursor to the invasion of Europeans; they got to the tribes way before Europeans got there," said Dan O'Brien. "And they were a technological improvement. But, you know how those 'improvements' work out, sometimes."

The Great Plains became a contested meeting ground for more than thirty tribes converging from every direction—each of them increasingly relying on the bison for their sustenance and prosperity, and relying on the horse for their hunting and their defense against their enemies.

The burgeoning herds of horses also became new grazing competitors with the buffalo for the prairie grasses. "In order to successfully hunt bison, now you have to be a horse-mounted Indian," Sara Dant said:

And in order to be a horse-mounted Indian, you can't just have one horse; you have to have five, sometimes as many as thirteen, per capita, basically. Well, that's a lot of mouths that are eating the exact same thing that bison are eating. So, where you may have had a carrying capacity on the Great Plains of 30 million bison, you start adding horses onto that, and there's going to be a direct cause and effect. More horses, fewer bison.

Since the time of Columbus, European powers—the Spanish, French, Russians, and British—had been locked in their own contest over the destiny of the North American West. In 1803, the United States joined in, when President Thomas Jefferson's Louisiana Purchase extended his young nation's western boundary from the Mississippi all the way to the Rocky Mountains.

He dispatched the Lewis and Clark expedition up the Missouri River to study the animals and plants, to map the terrain and assess the land's potential, and to inform the Indians living there they had a new "White Father," with whom they should now trade exclusively. The expedition would last two and a half years, taking the explorers all the way to the Pacific Ocean and back. Along the way they encountered nearly fifty different Native American nations and recorded the first written descriptions of 178 plants and 122 animals previously unknown to science, though obviously well known to the Indigenous people who had lived with them for thousands of years. Buffalo were nothing new to science or to Euro-Americans, but the herds were much bigger than anyone had ever encountered in the colonies.

The information logged into the expedition's voluminous journals provides a marker of sorts, a vivid baseline measuring what that section of the American West was like before the nation Lewis and Clark represented followed them across the continent, and in less than a century changed it forever. "All these members of the expedition were from the East," Dan Flores noted:

> They were from places like Kentucky and Virginia. They began to see a whole host of creatures that none of these people had ever seen. They see their first mule deer, their first magpies, their first coyotes, their first prairie dogs, their first pronghorns [and] grizzly bears. One animal after another that no one [in the East] had any inkling actually existed in North America is suddenly showing up in front of them.
>
> And one of the things they began seeing, of course, are increas-

ingly larger and larger herds of bison, stretching to those unfath-
omable distances across the horizon. So, what they preserve for us
in their journals is a glimpse into the America that had existed for
ten thousand years before us.

In what is now North Dakota, the explorers spent their first winter
among the Mandan and Hidatsa, who let them witness a sacred Buffalo Dance and participate in a snowy hunt. In March, they watched
the Hidatsas burn the nearby prairie to induce an early crop of grass
and draw the buffalo closer. They were fascinated by tales of buffalo
jumps, a hunting technique that horses were making obsolete. "The
part of the decoy I am informed is extremely dangerous," Lewis
wrote. "If they are not very fleet runners, the buffalo tread them
under foot and crush them to death, and sometimes drive them over
the precipice also, where they perish in common with the buffalo."
Before pushing farther west the next spring, Lewis sent Jefferson
seven buffalo robes, including one decorated with a depiction of a
battle between the Mandan-Hidatsa against the Lakota and Arikara,
which the president displayed in Monticello.

Back on the move in the spring of 1805, reaching the confluence of
the Yellowstone and Missouri Rivers, each of the expedition's journalists recorded the almost stupefying abundance and variety of the
wildlife that surrounded them in what John Ordway deemed "a hand-
some place . . . with a beautiful country around in every direction."
Patrick Gass called it "the most beautiful rich plains I ever beheld."
The men briefly made pets of some wolf pups; they saw their first
bighorn sheep; Lewis's Newfoundland dog, Seaman, caught an antelope in the river and dragged it to shore; beaver were so numerous,
the slapping of their tails on the water kept Clark awake at night.
Magpies, geese, trumpeter swans, pelicans, and cranes were in the
air or on the water. Lewis thought there were more bald eagles than
anywhere else in the country. (Ordway used the quill from one in
writing his daily journal.) After noting the profusion of red berries,
serviceberries, gooseberries, chokecherries, purple currants, rose-
bushes, and honeysuckle along the river bottoms, Lewis climbed a
hill and was transported into a reverie by the prospect before him:

The whole face of the country was covered with herds of buffalo, elk and antelopes; deer also abundant.

The buffalo . . . are so gentle that we pass near them while feeding, without appearing to excite any alarm among them, and when we attract their attention, they frequently approach us more nearly to discover what we are, and in some instances pursue us a considerable distance apparently with that view.

Although game is very abundant and gentle, we only kill as much as is necessary for food. I believe that two good hunters could conveniently supply a regiment with provisions.

"We eat an immensity of meat," Lewis wrote farther up the Missouri, as the thirty-three-member expedition battled the Missouri's insistent current, often trudging in shallow water and mud as they towed their heavy dugout canoes with a rope, simply to make ten or twelve miles before nightfall. The men were understandably famished from the exertion. Each one was consuming nine pounds of meat a day. "It requires four deer, an elk and a deer, or one buffalo to supply us plentifully 24 hours," Lewis calculated.

Toussaint Charbonneau, their French-Canadian interpreter (who brought along his wife, Sacagawea, and their infant son, Jean Baptiste), occasionally treated them to a concoction he called *boudin blanc*, which Lewis had fun describing in great detail: a freshly killed buffalo's intestine is steadily squeezed at one end to push out what Charbonneau euphemistically described as "that not good to eat" from the other end; chopped bison meat and kidneys were stuffed into the evacuated tube, and the whole thing was "baptized in the Missouri with two dips and a flirt" before being boiled in a kettle and then fried in bear's oil "until it becomes brown, when it is ready to assuage the pangs of a keen appetite." Lewis proclaimed it "one of the greatest delicacies of the forest."

For nearly four months, as they worked their way up the Missouri across the plains of what is now Montana, bison meat became the staple of the expedition's diet—and it was readily available. At different points, the captains estimated herds of ten thousand, twenty thousand, and thirty thousand within a single view. But when the expedition entered the western mountains in the fall of 1805, they nearly starved, reduced to eating a few of their horses—and even some of their candles—in the steep and snowy terrain; on the salmon-rich Columbia River watershed, they preferred buying dogs to eat from Native tribes, rather than the fish abundantly around them. On their return trip in 1806, once they reached the Great Plains, the men rejoiced to be back among the buffalo and a reliable supply of the meat they loved most.

Traveling down the Yellowstone, Clark described the bison as "astonishingly numerous," and, after halting his canoes for more than an hour as a herd swam across the river in front of them, he finally gave up attempting to reckon their numbers. "For me to mention or give an estimate of the different species of wild animals on this river, particularly buffalo . . . would be incredible," he wrote, spelling the last word "increditable," suggesting that he leaned toward a meaning of too extraordinary to be believed, rather than simply amazing. "I shall therefore," he concluded, "be silent on the subject further."

Lewis literally carried his memories of the American buffalo with him for the rest of his life. Three years after the expedition's return, as governor of the Missouri Territory, his mental state deteriorated, and he began a fevered journey from St. Louis to Washington, D.C., during which he had to be restrained from suicide at one point before continuing east. On October 10, 1809, he arrived at a small inn on Tennessee's Natchez Trace, where he spent his troubled last night on Earth. After declining the offer of a feather bed, Lewis unfolded a buffalo robe he had brought along and spread it out on the floor. He died on it early in the morning of October 11, after shooting himself two times.

THREE

Omen in the Skies

[These strangers] will be a people who do not get tired, but who will keep pushing forward, going, going all the time. They will keep coming, coming.

Follow nothing that [they] do, but keep your own ways that I have taught you as long as you can.

SWEET MEDICINE

AMERICAN INDIANS had been exchanging animal pelts for European trade goods for more than two centuries. When Lewis and Clark returned in 1806 with reports of rivers teeming with beaver, fur companies responded by sending squadrons of traders and trappers, called "mountain men," into every corner of the West, all to feed the demand in New York, Paris, and London for fashionable hats made of beaver fur. Second only to that of sugar, the fur trade was the most lucrative international business of the day, Elliott West said, "and this was really the first step in which Indian peoples of the Far West began to become enmeshed in this global economy."

By the late 1830s, most of the beaver had been trapped out—and the fashion changed to silk hats, ending the mountain-man era almost as quickly as it had begun. But there were still millions of buffalo. Only twenty years earlier, a single beaver pelt had been worth as much as three buffalo robes. Now, consumers in the East had developed a taste for salted buffalo tongues, and thick buffalo robes became popular for keeping people warm while they rode in their carriages.

Along the Missouri River and its tributaries, the fur companies established dozens of trading posts, where tribes bartered buffalo robes and tongues for goods manufactured in Europe and the East: metal pots to make their lives easier; decorative items like colorful glass beads; and guns for hunting or for fighting their enemies. Though it was officially forbidden by government policy, alcohol also worked its way into the barter system. A watered-down gallon of alcohol was worth five prime buffalo robes.

"Native peoples get caught up in the market in part to get at the things that they need to succeed in their subsistence lifestyle on the Plains that they can't provide for themselves," said Sara Dant:

> If you want to defend your hunting grounds, you need guns. You can't manufacture them; you've got to trade for them. And the market says hides are valuable, we'll trade hides for guns. You need ammunition. You need powder. All of that requires a trade in something that is deemed valuable by a market, and that valuable commodity becomes bison hides. Bison commodities, robes in particular, become the "cash" for much of the Great Plains.

In order to trade with farming Indians for things they no longer grew themselves, like corn and squash and tobacco, the semi-nomadic tribes were already killing more buffalo than they needed for their own subsistence. Now they began killing even more to meet the demand of white people far away.

In the early 1830s, large steamboats replaced smaller keelboats and canoes, and the volume of trade exploded. The first steamboat to ply the Missouri returned to St. Louis loaded down with buffalo robes and ten thousand pounds of tongues. In one five-year period, New Orleans handled more than 750,000 buffalo robes, bound for eastern markets.

To prepare a robe for market took time and hard work—from painstakingly scraping away the flesh and fat on the hide of a freshly killed bison to softening the hide by patiently rubbing it with cooked bison brains—tasks traditionally entrusted to women. In a year's time, one woman could dress ten good robes. But a mounted hunter could easily kill many more than ten bison, and in the new robe economy there was every incentive to do so. In some tribes, Andrew Isenberg said, the practice of polygyny increased; the most prosperous men now might have nine wives.

"The robe trade was a very lucrative market," Elliott West said. "It provided enormous income for these Indian peoples. But, at the same time, this was a huge step toward further plugging them into this international, mercantile-capitalist market economy. And, so, it made them vulnerable in ways that they could not possibly have anticipated."

Many Plains tribes kept a pictorial calendar, often called a "winter count," of each passing year: a single painted image, usually on a buffalo hide, depicting the event they remembered most vividly. In any individual year, for some it might be a battle with their enemies, or a successful hunt, or the outbreak of a disease. But in 1833, they all recorded the same thing. They remembered it as "the year the stars fell."

In the dark, early hours of November 13, the largest meteor shower ever recorded—an estimated 72,000 shooting stars per hour—burst over much of North America. Townspeople on the East Coast were astonished at the display. For people living in tepees on the open prairie, the spectacle was overwhelming. N. Scott Momaday recounted the story passed down to him:

The Kiowas were camped in the Wichita Mountains, and it seemed that the world was coming to an end. They were awakened by the light of flashing stars. They ran out into the false day and were terrified. And they think of the year and the event as being an omen. Bad things came after that. Lots of things happened that were harbingers of the end of the culture.

The United States was pushing westward. Within fifteen years its boundary would stretch to the Pacific. To get there, all of the overland trails had to cross the Great Plains, still controlled by the Native nations who inhabited it. Americans had different motives for their migrations—for better farmland, for gold, for commerce, for art, for their religious beliefs—but the bison herds played a role in everyone's journey.

In 1836, Narcissa Whitman was on her way to the Pacific Northwest to help her missionary husband convert Indigenous people to Christianity. Following the Platte River, they ate buffalo meat every day, she said:

> I never saw anything like buffalo meat to satisfy hunger. We do not want anything else with it. We have meat and tea in the morn, and tea and meat at noon. . . . So long as there is buffalo meat I do not wish anything else.
>
> Our fuel for cooking since we left timber has been dried buffalo dung; we now find plenty of it and it answers [a] very good purpose, similar to the kind of coal used in Pennsylvania.

In 1843, the famous artist and naturalist John James Audubon embarked to the West on his last expedition—this time to paint the animals, not birds, of America. As his riverboat approached the confluence of the Yellowstone and Missouri Rivers, he was amazed by the array of wildlife on the shores: wolves, elk, bighorn sheep, grizzly bears, and buffalo. "It is impossible," he wrote of the bison, "to describe or even conceive the vast multitudes of these animals that exist even now, and feed on these ocean-like prairies." But he also noted the "immense numbers that are murdered daily," and he chastised himself after he and his companions killed four of them, taking only their tongues: "What a terrible destruction of life, as it were for nothing, or next to it."

Three years later, twenty-three-year-old Francis Parkman launched his career as a writer and historian with a two-month adventure on the Great Plains, which he described in his first book, *The Oregon Trail.* Along the Arkansas River in the southern Plains, he wrote, "from the river bank on the right, away over the swelling prairie on the left, and in front as far as we could see, extended one vast host of buffalo. In many parts they were crowded so densely together that in the

distance their rounded backs presented a surface of uniform black-
ness." Hunting on horseback, he told his readers, "goes by the name
of 'running,' [and] of all American wild sports, this is the wildest."

Bound for California in 1846, the ill-fated Donner Party feasted
on bison as they crossed the Plains. The steaks broiled over buffalo
dung, Tamsen Donner wrote, "had the same flavor they would have
had upon hickory coals." Farther west, after taking what they had
been told was a "shortcut" across what is now Nevada, they would be
trapped by snows in the Sierra Nevada. Some turned to cannibalism
as others starved to death.

A merchant traveling the Santa Fe trail through Kansas reported
that his wagon train spent three full days moving through one
immense herd. An overlander on his way from Illinois to Oregon
described buffalo "as thick as sheep ever seen in the field." Driven
out of Missouri and Illinois, thousands of Mormons sought sanctuary from religious persecution in the deserts near the Great Salt
Lake in what is now Utah. On the way, their leaders used bleached
buffalo skulls as signposts to leave instructions to those following
behind and to indicate prime camping places. "Camped here, June 3,
1847," Brigham Young painted on one skull. "Making 15 miles today.
All Well." Young also warned the Mormon pioneers against needless
killing of the buffalo along the trail. "If we do slay when we do not
need, we will need when we cannot slay," he told them, "for it is a sin
to waste life and flesh."

Aristocrats from Europe and Great Britain were also showing up.
Sir William Drummond Stewart, a Scottish baronet, made repeated
trips in the 1830s, attending the raucous summer rendezvous of the
mountain men and bringing along the painter Alfred Jacob Miller
to record his adventures. Prince Maximilian of Wied, a German
explorer and ethnographer, went up the Missouri to study the Indians and hired the Swiss artist Karl Bodmer to illustrate his detailed
report.

Sir St. George Gore of Ireland came merely to hunt. His extravagant expedition, which cost him a quarter of a million dollars,
departed Missouri in a fleet of wagons carrying tons of supplies and
equipment—including a steel bathtub embossed with the Gore fam-

ily crest, a brass bed frame, an oak dining table, a library of leather-bound books, and a fur-lined commode. There were seventy-five horses and oxen, along with two cows to provide milk for Lord Gore's breakfast porridge; a retinue of forty hired workers, including his personal cook, who embellished the meals with French wine, English gins, and Irish whiskey; an arsenal of one hundred firearms and kegs of gunpowder; and fifty dogs (eighteen English foxhounds trained for tracking and thirty-two greyhounds for the chase).

During his three years traversing the West, Gore killed fifteen hundred elk, two thousand deer, more than five hundred antelopes, five hundred bears, and four thousand bison—often leaving their carcasses on the prairie unless he considered part of the dead animal worthy of being shipped home as a trophy. Many of the frontiersmen he had hired were offended by Gore's wanton destruction of wildlife, and Native tribes protested to federal officials. "We punish an Indian for killing a settler's cow for food," said a letter to Washington in support of their complaints. "How can such destruction of their game be permitted by their friends in the government of the United States?"

In the end, Native people, not the Office of Indian Affairs, brought Gore's escapade to its conclusion. After sending his cargo down the Missouri River to St. Louis, Gore decided to lead a small group to the Black Hills, which at the time was marked "Unexplored" on some government maps. The Lakotas considered the region, which lay at the heart of their prized hunting grounds, sacred. More than a hundred warriors confronted Gore and his dozen men when they approached it. Written accounts of what happened next differ in some details, but none of them describe any violent fight; all of them record that Gore and his men showed up back on the Missouri without their horses and supplies. A few add a note of even sweeter revenge: that the Lakotas had given the intruders a choice of either fighting to the death or surrendering their guns, their horses, their supplies, *and their clothes.* According to these accounts, one of the West's most profligate hunters and his men ended up walking, naked, more than two hundred miles, surviving on roots, berries, and birds' eggs, until they came across some Hidatsa Indians, who took pity on them and saved them. Totally unrepentant, Gore returned to his grand hunting lodge in Scotland to admire the trophies from his Great Plains safari and began planning a trip to Florida's Everglades to shoot egrets and alligators.

The artist George Catlin developed much better relations with the people who called the West home. Hoping to revive his faltering career, Catlin spent six years crisscrossing the West to paint portraits of Native people and their environment. He thrilled at joining the Lakotas in a bison hunt. The "extraordinary and inexpressible exhilarations of chase," he wrote, "seem to drown the prudence alike of instinct and reason, both horse and rider often seem rushing to destruction, as if it were...a delightful dream, where to have died would have been to have remained, riding on, without a struggle or a pang."

But Catlin also feared that both the buffalo and the Indians would soon meet their destruction "at the approach of civilized man— and...in a very few years [will] live only in books or on canvass:

> It is a melancholy contemplation for one who has traveled as I have through these realms and have seen this noble animal in all its pride and glory, to contemplate it so rapidly wasting from the world, drawing the irresistible conclusion...that its species is soon to be extinguished, and with it the peace and happiness (if not the actual existence) of the tribes of Indians who are joint tenants with them, in the occupancy of these vast...plains.
>
> And what a splendid contemplation, too, when one...imagines them as they might in future be seen (by some great protecting policy of government) preserved in their pristine beauty and wildness [in] a magnificent park...a nation's park containing man and beast, in all the wild and freshness of their nature's beauty.

No one heeded Catlin's call for a "nation's park," but in eastern cities, thousands of people soon thronged to see his "Indian Gallery," which featured his paintings, speeches by the artist dressed in Indian clothes in front of a tepee—and sometimes real Indians. He brought his pageant to England and Europe, and even performed for the king of France.

Catlin's success caught the attention of the great showman and huckster P. T. Barnum. On August 31, 1843, twenty-four thousand people rode the ferry from New York City to Hoboken, New Jersey, where Barnum had promised a "Grand Buffalo Hunt," with free admission. Instead of a "grand hunt," what they witnessed was fifteen bison calves huddled in a field, refusing to move when an attendant on horseback, dressed as an Indian, prodded them with a stick. The immense crowd's laughter and taunts frightened the calves, who stampeded through a fence into a nearby swamp. Barnum himself had the last laugh: he had secretly cut a deal with the operators of the ferry and cleared $3,500 for the day from toll receipts.

Decades earlier, the bison had been extirpated in the East, but Barnum and Catlin both demonstrated that the public's fascination with the animal had, if anything, been heightened by its absence. "The West is where the American identity is," Elliott West said. "What are the things that stand distinctively for that West, and, therefore, stand distinctively for the American people, who we are? What sets us apart from the Old World? And they settle more than anything else upon these two images, these two characters of the Far West— the American Indian; and the American buffalo. They became sort of the symbols of who the emerging Americans were."

The un-transacted destiny of the American people is to subdue the continent—to rush over this vast field to the Pacific Ocean . . . to change darkness into light and confirm the destiny of the human race.

The American realizes that "Progress is God." Divine task! Immortal mission!

The pioneer army perpetually strikes to the front. Empire plants itself upon the trails.

WILLIAM GILPIN, explorer and politician

Back on the Plains, the nation's relentless movement westward was beginning to hem in the bison—and the Native people who relied on them. White settlements and farms were steadily filling the prairies between the Mississippi and Missouri Rivers, and although the government had designated the territory just beyond as the exclusive reserve for Indians, the overlanders bound for Oregon and California had noticed how fertile some of its land was. A collision between two different cultural belief systems about human beings' place in nature had occurred two centuries earlier, when the first colonists arrived on the Atlantic Coast. Now it would play out on the Great Plains.

"There is a difference between the way Indigenous people view the natural world and the way Europeans and then Americans view the natural world," the historian Rosalyn LaPier said. "Indigenous people, for the most part, [describe] this relationship between the supernatural realm and humans, and there's a reciprocity. But then, there's also sort of a responsibility—a responsibility of humans maintaining that relationship."

The newcomers to the continent, on the other hand, brought with them a divergent view. "A lot of their sense of it comes from faith and the Bible, which tells them to subdue the Earth and have dominion over every living thing," Sara Dant said. "There's this sense of separateness, this sense that, somehow, humans and nature are separate from one another, that God put Earth and all of its resources there for his chosen people. There's tremendous variety here, but, in general, Native peoples very much saw themselves as part of the natural world, rather than removed from it."

When he visited the United States in the 1830s and produced his analysis of the American people and their nascent experiment in democracy, the French diplomat and political scientist Alexis de Tocqueville found much he admired, but noted:

They are insensible to the wonders of inanimate nature and they may be said not to perceive the mighty forests that surround them till they fall beneath the hatchet. Their eyes are fixed upon another sight . . . the march across these wilds, draining swamps, turning the course of rivers, peopling solitudes, and subduing nature.

They will habitually prefer the useful to the beautiful, and they will require that the beautiful should be made useful.

Though the Americans streaming across the continent in the nine-teenth century did so for disparate reasons, "the search for American identity came to focus, increasingly, on our conquest of the West," Elliott West said, and it came to be portrayed, especially by some pol-iticians, as part of a larger plan that superseded any individual desires:

> Manifest Destiny—that it was God, or history, or fate, or whatever, that determined that the United States was destined to expand to the Pacific Coast. These people were intent on transforming the environment of the Great Plains in ways that the Indians had never done. It was in the interest of Native peoples to keep that environ-ment as much as possible as it had been. It was the interest of these newcomers to transform it, to bring domesticated grasses, like corn and wheat, to replace the native grasses that supported the bison.

American Progress, a famous nineteenth-century painting by John Gast, captures this idea without saying a word. "Progress" is per-sonified by a blond-haired woman in a diaphanous gown, floating serenely over the prairie, the Star of Empire on her forehead. She cradles a school book in her right hand, while with her left hand she slowly uncoils a telegraph wire that is connected to the posts that have sprouted behind her. In the far background is an eastern city that resembles Manhattan, bathed in the light of a rising sun. She is followed by railroad trains, a stagecoach, and a farmer plowing a field near a cabin; accompanying her are a covered wagon pulled by oxen, and miners walking forward with shovels and guns. Ahead of her, the scene is darker, shadowed, as yet unlit by the sun: the snow-covered mountains of the West; a grizzly bear skulking away as it looks back and snarls; a group of Native Americans also looking over their shoulders at her advance; and a herd of buffalo stampeding into the deep shade at the edge of the frame. (Two buffalo skeletons are also depicted, one being picked over by coyotes and one with an arrow in its side.) "Now, the bison are not fleeing Indians who are hunting them," West pointed out. "The bison now are fleeing us."

George Horse Capture Jr. summarized the painting's meaning for Indigenous people: "With the westward expansion, everything had to get out of the way. And it doesn't matter what continent. When the Europeans come in, everything that's natural has to get out of the way. It's just a matter of fact."

More than a million cattle and sheep had accompanied the wagon trains to California, Oregon, and Santa Fe, devouring the same grasses that nourished the buffalo, and doing more damage than the loss of whatever number were shot for food by the westering pioneers.

The wagon trails followed river valleys, said Andrew Isenberg, "and what this does is, it effectively ruins [them] as a habitat for bison. The livestock have grazed out most of the grass. The river valleys have also been denuded of trees, and bison had gone there in the winter to get some respite from the elements. So, there's a really large barrier through the middle of the Great Plains that is no longer suitable for bison." The Shoshone chief Washakie, whose people lived along the overland trails, explained the impact of it all:

> This country was once covered with buffalo, elk, deer and antelope, and we had plenty to eat, and also robes for bedding and to make lodging.
>
> But now, since the white man has made a road across our land and has killed off our game, we are hungry, and there is nothing for us to eat.
>
> Our women and children cry for food and we have no food to give them.

The domesticated cattle and sheep also spread foreign diseases—like anthrax, bovine tuberculosis, and other diseases—to the buffalo. And, in a repeat of the "Great Dying" that had transpired more than a century earlier, further epidemics of European sicknesses—smallpox and then cholera and measles, brought into the region by the wagon trains and steamboats—had ravaged the Plains tribes. The Pawnee lost half their population to smallpox, which hit the Mandan, Assiniboine, and Blackfeet even more severely: in some cases only one-tenth of their people survived. Kiowa calendars noted one year as the "Smallpox Winter." The summer of 1849 was remembered as the "Cramp Sun Dance," in which half of them perished from cholera, while others died by suicide in pain and despair. The diseases "came in waves," said Germaine White. "They came invisibly, because it came through intertribal gifting and exchange where our neighbors brought it to us. One in the family got it, then another, and another, and another, and it was devastating. They had a continuous grave."

The federal government, meanwhile, was forcibly removing tens of thousands of Native Americans from their homelands in the Midwest and the Southeast—including the Sauk and Fox and Ottawa, the Seneca and Shawnee, the Cherokee, Choctaw, Chickasaw, Creek, and Seminole—transplanting them into a newly declared Indian Territory in eastern Kansas and what is now Oklahoma. Some of them began hunting buffalo, too, placing yet another strain on the herds.

In the southwestern Plains, New Mexican *ciboleros*—descendants of Spanish settlers—were making annual forays into the Texas Panhandle to hunt buffalo. Like their ancestors, they used lances as their weapon of choice, and brought the meat and hides of nearly 25,000 bison a year back to their settlements along the Pecos River.

And from Canada, large brigades of the Métis—descendants of Europeans and Native tribes, who had settled along the Red River in Manitoba—were expanding their buffalo hunts across the border into the Dakotas. One hunt in the early 1840s included sixteen hundred people and twelve hundred two-wheeled carts. It brought back five hundred tons of dried meat and pemmican.

Compounding the difficulties for the bison, some of the most powerful tribes of the Great Plains came to terms over their long-standing rivalries. For years, the area between the forks of the Platte River all the way down to the Arkansas had been a contested war zone. The alliance between the Lakota, Cheyenne, and Arapaho competed with the Comanche-Kiowa alliance to the south for control, but neither side was dominant enough to occupy it. Small hunting parties made forays into it at great risk and never lingered for long periods of time. Tribes that weren't part of either alliance also needed to be careful and only made limited hunting forays. "What that means for game, generally, and for bison in particular, is that this 'buffer zone' becomes a kind of game reserve," according to Elliott West. "The animals sense that, and they gravitate to these areas where they are relatively safe. Consequently, you find these areas teeming with game." (In 1806, William Clark had noted the same thing during his expedition's return trip through the Great Plains. In what is now South Dakota, he came across what he believed to be the biggest herd he had ever seen, and added, "I have observed that in the country between the nations which are at war with each other, the greatest numbers of wild animals are to be found.")

But in 1840, the two major Plains alliances held a grand conference, exchanging gifts and promises to end the hostilities. With that agreement, some bands began wintering along the eastern slope of the central Rocky Mountains; and whole communities, including women and children, embarked on large and long summer hunts. Tribal peace, as Elliott West observed, in a sense was bad news for the buffalo.

Then, in the late 1840s, a decade-long drought began. The Little Ice Age (and its moister conditions) was ending, and the carrying capacity of the grasslands began shrinking. Already pressured by the lucrative buffalo-robe trade, the impact of the overland migrations, the increased settlement on the eastern prairies, and so much more, the bison herds diminished. A Lakota calendar commemorated a special ceremony meant to bring the buffalo back. The Kiowas prepared for a great antelope drive, because the supply of bison meat was insufficient. A Blackfeet band marked 1854 as "the year when we ate dogs."

By the end of the 1850s, the buffalo had been driven from all but the interior portion of the Plains—where, by the mid-1860s, an estimated 12 to 15 million of them still lived. "That's a lot of bison," Elliott West said. "Twelve to fifteen million animals. There were still a lot of bison to hunt. And there would remain to be a lot of bison there up until into the 1870s, when the real hammer fell."

On the Great Plains, "buffalo wallows" (top) became an important part of the ecosystem, and river valleys (above) were crucial habitat for the animals. Like all tribes, the Mandan had sacred ceremonies (opposite) meant to assure successful hunts.

Many tribes, like the Lakota (opposite, top), held a yearly Sun Dance featuring a bison skull or head, to renew their relationship with the spiritual life force permeating the universe. A Quapaw dance robe (opposite, bottom) and an Assiniboine shrine (above) also show how central the buffalo were to Native people's beliefs.

Without horses, hunting tactics included creeping up on herds in disguise (opposite, top); pursuing them into snowdrifts (opposite, bottom); or decoying them and then stampeding them over cliffs called "buffalo jumps" (above, below).

Buffalo hides were painstakingly scraped for a variety of uses, from clothing and tepee covers (above) to bowl-like boats (right) for crossing rivers.

y matan vn cauallo, quando ellos se embrauecen,
y enojã: finalmẽte es animal feo y fiero de rostro,
y cuerpo. Huyen dellos los cauallos por su mala
catadura, o por nunca los auer visto. No tienẽ sus
dueños otra riqueza, ni hazienda, dellos comen,
beuen, visten, calçan, y hazen muchas cosas: de
los cueros, casas, calçado, vestido y sogas: delos hu
essos, punçones: delos neruios, y pelos, hilo: de
los cuernos, buches, y bexigas, vasos: delas boñi-
gas, lumbre: y delas terneras, odres, en que traen
y tienen agua: hazen en fin tantas cosas dellos
quantas han menester, o quantas les bastan para
su biuienda. Ay tambien otros animales, tã gran-
des como cauallos, que por tener cuernos, y lana
fina,

BUFFLE.

BUFFEL.

Written accounts from explorers like Francisco Vásquez de Coronado prompted European artists to attempt depicting an animal they had never seen.

When Daniel Boone led the first white settlers through the Cumberland Gap into Kentucky (left), he wrote that buffalo were "more frequent than I have seen cattle in the settlements." By the early 1800s, nearly all the bison east of the Mississippi River were gone, but perhaps 30 million of them still roamed on the Great Plains (below).

The Spanish had brought horses back to North America, remembered in a pictograph in the Southwest (opposite, top). With horses, Native people no longer relied on dogs to transport their belongings on travois (opposite, bottom), could venture farther into the Plains (above), and could hunt buffalo more easily (top).

The horse utterly transformed life for Indigenous
people in the West. Some tribes abandoned
their villages on the edges of the Great Plains to
become semi-nomadic hunters in its interior—
and more dependent than ever on the buffalo.

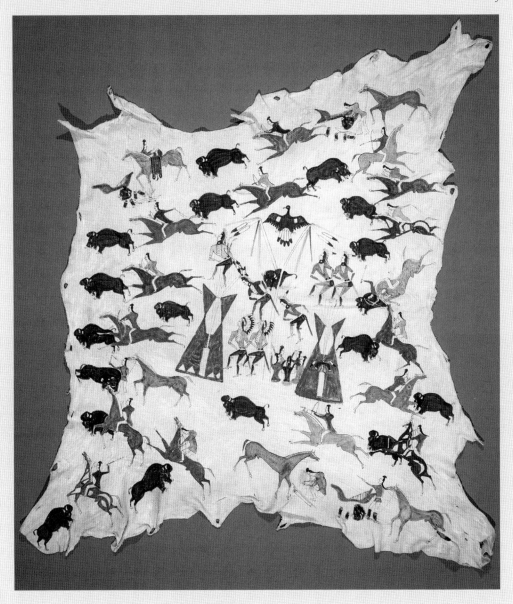

As the Lakota painting (opposite, top) and the
Shoshone hide painting (above) demonstrate,
horses became essential to many tribes'
cultures—for hunting buffalo and fighting
enemies. In the 1800s, a Lakota named Lone
Dog drew images on a buffalo hide (opposite,
bottom) to keep a "winter count" of each year's
most important event. On it, he recorded treaties,
diseases, conflicts, and the meteor shower of 1833
(center, far right on the hide).

The Lewis and Clark Expedition of 1804–1806 was the United States' first official venture into the West. Amazed by the size of the buffalo herds they continually encountered on the Plains— including one that blocked their passage down the Yellowstone River for more than an hour— they ate "an immensity of meat," Lewis wrote; it took about one buffalo per day to keep the men well fed.

Rising demand for buffalo robes in
the East brought more traders west.
Steamboats increased the capacity for
transporting them, and the hard work
of preparing robes for the market
intensified.

George Catlin (left) painted hundreds of western scenes in the 1830s, including a portrait of a dying bison (below) and of a Pawnee warrior named Buffalo Bull (right).

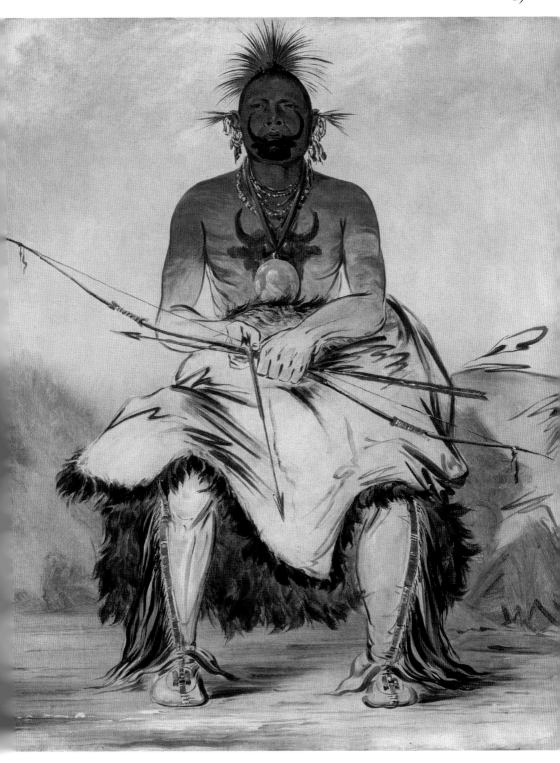

The overland migrations of settlers and gold-seekers in the 1840s and 1850s were depicted in numerous paintings, but none became more famous than John Gast's *American Progress* (above), a triumphalist rendering of "Manifest Destiny," in which Native Americans and buffalo are being pushed out of the way of the nation's relentless movement across the continent.

On the Great Plains, new waves of epidemics decimated Native tribes (left, above). *Ciboleros* from New Mexico (opposite, bottom) ventured eastward to hunt buffalo, while the Métis from Canada (below) came south to expand their hunts into the Dakotas.

Albert Bierstadt's *The Last of the Buffalo*. By the end of the 1850s, the 30 million bison that had roamed the Plains half a century earlier had been reduced to an estimated 12 to 15 million. The pace of change was about to accelerate even more.

FOUR

THE IRON HORSE

We saw the first train of cars that any of us had seen. We looked at it from a high ridge. Far off it was very small, but it kept coming and growing larger all the time, puffing out smoke and steam; and as it came on, we said to each other that it looked like a white man's pipe when he was smoking.

PORCUPINE, Cheyenne

In the ripeness of time, the hope of humanity is realized.... This continental railway will bind the two seaboards to this one continental union like ears to the human head; [and plant] the foundation of the Union so broad and deep that no possible force or stratagem can shake its permanence.

WILLIAM GILPIN, governor of Colorado Territory

THE CATACLYSM of the Civil War tore the nation apart, causing the death of 750,000 men, more than 2 percent of the population. But when the war was over, and the North and South were reunited, Americans set out with renewed energy to unite the nation, East and West. To do it, they began extending railroads to span the continent—opening up vast areas beyond the Missouri River for homesteaders, creating easier access to distant metropolitan markets for crops and cattle, and servicing the demands of boomtowns that had sprung up after gold discoveries in the mountains of Colorado and Montana. In the Great Plains, the pace of change quickened as never before, and on a scale that made the spread of the horse culture in the 1700s and the arrival of steamboats in the 1830s pale by comparison. Native people called this newest agent of transformation the "Iron Horse."

"What we see happening in the Great Plains, in the years after the Civil War, is different from what had been going on earlier," said the historian Andrew Isenberg. "In the beginning of the nineteenth century, there's trade between Native people and Euro-American fur traders. They're consuming beaver pelts and they're consuming bison robes. That's very different from this industrial society in the post–Civil War period that encounters the Great Plains—an industrial society that is much more interested in consuming resources."

As the Union Pacific pushed west across Nebraska, heading toward California, the Kansas Pacific aimed for Denver from Kansas City, piercing into the heart of the buffalo range of the central Plains. To feed the hungry crews laying track, the railroad company hired an ambitious and flamboyant twenty-one-year-old Union veteran, paying him $500 a month to keep them supplied with the meat from twelve buffalo a day. His name was William F. Cody. By his own account, he killed 4,280 bison during a year and a half to fulfill his contract. Within a few years—thanks in part to his talent for self-promotion and his incorrigible habit of embellishing his actual exploits—he would become one of the nation's most famous westerners, but under a different name: "Buffalo Bill" Cody.

Homesteaders along newly completed sections of the railroad lines also discovered that bison could be useful for getting ahead in life. Some hunted buffalo to feed their families or to supplement their meager incomes by hauling buffalo meat to railroad depots for passengers to feast on. Nearly all of them gathered the ubiquitous dried manure piles (called "buffalo pies" or "buffalo chips") to burn in their stoves and fireplaces for cooking their meals and keeping their sod houses warm.

Railroad passengers often amused themselves by firing at the herds that sometimes slowed a train's movement. "[It] was the greatest wonder that more people were not killed, as the wild rush for the windows, and the reckless discharge of rifles and pistols, put every passenger's life in jeopardy," wrote Elizabeth Custer, traveling to join her husband, an Army officer stationed in Kansas. To publicize its progress across the Plains, the Kansas Pacific even promoted excursion trips for passengers eager to see—and shoot at—the buffalo they were sure to encounter. "In estimating the number," a satisfied customer reported, "the only fitting word was 'innumerable;' one hundred thousand was too small a number, a million would be more correct."

A church group from Lawrence organized a special two-day outing to raise money for the congregation. Three hundred people signed up—and brought along a cornet band. On the second day, they came upon a herd, according to an account by E. N. Andrews:

> [The buffalo] kept pace with the train for at least a quarter of a mile, while the boys blazed away at them without effect. Shots enough were fired to rout a regiment of men.
>
> Ah! See that bull in advance there; he has stopped a second; he turns a kind of reproachful look toward the train; he starts again to lope a step or two; he hesitates; . . . a pail-full of blood gushes warm from his nostrils; he falls upon the right side, dead.
>
> The train stopped, and such a scrambling and screeching was never before heard on the Plains, except among the red men, as we rushed forth to see our first game lying in his gore.
>
> [I] had the pleasure of first putting hands on the dark locks of the noble monster who had fallen so bravely. . . . Then came the ladies; a ring was formed; the cornet band gathered around, and . . . played "Yankee Doodle." I thought that "Hail to the Chief" would have done more honor to the departed.

Such excursion trips made good copy for newspapers and may have helped the railroads advertise their progress across the Plains, but they did not reduce the bison population appreciably, Elliott West said: "There are these images of people shooting bison from railroad cars, and, as you hear with the overlanders, that's sometimes given as a reason for the decline of the bison. Well, of course not. I mean, were you really going to kill that many animals shooting at a moving target from a train?" More significant was the way the railroads accelerated the encroaching settlement of eastern Kansas and Nebraska, which were no longer reserved as part of Indian Territory. Cattle drives had begun, trailing thousands of cows (some carrying a disease called Texas tick fever) from Texas north to reach the railroads, for shipment to eastern stockyards and slaughterhouses. The buffalo range contracted some more.

In only one way did the bison seem to welcome the arrival of the Iron Horse. Along the new tracks, telegraph lines were strung from wooden poles. The buffalo—always looking for a rough surface to rub up against on the treeless Plains—found them to be perfect scratching posts. They toppled so many poles, the company decided to attach bradawls, a metal tool with sharp points, to dissuade them. It didn't work. "[The buffalo] would go 15 miles to find a bradawl," *The Leavenworth Daily Commercial* reported. "They fought huge battles around the poles containing them, and the victor would ... scratch himself into bliss until the bradawl broke, or the pole came down. There has been no demand for bradawls from the Kansas region since the first invoice."

> When the white man wanted to build railroads, or when they wanted to farm or raise cattle, the buffalo protected the Kiowas. They tore up the railroad tracks and the gardens. They chased the cattle off the ranges.
>
> The buffalo loved their people as much as the Kiowas loved them.
>
> There was a war between the buffalo and the white men. The white men built forts in Kiowa country ... but the buffalo kept coming on, coming on. ... Soldiers were not enough to hold them back.
>
> OLD LADY HORSE

Even before the Civil War's end, Native tribes had successfully resisted the relentless incursions onto their homelands, and the Army had built forts in response. Now, more forts were established, and more troops were dispatched to man them. Buffalo Bill Cody signed up to act as an Army scout and to help supply the posts with buffalo meat. Officers and enlisted men spent some of their idle time firing at bison for pleasure. At one fort in Kansas, the captain issued an order: "Item No. 1. Members of the command will, when shooting at buffaloes on the parade ground, be careful not to fire in the direction of the Commanding Officer's quarters."

George Armstrong Custer had been a celebrated cavalry hero during the Civil War. His impulsive bravery in a series of battles made him, at the age of twenty-two, the Union's youngest general. Eleven horses had been shot out from under him. Posted now at Fort Riley, Kansas, with the newly formed Seventh Cavalry, he rode out one day to kill his first buffalo. Galloping up next to a bull, he aimed his revolver—and somehow managed instead to shoot his horse through the head. On foot, bruised, and totally lost, he had to be rescued by his own men. Adding to the humiliation, the dead horse was one he had taken from Confederates at Appomattox, named Custis Lee, and given to his wife. He had to explain to Elizabeth that he had killed her favorite mount.

The soldiers were there to deal with what was called "the Indian problem," not to hunt buffalo for sport. For Custer and all the other Army officers, vanquishing the western tribes was proving frustratingly difficult. Native American warriors attacked railroad survey crews and road gangs, occasionally even derailed trains. The Army's retaliations proved ineffective—and sometimes disastrous for both sides. The Plains seemed aflame with skirmishes, raids, and occasional massacres. In 1867, Congress decided to try a different approach. Delegations were dispatched to pursue "the hitherto untried policy of conquering with kindness."

That October, more than five thousand Kiowas, Comanches, Arapahoes, and Southern Cheyennes gathered at Medicine Lodge Creek in Kansas to hear a proposal from U.S. officials to end the violence on the southern Plains. The treaty council nearly ended before it began. The Indians learned that on the way, and despite explicit orders from their officers, some soldiers had killed buffalo for their tongues and left the carcasses to rot. "Has the white man become a child, that he should recklessly kill and not eat?" a Kiowa chief asked. The offending soldiers were placed under arrest, and the negotiations commenced.

The government proposed that the United States be allowed to build railroads to the Colorado gold mines and encourage settlement north of the Arkansas River. The Native tribes would move onto reservations in what is now southwestern Oklahoma, where they would be supervised by agents drawn from Christian denominations like the Quakers. They would receive food and supplies for thirty years, be provided schools for their children, and be taught how to farm. The Kiowa chief Satanta objected:

> I love the land and the buffalo and will not part with it. I want you to understand what I say. Write it on paper.
> I don't want to settle. I love to roam over the prairies. There I feel free and happy, but when we settle down we grow pale and die.
> A long time ago this land belonged to our fathers; but when I go up the river I see camps of soldiers on its banks. These soldiers cut down my timber; they kill my buffalo; and when I see that, my heart feels like bursting. I have spoken.

"Do not ask us to give up the buffalo for the sheep," Ten Bears of the Comanche added. "Do not speak of it more:

> I was born upon the prairie, where the wind blew free, and there was nothing to break the light of the sun. I was born where there were no enclosures, and where everything drew a free breath. I want to die there, and not within walls.
> I have hunted and lived over that country. I lived like my fathers before me, and like them, I lived happily. So why do you ask us to leave the rivers, and the sun, and the wind, and live in houses?

The peace commissioners promised that, south of the Arkansas River, non-Indians would be prohibited from settlement, and the tribes could exclusively continue hunting there "so long as the buffalo may range thereon in such numbers as justify the chase." Though not every band of each tribe was represented, the treaty was signed and sent to Congress. The Kiowa calendar for that year showed an Indian and a white man shaking hands near a grove of trees.

A year later, farther north at Fort Laramie on the Platte, a similar treaty was signed by some of the Lakota Sioux. In exchange for the government's abandoning its Army forts in Wyoming's Powder River country, an expansive Great Sioux reservation was created, encompassing half of present-day South Dakota, including the sacred Black Hills. The treaty also contained a clause stating that the Lakotas were free to hunt outside the reservation—so long as there were buffalo.

General William Tecumseh Sherman, now in command of the Army in the West, reluctantly agreed to the hunting concession. "This may lead to collisions," Sherman wrote his brother, "but it will not be long before all the buffaloes are extinct near and between the railroads."

General Sheridan,

As long as buffalo are up on the Republican [River], the Indians will go there. I think it would be wise to invite all the sportsmen of England and America . . . for a Grand Buffalo hunt, and make one grand sweep of them all.

Until the buffalo and consequent[ly] Indians are out [from between] the roads, we will have . . . trouble.

GENERAL WILLIAM T. SHERMAN

Early on the morning of January 13, 1872, a train pulled up to the Union Pacific railroad platform at North Platte, Nebraska, flying the flags of the United States and Russia, and carrying a special passenger. Grand Duke Alexis Alexandrovich, the fourth son of Czar Alexander II, was in the midst of a goodwill tour of America that had already created a media sensation with massive parades and elegant receptions in cities up and down the East Coast. He had come west to hunt buffalo.

His host, Lieutenant General Philip Sheridan, was overseeing the elaborate details for the outing. Troops of soldiers, even a cavalry band, had already set up "Camp Alexis" a day's ride south, with a walled tent, floored and carpeted for the guest of honor, and wagon-loads of provisions that included plenty of champagne. Buffalo Bill Cody was on hand, having selected a campsite he was sure would be near a buffalo herd. Cody had recently guided a number of news-paper owners and wealthy businessmen on what was dubbed in the press as the "millionaire's hunt" in the same area. To accompany Rus-sia's young aristocrat, Sheridan selected George Armstrong Custer, now a lieutenant colonel. Despite his disastrous first encounter with a buffalo, Custer had developed a love for chasing game across the Plains and had also hosted hunts for English nobility, journalists, and influential easterners. "Buffalo hunting," he said, is "the most exciting of all American sports."

The hunt began on January 14—the Grand Duke's twenty-second birthday—and Alexis was accorded the privilege of the first kill. Equipped with a pearl-handled revolver, made especially for him by Smith & Wesson, and after some coaching from Custer, he rode up alongside a bull and fired several shots. But the bull was only wounded. In his own embroidered account of the moment, Buffalo Bill placed himself at the center of the action, claiming that Alexis was riding his horse, Buckskin Joe:

> I rode up to him, gave him my old reliable [rifle] "Lucretia" and told him…I would give him the word when to shoot.
>
>   At the same time I gave old Buckskin Joe a blow with my whip, and with a few jumps the horse carried the Grand Duke within about ten feet of a big buffalo bull.
>
>   "Now is your time," said I. He fired and down went the buffalo.

Alexis jumped down, cut off the buffalo's tail as a souvenir, and "let go a series of howls and gurgles like the death song of all the foghorns and calliopes ever born." In celebration, bottles of champagne were distributed to everyone. Later, when the Grand Duke shot a second bison, out came a second round of champagne. "I was in hopes that he would kill five or six more before we reached camp," Buffalo Bill recalled, "especially if a basket of champagne was to be opened every time he dropped one."

That night, Sheridan presented his guest with another gift. With the promise of thousands of rations of flour, sugar, coffee, and tobacco, he had lured Chief Spotted Tail and nearly six hundred members of his Lakota tribe to join them. The next day, nine of the Lakotas took part in the hunt. One of them, named Two Lance, demonstrated how Indians could bring down a buffalo with a single arrow. Two Lance's passed clear through the animal's chest. He then presented the arrow to the Grand Duke as a parting remembrance of his adventure.

"I think I may safely say," Sheridan proudly reported to Washington, that the hunt "gave more pleasure to the Grand Duke than any other event which has occurred to him since he has been in our country." Alexis took the train to Denver for a grand ball, then for another hunt with Custer in eastern Colorado Territory. On their way through Kansas, he shot a bull from the window of his passenger car. Later, the Grand Duke and Custer posed for portraits together. Not to be forgotten, Cody had copies of the photograph reproduced—with an image of himself superimposed to make them a trio.

As Alexis headed home to Russia, Buffalo Bill left the Plains for New York City. A dime novel about him had been turned into a play—and the breathless newspaper accounts of his time with the Grand Duke had made him even more of a celebrity. Once he saw the gaudy melodrama, he decided to join the cast. If money was to be made playing Buffalo Bill onstage, he might as well get some of it himself.

We want to go on the buffalo hunt so long as there are any buffaloes—we are afraid when we have no meat to offer the Great Spirit he will be angry and punish us.

> Those buffalo are mine... We sold the land to the whites, but reserved the buffalo.   PE-TA-NA-SHARO, Pawnee

That same year of 1872, a different hunt took place in southwestern Nebraska. Under the government's "Peace Policy," the Pawnees had been placed on a reservation, but were given permission to leave it in their annual search for bison herds—provided they were chaperoned by white men, whose job was to make sure there were no troubles with settlers now living on the Indians' old homelands.

Joining the Pawnees' hunt was a twenty-two-year-old from New York City, George Bird Grinnell, the son of a prominent Wall Street banker. Two years earlier, as a senior at Yale, he had ventured west for the first time as part of a paleontology expedition that unearthed the bones of one hundred species of extinct animals—including a pterodactyl and a tiny eohippus, the world's first known horse. Around the campfire, Grinnell's group and the expedition's Pawnee scouts had entertained each other. "They sang the buffalo song," he remembered, "and we sang some college songs."

At the time, the theory of species extinction was still relatively new. "It wasn't until the late 1700s that scientists realized that it was possible for a species to go extinct at all," Michelle Nijhuis said. "Before then, scientists in North America and Europe believed that species were just unchanging entities. We had always had the same number of species that we had, and would continue to have, forever." But as skeletons of animals like mastodons and mammoths were discovered, and fossils of even more ancient species were uncovered in rock sediments, it became clear that many animals that had once populated the Earth no longer existed. In his landmark book about evolution, *On the Origin of Species*, Charles Darwin attributed it to his theory of "natural selection; for old forms will be supplanted by new and improved forms" over time. "Even after people realized extinction was possible, it took decades for them to understand that human activities could drive species extinct in the here and now," Nijhuis said. In 1844, the overhunting of the great auk, a flightless bird in the North Atlantic, proved that extinction could also occur by human hands.

Grinnell's paleontology expedition in 1870 altered the arc of the young man's life, according to his biographer Michael Punke. "He'd been kind of an aimless person before that," Punke said. "He's out there digging up dinosaur bones, and he has this incredibly hands-on, tangible experience where they discover a hundred extinct species. So, for somebody of that era, he understands, in a very unique way, that extinction is something that's possible."

When Grinnell returned to the West again in 1872, the Pawnees introduced him to some of their sacred rituals before going after the bison. "The success of the hunt," he wrote, "was supposed to depend largely upon the respect shown to the buffalo." He marveled at how disciplined the Pawnee hunters were, making sure no one rode ahead and scared off the herd, until the leader gave the signal for everyone to charge; how skillfully they handled their horses, riding bareback and bringing down their prey with bows and arrows; and how the whole tribe celebrated after the successful hunt.

"Grinnell was somebody who, throughout his life, could see what was coming before most other people," Punke said, and that night, he experienced "an epiphany." His time with the Pawnee, Grinnell wrote, "[started me] musing sadly upon the future of the Indian and the buffalo:

> Their days are numbered, and unless some action on this subject is speedily taken not only by the states and territories, but by the national government, these shaggy brown beasts, these cattle upon a thousand hills, will ere long be among the things of the past.

FIVE

KILLS TOMORROW

IN THE FALL OF 1872, tracks for a new railroad—the Atchison, Topeka and Santa Fe—reached a small settlement that had grown up around Fort Dodge, on the north shore of the Arkansas River in southwestern Kansas. Town builders had originally hoped to name it Buffalo City, but the postal service turned them down, since Kansas already had a town by that name. So they christened it Dodge City, in honor of the nearby fort.

Buffalo were everywhere. One merchant shot them from the fence of his corral for his hogs to feed on. Another resident had tamed two calves that he allowed to meander through town. The pair soon became a nuisance, poking their noses into kitchen windows for scraps of food, and an ordinance was passed prohibiting locals from letting bison loose on the streets. "When the railroad hit Dodge City," Steven Rinella said, "there were so many so close to town, they were killing them so fast, that residents began to complain about the stench of rotting buffalo surrounding the town." The first construction train into Dodge City was delayed two hours, waiting for a herd three miles long to pass in front of it.

J. Wright Mooar, a young Vermonter, had been supplying the work crews with buffalo meat for three cents a pound, but news from the East was about to transform his life—and everyone else's on the southern Plains. Commercial tanners in Europe, England, and Philadelphia had developed a way to efficiently process stiff buffalo hides into a supple but durable leather as good as a cow's hide—and suitable for the belts used to drive industrial machines. "There's a shortage of leather in the United States in the years after the Civil War," said Andrew Isenberg. "Leather is the fifth-largest industry in the United States. So, one of the reasons why this industrial society reaches out into the Great Plains to consume bison hides is just to feed this appetite." Bison had become one more necessary component in the Industrial Revolution.

Dealers were clamoring for as many hides as they could get—and offering more than three dollars for each one. Mooar brought in 305 hides in a month's time and made more than $1,000—roughly twice what an average day worker back east made in a year. Word of the lucrative market in hides spread quickly and soon brought more men to Dodge City—two thousand of them, according to one newspaper, each dreaming of striking it rich. In its first three months after reaching Dodge City, the Santa Fe railroad carried out 43,029 buffalo robes and 1,436,290 pounds of meat.

The same thing was occurring at other rail centers in Kansas and western Nebraska. Thousands of other hunters swarmed in, especially in 1873, when the sudden collapse of railroad bonds triggered the failure of a hundred banks and ushered in a financial depression. Across the nation, a million workers were unemployed, and those with jobs had their wages cut. Hunting buffalo was one of the few booming businesses.

Many of the men were newcomers to the West and unprepared for the challenges of surviving on the Plains. During the harsh winter of 1872–73, an estimated one hundred of them froze to death along the Arkansas River; the surgeon at Fort Dodge performed seventy amputations. Still, the prospect of easy money was too alluring, and the number of hunters kept increasing.

"The whole western country went buffalo-wild," remembered Frank Mayer, a twenty-two-year-old from Pennsylvania. "It was like a gold rush. Men left jobs, businesses, wives, and children. There were uncounted millions of the beasts. They didn't belong to anybody. If you could kill them, what they brought was yours. They were like walking gold pieces." Mayer sank everything he owned into a hunting outfit—wagons, mules, camp equipment, and firearms—and contemplated the fortune that awaited:

When I went into the business, I sat down and figured that I was indeed one of fortune's children.

Just think! Each [hide was] worth at least $3. Cartridges cost 25 cents each, so every time I fired one I got my investment back twelve times over. I could kill a hundred a day. That would be $6,000 a month—[more than] what was paid the President of the United States, and a hundred times what a man with a good job... could be expected to earn.

Was I not lucky? I thought I was.

Like the other hide hunters fanning out across the southern Plains, who preferred to call themselves "buffalo runners," Mayer learned quickly that chasing bison on horseback—as depicted in popular dime novels—was "a bad gamble." "Shooting from the back of a running horse was always uncertain," he said. It meant too many wasted shots; too many wounded buffalo; too many carcasses of whatever bison he managed to kill scattered across greater distances, which made skinning them more time-consuming. And the rifles they used often required several shots to bring a buffalo down. "I was a businessman," he wrote. "I wanted efficiency. The thing we had to have, we businessmen with rifles, was one-shot kills. We couldn't afford to miss; [we needed] nine in ten dropped instantly, within a space of one hundred feet."

J. Wright Mooar sent a letter to the Sharps Rifle Manufacturing Company in Connecticut asking for a gun with more stopping power—and greater range. Sharps and other manufacturers responded with a series of new models. They weighed twelve to sixteen pounds, featured longer and wider barrels that could handle larger amounts of gunpowder to fire heavier slugs of lead with great accuracy over a distance of four hundred yards—and could even reach targets more than a thousand yards away.

Native people who saw the new buffalo guns in action, Mooar reported, said it "shoots today and kills tomorrow"—referring to the extreme distance the bullet traveled. But the phrase would soon assume a more profound meaning: for the bison and for the Native people, "tomorrow"—the future itself—was being killed.

Replacing horse-mounted chases, the most effective technique was called a "stand." A hunter carefully positioned himself about two hundred to three hundred yards downwind from the herd so the animals couldn't smell him. Then, kneeling or sitting, his heavy rifle barrel resting on the crook of two sticks bolted together, and sometimes peering through a telescopic sight, he picked out a lead buffalo, took careful aim, and fired, usually aiming for the lungs. "A buffalo shot through the lungs immediately sank to his haunches, rocked sidewise, as his air passages filled with blood, and finally he rolled over and expired," Mooar wrote. "If you shot him through the heart, he'd run about 400 yards before he'd fall, and he'd take the herd with him." According to Mayer, "The rest of [the] herd, whether it was three or thirty, would gather around . . . and stupidly 'mill.' They were completely bewildered. All you had to do . . . was pick them off one by one, making sure you made a dropping kill at every shot." What Mayer considered the bison's stupidity for clustering together as one after another dropped to the ground was not that at all; the sudden appearance of long-range lethality had short-circuited more than ten thousand years of evolutionary defense mechanisms. "Adventurous?" Mayer wrote. "No more than shooting a beef critter in the barnyard. It was a harvest. We were the harvesters."

Firing too fast could overheat a rifle barrel and ruin its accuracy. To cool it down, hunters used their canteen water; if the water ran out, they urinated down the barrel and kept shooting. Some hunters recorded "stands" in which they killed upward of a hundred buffalo from the same location before stopping. Mooar brought down 96 in one; "Doc" Zahl, 120. In 1873, Tom Nixon gathered a crowd to watch him shoot 120 buffalo in just forty minutes; in a later "stand" he killed 205. Frank Mayer's biggest total was 59, but he was usually done hunting for the day by noon, when he reached 25 downed bison. While his skinners went to work, he went back to camp and cleaned his rifle, hand-loaded cartridges with powder by hand (he said it cut the cost by half, compared to store-bought ammunition), and then scouted for the next day's shoot. "We never killed all the buffalo we could, but only as many as our skinners could handle," he explained.

"Killing more than we could use would waste buffalo, which wasn't important; it would also waste ammunition, which was."

The skinners' job—"dirty, disagreeable, laborious, uninspiring," according to Mayer—was to strip the hides off the carcasses from the neck down. Occasionally, some attached ropes to the hide and pulled it off with their wagon, but that too often damaged the hide, so they usually did the work entirely by hand. Experienced skinners with well-sharpened knives could get it done in about twenty minutes. Some outfits—like J. Wright Mooar's—also took some meat back for sale. But most just removed the tongues, worth twenty-five cents each, and left everything else—six hundred to eight hundred pounds of meat, along with the hooves and the head and the horns—to rot. The hides would be carted back to camp and staked out to dry for about ten days, then folded and stacked into bales on the freight wagon for transport to the nearest railroad.

The Industrial Revolution had transformed the Great Plains into a factory floor. Instead of assembling something, however, the workers were disassembling something. They took only the bison's most valuable component part before placing it on a conveyer belt, the railroad, so the disassembled part could be used to run a machine on the East Coast. Since it was a buffalo's hide—not a thick winter coat—they were after, the "factory" could run year-round, which impeded the bison's regeneration during the summer mating season. "The constant pressure of these hunters," Andrew Isenberg said, "was upsetting the bison's patterns of reproduction, of grazing, and so they're putting a dent into the bison population that's not just measured by the hides they ship."

And despite Frank Mayer's focus on efficiency, there was considerable waste. "If they had shot the buffalo more than once, that could destroy the hide," Michael Punke said:

> If the skinners were not good at their work, the skinners could destroy the hide. If the hides were staked out and there was a rainstorm, the hides could rot. Insects came along and chewed on the hides. By one estimate, you had to kill about four buffalo to get

one hide to market. So, not only was the carcass wasted, but even the hides were wasted in this industry.

Uncounted numbers of wounded buffalo wandered off and died. So did motherless calves. Even so, more than a million hides made their way east from the southern Plains before the end of 1873, indicating that more than 4 million bison had possibly perished.

But Frank Mayer's dream of getting rich as a "buffalo runner" was evaporating, as he calculated the receipts and expenses of his "small, tidy little organization." "I didn't make a fortune, I just got by," he admitted:

> Within a year or a year and a half after I got into the business, we hit what I now know is called diminishing returns. We called it a scarcity of buffalo.
>
> With 5,000 rifles a day levelled at him, it wasn't long until there was very little of him, or her, left to shoot. So we had to spend more and more time in the wagons exploring one range after another—riding miles and miles and miles...over the uncharted plains, looking into every gulley and prowling around every stream bed, on the off chance that we would find a herd that some other runner had overlooked.
>
> All of this took days of time, and expenses went on, even if the barrel of my rifle was cold for weeks on end. And my dreams of fortune—they grew dimmer and dimmer as the months went by.
>
> I was fast becoming a bankrupt. But I stuck. I was no quitter.

The hunters adapted their tactics, and began to work cooperatively. "They would use fires at night to ward the bison off of water sources, to prevent them from coming at night to quench their thirst, knowing that [these] thirst-crazed animals would just have to come to water in the daylight hours," Steven Rinella said. "And you could wait at the water just to shoot them. It was a business, and the animal wasn't even imagined as an animal. It was just imagined as a natural resource." Going between two Army posts in Kansas, Colonel Richard Irving Dodge had once driven a wagon for twenty-five miles through what he described as "one immense herd" of buffalo. But that was no longer the case, he wrote: "Where there were myriads of buffalo the year before, there were now myriads of carcasses. The air was foul with a sickening stench, and the vast plain, which only a short twelve months before teemed with animal life, was a dead, solitary putrid desert."

The hide yards at Dodge City now stood empty. But south of the Arkansas River—in the area reserved by the Medicine Lodge Treaty for Indian hunting—big herds still roamed. J. Wright Mooar crossed over to investigate. "For five days," he said, "we [rode] through and camped in a mobile sea of living buffalo." Back at Fort Dodge, he and other hunters asked the commander what the Army would do if they trespassed into the treaty lands. "Boys," the officer replied, "if I were a buffalo hunter, I would hunt buffalo where the buffalo are."

The hide hunters took it as a signal that American soldiers wouldn't stop them, though they would be on their own against any Native warriors who responded to their trespass. "The Arkansas was called the 'dead line,' south of which no hunter should go," Billy Dixon, one of hunters, recounted. "But as buffalo grew fewer in number, we gazed longingly across the sandy wastes that marked the course of the Arkansas. The oftener we looked, the more eager we became to tempt fate. Even the sky looked more inviting in that direction.... So we crossed over."

Back east, as early as 1872, bills had been introduced in Congress to protect the buffalo and other wild animals from "indiscriminate slaughter and extermination." None of them passed. By 1874, reformers had been galvanized by increasing reports of the slaughter under way on the southern Plains. *Harper's Weekly* had illustrated one account with a cartoon by Thomas Nast, entitled "The Last Buffalo," showing a bison standing up, stripping off its hide, and telling a hunter, "Don't shoot, my good fellow! Here, take my robe, save your ammunition and let me go in peace."

Representative Greenbury Lafayette Fort of Illinois proposed legislation making it "unlawful for any person who is not an Indian to kill, wound or in any way destroy any female buffalo, of any age, found at large within the boundaries of the Territories of the United States." In the debate, Fort and others read into the record newspaper editorials and statements by some Army officers stationed in the West who supported the measure, because they thought the scale of destruction was exacerbating already tense relations with Indian tribes. The American Society for the Prevention of Cruelty to Animals was also campaigning for something to be done.

But the secretary of the Department of the Interior, Columbus Delano, had already made his position clear in the department's annual report, linking the fate of the bison with efforts to keep western tribes on their reservations and teach them to be farmers: "I would not seriously regret the total disappearance of the buffalo from the western prairies, in its effect on the Indians, regarding it rather as a means of hastening their sense of dependence upon the products of the soil and their own labors." Arguing against the protection bill's passage, Representative James Garfield of Ohio contended that eliminating the buffalo herds would "be the best thing which could happen for the betterment of our Indian question." "It may be possible," he added, that "in our mercy to the buffalo, we may be cruel to the Indian." To Fort, that argument was absurd. "I am not in favor," he said, "of civilizing the Indian by starving him to death."

In the end, the House passed the buffalo protection bill and sent it to the Senate, which also voted in favor of it. But President Ulysses S. Grant, who had remained silent on the issue, quietly killed the bill—using a so-called pocket veto, by refusing to sign it when Congress adjourned. Two years later, a similar bill would pass the House but die in a Senate committee. During this time, some territories passed measures imposing certain closed seasons for hunting buffalo and other game, but they all proved unenforceable. A few states also adopted bison protection legislation—though always *after* the buffalo had disappeared from within their borders.

For more than a century, historians have debated whether the federal government and its military deliberately set out to eradicate the buffalo in the late 1800s. The evidence is mixed—as the congressional debate, passage, and ultimate fate of Fort's protection bill attests.

One of the most-repeated stories in the literature of the American buffalo is of General Philip Sheridan hurrying to Texas in 1875, when state legislators were considering their own law to protect the bison. Sheridan was against it. The hide hunters, he told them, "have done more in the last two years and will do more in the next year to settle the vexed Indian question than the entire regular Army has done in the last thirty years.... Send them powder and lead, if you will; for the sake of lasting peace, let them kill, skin, and sell until the buffaloes are exterminated. Then your prairies can be covered with speckled cattle, and the festive cowboy, who follows the hunter as a second forerunner of an advanced civilization."

The problem with this "smoking gun" speech, the historian Dan Flores discovered, is that there is no record of Texas ever considering such a bill, nor of Sheridan ever testifying before its legislature. The Texas delegation in Congress had opposed Fort's bill, Flores points out, in his book *Wild New World;* and in 1878, Sheridan actually sent a telegram to the War Department decrying the market destruction of the bison. "I consider it important," the general wrote, "that this wholesale slaughter of the buffalo be stopped." The anecdote about Sheridan's purported Texas speech first appeared in a 1907 memoir by a hide hunter, who prefaced the story with "It is said" and never identified his source. Flores contends that the account was fabricated, meant to focus the narrative of the bison's demise away from disparaging the market hunters, who could then be portrayed as simply agents, perhaps even heroes, of a larger—and officially sanctioned—national effort.

Still, there is plenty in the record suggesting that there were many people in positions of authority who wanted the huge herds gone. Although "the Army never pursued a policy themselves to destroy those animals," Elliott West said, "the military in the West certainly had a motive to do what they could to eliminate as many bison as they could, because they understood the obvious: that the bison were key to the Native economy. They didn't do it themselves, but they certainly helped it and supported it." The federal government, Andrew Isenberg said, "observed the decline of the bison and it endorsed the decline of the bison. It's not as if the United States sent hunters out or soldiers out, to kill as many bison as they could so that the Native people who relied on the bison would have to surrender to the reservation system. They didn't command these hunters, but they certainly commended the work of these hunters." Michael Punke, not only a writer but someone with a long career in government, came to a similar conclusion. "It was not something that they wrote down and propagated through legislation," he said, "but I think through all sorts of informal practices and lots of winking and nudging, the destruction of the buffalo is something that was very much encouraged by the U.S. government."

From the point of view of Native people, who had the greatest stake in the matter, the issue seemed clear, expressed by Germaine White, of the Confederated Salish and Kootenai in Montana. "When there was a desire to connect the East Coast and the West Coast, there were two great impediments," she said. "One was bison. The other was Indigenous people. And they thought they could solve the second by eliminating the first. It was kind of a 'twofer.' "

Whether it was an official policy or a secret policy or, perhaps as likely, no policy at all, it had the same effect for the bison, who were eliminated, and for the Native people who, for thousands of years, had depended on them. But one thing was indisputable: The federal government was not going to *defend* the buffalo.

Your people make big talk, and sometimes make war, if an Indian kills a white man's ox to keep his wife and children from starving.

What do you think my people ought to do when they see *their* cattle—the buffaloes—killed by your race when they are not hungry?   LITTLE ROBE, Cheyenne

[The Indians] sensed that we were taking away their birthright and that with every boom of a buffalo rifle their tenure on their homeland became weakened, and that eventually they would have no homeland and no buffalo.

> So they did what you and I would do if our existence were
> jeopardized: they fought.   FRANK MAYER

The so-called Peace Policy that began with the Medicine Lodge and Fort Laramie treaties had never brought peace to the Great Plains. In 1874, things got worse. George Armstrong Custer led an expedition into the Black Hills, an area that had been reserved exclusively for the Lakota, who considered the area sacred. A prospector Custer brought along started searching for gold there. At the same time, farther south, hide hunters had crossed the Arkansas River into the buffalo range supposedly off-limits to whites—and brazenly established outposts to keep themselves supplied with ammunition and whatever else they needed to continue their deadly business.

"The government made treaties with the Indians when they wanted something and it was convenient," Michael Punke said. "And the second that the treaty was inconvenient, and they wanted something else, they broke the treaty. That pattern permeates the history of the United States government with Indigenous peoples. There's another element, and that is, once violence starts, it's incredibly difficult to stop. Violence incites more violence, and that cycle's incredibly difficult to break." Incensed by the treaty violations in the southern and northern Plains, warriors from the Lakota, Cheyenne, Arapaho, Kiowa, and Comanche struck back.

Among the Quahada band of Comanches, a tall twenty-six-year-old, who had already distinguished himself with his fearless courage, was rising in leadership. His name was Quanah. He had been born near the Wichita Mountains, the oldest son of a prominent chief, Peta Nocona, and a white woman, Cynthia Ann Parker, who had been taken captive as a child and adopted into the Comanche tribe. In 1860, while Quanah and his father and most of the other warriors were gone, Texas Rangers overran their village, killed a number of people, and took his mother and baby sister into custody. "It wasn't a famous thing you read about in Texas history. It was a massacre," said Ron Parker, a great-grandson of Quanah. "They eventually took her back to her people [in the white settlements]. She didn't want to go, but they took her anyway. She never wanted to go back, because she was Comanche, because that's all she knew, the Comanche way, and she loved the way." Dustin Tahmahkera, Quanah's great-great-grandson and a cultural historian, said that although Cynthia Ann's capture "was being hailed as a rescue, it's really another abduction. In those few remaining years of her life, it's said that she was just very distressed, very broken-hearted." After she lost her daughter to pneumonia, Cynthia Ann tried in vain several times to rejoin the Comanches. She died in despair, still forced to live among the whites.

By age fifteen, Quanah was leading raids into Mexico and attacks on Texans, against whom he harbored an implacable hatred. At eighteen, he attended the Medicine Lodge Treaty negotiations, which the Quahadas refused to sign. For seven years, they had stayed away from the reservation, and Quanah took part in skirmishes with the soldiers sent to force them in. "There were more raids to continue; there were more battles to fight," Tahmahkera said. "There was still more of a buffalo-centered way of life, and a horse way of life, that they needed to defend."

In the summer of 1874, Quanah joined a war against the hide hunters. At the yearly Sun Dance, a medicine man named Isatai announced that in a vision he had been given the power to raise the dead, stop the white man's bullets, and help the tribes retake their homelands and restore the old ways. Quanah later recalled the moment:

> Isatai [was making] big talk at that time. He says, "God [told] me we [are] going to kill lots of white men. I [will] stop the bullets in their guns. Bullets [will] not pierce our shirts. We [will] kill [them] all...."
>
> Everybody saddled up; took their war bonnets and shields.

With Quanah and Isatai leading, more than three hundred Comanche, Kiowa, and Southern Cheyenne warriors set off for Adobe Walls, a trading post in the Texas Panhandle provisioning the buffalo hunters. "Quanah knew that they had to destroy the buffalo hunters,"

Tahmahkera said. "It becomes a matter of defending your people, of defending your family, of defending the buffalo."

Twenty-nine people were there when the Indians attacked at dawn on June 27, 1874. Two white men were killed in the early moments, as hide hunters who had been sleeping under their wagons scrambled to defend themselves before taking shelter in the buildings. Quanah was wounded when a bullet ricocheted into his neck, but he kept fighting. "We charged pretty fast on our horses, throwing up dust," he recounted. "I got up [onto] the adobe houses with another Comanche. We poked holes through the roof to shoot." Billy Dixon, one of the hide hunters inside, helped drive off the attack:

> For the first half hour the Indians were reckless and daring enough to ride up and strike the doors with the butts of their guns. Finally, the buffalo hunters all got straightened out and were firing with deadly effect.
>
> The Indians stood up against this for a while, but gradually began falling back, as we were emptying rawhide saddles entirely too fast for Indian safety.

"They had better guns than the Natives; they could shoot farther," Ron Parker said. The attackers "were outgunned, really, is what it was." The battle evolved into a siege for several more days. But as the Indians rode in ever-expanding circles around Adobe Walls, Dixon said, "our guns had longer range than theirs [and] we began picking them off."

Seeing a group of Indians on a bluff more than three-quarters of a mile away, the hunters urged Dixon to take a shot with his big Sharps buffalo rifle. "I took careful aim and pulled the trigger," he said. "We saw an Indian fall from his horse." The bullet had struck before the rider heard the sound of Dixon's rifle.

Fifteen of the warriors who had followed Isatai and his vision had died in the initial attack, and now more were dead or wounded. "All [the] Cheyennes [were very] mad at Isatai," Quanah remembered. They shouted, "What's the matter with your medicine!" One Cheyenne beat him with a riding whip.

·   ·   ·

In the wake of the battle of Adobe Walls, Comanche, Kiowa, Cheyenne, and Arapaho warriors regrouped and embarked on raids across Texas, Colorado, and parts of New Mexico and Kansas that left 190 white people dead. President Grant put the reservations under military control. Any Indians who did not return were to be considered "hostile" and hunted down. Generals Sherman and Sheridan devised a massive five-pronged offensive to destroy resistance on the southern Plains forever—and for three months what was called the Red River War resulted in a number of skirmishes and casualties on both sides. Billy Dixon, who had given up bison hunting and joined the Army, barely escaped from another attack; crouching in a buffalo wallow for protection, he and his scouting party held off mounted warriors until a relief column arrived. By late September, more than four thousand Indians—twelve hundred of them warriors—still remained at large.

On the morning of September 28, 1874, Colonel Ranald S. Mackenzie and thirteen companies of cavalry and infantry reached the rim of Palo Duro Canyon in the caprocks section of the Texas Panhandle. Peering down, Mackenzie saw an array of Indian encampments spread along the canyon floor. He had been chasing off-reservation Comanches for years without success. In one engagement, Quanah had led a midnight raid on Mackenzie's camp and had run off with many of the cavalry's horses, including the colonel's prized gray pacer. Now, it was Mackenzie who had the element of surprise.

He ordered his men down a narrow trail, and they began their charge. The villagers abandoned their tepees and fled up the canyon walls, while their warriors covered their retreat. As a battle, the fight in Palo Duro Canyon resulted in few casualties: three Native Americans and one cavalry trooper were killed. But the Army had captured the possessions the Indians left behind: more than two hundred tepees, hundreds of robes and blankets, and thousands of pounds of dried buffalo meat—their winter food supply. Mackenzie ordered it all piled in a mound on the canyon floor and burned.

The next morning, Mackenzie dealt another devastating blow. The soldiers had also captured most of the villagers' huge herd of horses. After distributing nearly 350 of them to his Tonkawa Indian scouts, he had the remainder—more than a thousand horses—driven into a box canyon, lined its rim with soldiers, and commanded his men to shoot them all. Only a century earlier, the horse had made a new way of life possible for the Comanches and other Plains people. In ways both literal and symbolic, nothing Mackenzie could have done to illustrate that a way of life was ending said it more clearly than the shooting of their horses. "We have elders today," said Dustin Tahmahkera, "who say that if you go to that site that you can still hear those horses, and the destruction, and the crying that went forth so long ago."

For the rest of the fall—and into the winter—the Army's columns patrolled the Panhandle, ceaselessly pursuing any straggling bands who didn't return to the reservation at Fort Sill. Many of them, reduced to eating roots and rodents to survive, began to starve. In February 1875, the last of the Kiowas came in. Then the Cheyennes in March, followed by some Comanches. By May, only Quanah and his four hundred Quahadas—who still had their horses—remained free. As their leader, Quanah had a decision to make, Tahmahkera said:

> It's said that Quanah went up on a hill and drew a buffalo robe over his head and was waiting for signs, for direction.
>
> It's said that a wolf came along and howled, and took off in the direction of Fort Sill. It's said that an eagle flew overhead and began flying in the direction of Fort Sill. Quanah took those as signs to finally go to Fort Sill with other Quahadas.

For the sake of his people, Quanah decided that their survival required him to turn himself in. At Fort Sill, he began a new life on the reservation he had fought so long to avoid. He asked Mackenzie about his mother and little sister. Mackenzie made inquiries and reported that they had both died among the white people in Texas.

SIX

A DEATH WIND
FOR MY PEOPLE

WITH THE INDIANS of the southern Plains confined to reservations, the hide hunters—three thousand of them, by
one estimate—went back to work. J. Wright Mooar called 1876 "a
banner year for buffalo in this part of Texas." Another hunter said
the skinned bison carcasses looked "like logs where a hurricane had
passed through a forest" and glistened in the sun "like a hundred
glass windows."

John Cook, who had left Kansas to join the hunt in the Texas Panhandle, killed eighty-eight buffalo in one stand, alternating between
two rifles when one overheated. "As I walked through where the carcasses lay the thickest," he later recounted, "I could not help but
think that I had done wrong to make such a slaughter for the hides
alone:

> A slight feeling of remorse would come over me for the part I was
> taking in this greatest of all hunts to the death.
>
> Then I would justify myself . . . and pictured to myself a white
> schoolhouse on that knoll yonder where a maid was teaching
> future generals and statesmen the necessity of becoming familiar
> with the three R's.
>
> Back on that plateau I could see a courthouse of a thriving
> county seat. On ahead is a good site for a church. . . . Down there
> where those two riverines come together would be a good place
> for a country store and post office.
>
> Some of these days we will hear the whistle and shriek of a

locomotive as she comes through the gap. And not long until we can hear…the lowing of [cattle] and the bleating sheep, and the morning crow of the barnyard [rooster].

Then Cook remembered a song he said was being "sung all over the range with as much vim as the old-time 'John Brown's Body':

> It had a very catchy tune, and with the melody from the hunters' voices it was beautiful and soul-inspiring to me. One stanza and the chorus is all that I can now recall of it. It ran thus: "O, give me a home, where the buffalo roam, where the deer and the antelope play, where seldom is heard a discouraging word, and the sky is not cloudy all day."

It was Cook's memoir, *The Border and the Buffalo*, published in 1907, that first recounted the speech that Philip Sheridan apparently never gave in Texas, and his own self-justifying reverie about the bright future of the valley strewn with the carcasses of the bison he had just killed deploys similar oratorical flourishes. The emotions he described as having felt in 1876 may have actually come to him thirty years later, as he wrote his book. But the song he quotes, now known as "Home on the Range," is rooted in the historical moment. After President Franklin D. Roosevelt called it his favorite song in 1934, and many famous artists began performing it on the radio, a couple from Arizona claimed they had written it in 1904 as "An Arizona Home" and filed a copyright suit for half a million dollars. A lengthy investigation eventually traced its origin to a poem, "My Home in the West," written by Brewster M. Higley, a physician and homesteader in Kansas in the early 1870s, and set to music by Daniel E. Kelley for a local quartet. It spread quickly, often changing as it traveled. Many people remembered hearing it before 1880, in multiple versions, including one called "Colorado Home." The folklorist John A. Lomax, collecting material for his book *Cowboy Songs and Other Frontier Ballads*, first recorded it in 1908, sung by an African American saloon keeper in San Antonio, who said he learned it as a cowboy on the Chisholm Trail.

Unlike John Cook, Frank Mayer was less sentimental about the carnage the hide hunters wreaked on the southern Plains. "A couple of years before it was nothing to see 5,000, 10,000 buffalo in a day's ride; now if I saw 50 I was lucky," he wrote:

> Presently all I saw was rotting red carcasses or bleaching white bones. Millions of pounds of buffalo meat, carrion now, was piled up on the ranges, and the stench was so great that at a mile away from a stand you could smell it and be forced to hold your nose. Only the coyotes and wolves didn't seem to mind. We had killed the golden goose.
>
> Maybe we runners served our purpose in helping abolish the buffalo; maybe it was our ruthless harvesting of him which telescoped the control of the Indian by a decade or maybe more.
>
> Or maybe I am just rationalizing. Maybe we were just a greedy lot who wanted to get ours, and to hell with posterity, the buffalo, and anyone else, just so we kept our scalps on and our money pouches filled.
>
> I think maybe that is the way it was.

By 1877—only three years after the fight at Adobe Walls—the immense herds south of the Arkansas had been reduced to a few scattered bands. A year later, even those were disappearing. Cattle ranches, homesteads, and small towns were starting to fill what had been the buffalo's domain. For every Indian in the West, there were now forty whites. The hide hunters' trading posts in Texas began closing. Dodge City was turning into a raucous cow town, where live cattle—not buffalo hides—were being loaded onto the railroad cars, and cowboys coming off trail drives spent their earnings in the town's saloons.

To bolster his reservation's paltry food supply, Quanah obtained permission to lead three hundred Comanches and Kiowas on a hunt. They moved south, across familiar territory that now seemed an alien landscape littered with buffalo carcasses. "It's in such a short span of time where the buffalo are plentiful, where that way of life is going so strong," said Dustin Tahmahkera. "I can only imagine the scenes, the rotting smells, while en route to search for buffalo. And so, on our lands are all these visual reminders of what others had done to us and to a way of life."

Some of N. Scott Momaday's Kiowa ancestors were part of the sad passage across the Staked Plains. "To see the buffalo slaughtered and left to waste upon the Plains must have been almost unbearable," he said. "This was not only a violation, not only a crime, but a tortuous devastation of the soul, the spirit. Their reaction to it was what you might imagine, although it is unimaginable. It was a wound that would be very, very hard to heal, if it could be healed at all. Life was over, in a sense. To see such a thing is to see the death of a god."

In disbelief, Quanah's party pushed on to Palo Duro Canyon, which had always been a reliable refuge for the bison. Instead of buffalo, they found a herd of cattle. The rancher who owned it rode out to parley.

Charles Goodnight had fought against Indians as a Texas Ranger and had blazed some of the early cattle trails north to the railroads. After the Red River War, he had established the first cattle ranch in Palo Duro Canyon, moving his herd there from Colorado. "He knew that Comanches respected bravery, they respected that kind of strength, and he rode out, hopefully, to avoid any certain violent conflict," Dustin Tahmahkera said.

Goodnight, whose partner Oliver Loving had been killed by Comanches during a trail drive, knew of their intense hatred of Texans and told Quanah's group that he was from Colorado. That was "not totally a lie," Tahmahkera said, "but they also made sure to quiz him on that in the moment, and they started asking him about different geographical locations. And he passed the quiz. So, Goodnight and Quanah start talking with each other and they eventually set up something of their own treaty."

Goodnight also neglected to mention that he had been part of the group that had captured Quanah's mother and baby sister nearly two decades earlier. He did tell Quanah's group there were no longer any buffalo in the canyon, but they could continue their hunt to see for themselves. In the meantime, he said, if they stayed peaceful, they could kill two of his cows every other day so they had something to eat. They encamped for several weeks, scoured the Palo Duro, returning each time empty-handed. "Quanah went up to look for the buffalo, and there was none," said Ron Parker, "and then he realized that his way of life, and what they depended on, was no more."

Quanah led the band of Comanches and Kiowas back to the reservation, where the Kiowas recorded the summer of 1879 as the "horse-eating" time by depicting a ghoulish drawing of a horse head over the medicine lodge used for their Sun Dance. "I think their failures in finding buffalo the past year," the reservation agent reported, "will have a good effect in causing them to abandon their idea of subsisting this way and to look to their crops and stock for a support. As [the] supply [of buffalo meat] is cut off, the Indian must go to work and help himself or remain hungry on [government] rations."

In her oral history describing the Kiowa's ancient and intimate relationship with the buffalo, Old Lady Horse recounted a story about this traumatic turning point that was passed down among her people for generations:

The buffalo saw that their day was over. They could protect their people no longer. Sadly, the last remnant of the great herd gathered in council and decided what to do.

The Kiowas were camped on the north side of Mount Scott, those of them who were still free to camp. One young woman got up very early in the morning. The dawn mist was still rising from Medicine Creek, and as she looked across the water, peering through the haze, she saw the last buffalo herd appear like a spirit dream.

Straight to Mount Scott the leader of the herd walked. Behind him came the cows and their calves, and the few young males who had survived. As the woman watched, the face of the mountain opened.

Inside Mount Scott the world was green and fresh, as it had been when she was a small girl. The rivers ran clear, not red. The wild plums were in blossom, chasing the red buds up the inside slopes. Into this world of beauty the buffalo walked, never to be seen again.

"Old Lady Horse, I want to cry when I think of her," said N. Scott Momaday. "I see what she saw. Or, I *try* to see what she saw. But, what I really see is her seeing. This is the equation of tragedy. It was a farewell of tragic significance: a dark, massive animal vitality moving inexorably away from existence. It's a shadow within a shadow. And it has, for every Native American—man, woman, and child—a significance that probably is ineffable."

> I will remain what I am until I die, a hunter, and when there are no buffalo or other game, I will send my children to hunt and live on prairie mice, for where an Indian is shut up in one place his body becomes weak.
>
>   I want to hunt in this place. I want you to turn back from here. If you don't, I will fight you.   SITTING BULL, Lakota

On the northern Plains, where the railroad had not yet arrived, the buffalo were still plentiful. In 1873, the Northern Pacific Railway had crossed the Missouri River at Bismarck in Dakota Territory, but its plans to push farther west to the Yellowstone and then on to the Pacific Ocean had stalled because of the national financial depression. Steamboats and freight wagons remained the principal modes of transporting goods in and out of the region for the rest of the decade.

In 1874, George Armstrong Custer's expedition into the Black Hills had discovered gold. George Bird Grinnell, along as a naturalist to record the birds and animals, was in the camp when the prospector came in with his first samples. "Well, that will mean an Indian war, I expect," Grinnell had predicted. He was proved right. The resulting gold rush brought in swarms of miners and spawned boomtowns like Deadwood while the white population in the area reached about twenty thousand within a year—all in violation of the Fort Laramie Treaty that had promised the Black Hills in perpetuity to the Lakota.

Large bands of the Lakota, refusing to stay on their reservation, moved into the buffalo ranges of eastern Wyoming and Montana Territories—also promised to them as their exclusive hunting ground. They included the Hunkpapas, led by a chief whose name, *Tatanka Iyotake*, describes an intractable buffalo resolute in the face of his enemies—Sitting Bull. Survey crews were already at work, preparing to extend the Northern Pacific westward into the same area, and Lakota warriors began attacking them and their military escorts.

"The U.S. government does what it always does, when there's a conflict between a treaty, on the one hand, and an economic imperative on the other," said Michael Punke. "It goes to the Lakota and says, 'We want to renegotiate the treaty.' The Lakota said, 'No.' The government simply takes the Black Hills, orders the tribes onto a smaller reservation, and deems all of the tribes that are not compliant with that new edict to be 'enemies.'"

In 1876, a military campaign to drive them back to the reservation had resulted in disaster, when Custer and more than two hundred members of his Seventh Cavalry were annihilated on the Little Bighorn by Sitting Bull and his allies. (Grinnell had been invited to join the Seventh as a naturalist on that expedition, too, but didn't accept, sensing that it had little to do with science. Custer, he said, was "somewhat egotistical.") The Army's response to the humiliating defeat at the Little Bighorn was the same as it had been in the southern Plains after the battle of Adobe Walls: a relentless pursuit that by 1877 forced the surrender of one band after another.

But Sitting Bull and his Hunkpapas had escaped across the border into Canada, beyond the reach of American troops, where he intended to continue living off whatever buffalo remained there. By 1880, the Canadian herd was gone. Sitting Bull's people began to starve. In 1881, he led his band of 167 followers south into the United States and surrendered. At the Standing Rock reservation, near the spot where he was born, Sitting Bull composed his own song: "A warrior I have been," he sang. "Now it is all over. A hard time I have."

.   .   .

The same year that Sitting Bull surrendered, the Northern Pacific reached Miles City in Montana Territory. With the Indians no longer a threat, and with a railroad ready to provide easy access to the East, a ruinous reprise of the final slaughter in the southern Plains played itself out.

An estimated five thousand hide hunters and skinners spilled over the buffalo range from the Yellowstone River to the Upper Missouri, where they set up what one Army lieutenant called "a cordon of camps...blocking the great ranges...and rendering it impossible for scarcely a single bison to escape." Many of the hunters were veterans of the slaughter farther south. Vic Smith, originally from Buffalo, New York, was already there, having served as a scout and game provider for the Army during the Indian wars in Montana. As a hide hunter, in the winter of 1881–82 he killed nearly five thousand buffalo, including one stand that brought down 107 of them in an hour's time.

In New York, thirty-one-year-old George Bird Grinnell had become editor of *Forest and Stream*, a publication for hunters and fishermen that he was pushing to take on issues of conservation with more urgency. During the hide hunting on the southern Plains, he had advocated for policies he called "just" and "honest" toward Native Americans that would, he wrote, "conscientiously aid in the increase of the buffalo, instead of furthering its foolish and reckless slaughter." Now, Grinnell turned his attention to what was unfolding in Montana:

> There is nowhere in the world such systematic, business-like and relentless killing as on the buffalo plains.
>
> Up to within a few years [ago,] the valley of the Yellowstone River has been a magnificent hunting ground. The progress of the Northern Pacific Railroad, however, has changed all this. The Indians have been run out and the white men have had a chance to do what they could toward killing off the game.
>
> [The buffalo] will disappear...unless steps are taken to protect it there.

The killing continued—and grew more and more methodically efficient. For every ten buffalo killed, nine hides made it to market, shipped out by the hundreds of thousands. "This is the era of the myth of inexhaustibility, the belief that the West is so vast, that the resources are so vast, that they can never be exhausted," Michael Punke said. "But, it was so much in front of them what was happening that I think they began to figure it out. It became more and more difficult to find buffalo. And there were ominous signs. Weird things began to happen, like they would find herds that were comprised entirely of calves. But there also was a capacity to deny and to believe that they had just gone over the next ridge line, gone into the next territory. And, so, all of that kind of mixes together."

In 1883, word spread that a herd of ten thousand buffalo had moved east, near the Great Sioux reservation in Dakota Territory. The white hunters, including Vic Smith, hurried to find them for their hides. Sitting Bull and his Hunkpapas, with the reservation agent's permission, headed there too—for their meat. "When we got through [with] the hunt," Smith remembered, "there was not a hoof left."

In Miles City that fall, the hide hunters prepared for another winter on the Plains, believing there must still be plenty of buffalo between the Yellowstone and Missouri Rivers. They came back in the spring with almost nothing to show for their efforts, except some reports of seeing a few bison, but never enough to be considered a herd. "There are people in Miles City simply lolling around waiting for the return of the herds," Steven Rinella said. "They still thought there has to be some, somewhere. They're going to roll in from Canada and we'll resume the hunt. When they had finished, they didn't know they'd finished. They felt that, well, it can't be over. And it was over."

In 1884, the total number of hides brought to the Northern Pacific fit in a single boxcar. "One by one, we runners put up our buffalo rifles, sold them, gave them away, or kept them for other hunting, and left the ranges," Frank Mayer remembered. "And there settled over them a vast quiet punctuated at night by the snarls and howls of prairie wolves as they prowled through the carrion and found living very good. The buffalo was gone."

The hide hunters went broke. Some turned to killing other animals for the market—like antelope, elk, and grizzly bears. Many left to pursue other work, somewhere else. The Native people had no choice. They had to stay—and, without buffalo meat to supplement their meager government rations, many of them starved.

On the Blackfeet reservation, an inspector checked on twenty-three lodges in one village. He reported seeing a rabbit being cooked in one and a steer hoof in another; the other twenty-one lodges didn't have any food at all. Six hundred Blackfeet—a quarter of the tribe—perished during the winter of famine. The same sense of devastation and disbelief settled over other Plains tribes, as the Crow woman Pretty Shield recounted:

Nobody believed, even then, that the white man could kill all the buffalo. Since the beginning of things there had always been so many! And yet the white man did this—even when he did not want the meat.

Not believing their own eyes, our hunters rode very far looking for buffalo, so far away that even if they had found a herd we could not have reached it in half a moon.

"Nothing; we found nothing," they told us; and then, hungry, they stared at the empty plains, as though dreaming.

"I think it was, in fact, I *know* it was so devastating to our people, especially the ones who were supposed to take care of us, realizing they can't hunt for us anymore, realizing there was nothing there anymore," said Gerard Baker:

That would have been the most heartbreaking thing. I couldn't imagine the people, what they went through, especially a father, saying, "I've got to, I've got to take care of my children. I've got to take care of my clan. I've got to take care of my society and I can't do it." You're not a man anymore. Even though it's not your fault, this is the way the men think.

Marcia Pablo, a Pend d'Oreille–Kootenai, called it "a spiritual trauma; we had the songs, but no buffalo to sing them to." "A cold wind blew across the prairie when the last buffalo fell," Sitting Bull said, "a death wind for my people."

As Frank Mayer had noted, with all the bison carcasses decaying on the Plains, the wolves "found the living very good." But not for long. Wolf skins were worth two dollars each in New York City. From Montana Territory to the Texas Panhandle, teams of "wolfers" found the easiest way to kill their prey was to lace a buffalo carcass with strychnine. The poison proved as effective as it was hideous: a death by asphyxiation that convulsed its victim into frozen contortions. "There are horrific descriptions of some of the wolfers coming up on a carcass that they've poisoned and they began to find dead animals a mile, mile and a half, away from the carcass," said Dan Flores. "It's as if some centrifuge has spun carcasses out in a circle around every one of these bait spots they set up. The wolfers were never surprised to find as many as fifty dead gray wolves around a single bait station that they created."

Wolves, of course, were not the only animals that feasted on buffalo carrion, or that could be killed by strychnine. Coyotes, foxes, badgers, bobcats, skunks, vultures, magpies, ravens, eagles—all paid a deadly price for what the hide hunters left behind. Before it died, a wolf often vomited, poisoning the grass and creating more collateral damage when Indian horses grazed in the area. The wolfers "didn't really worry about what they mistakenly killed," said Dan O'Brien, "but they killed a lot of stuff." No figures exist for the total number of animals that perished, but Flores estimates it may have equaled the death toll of the buffalo.

When the wolfers were done, another buffalo business sprang up. There was money to be made in the bison's skeletons—and there were millions of them bleaching under the prairie sun. Millions more rested under the prairie sod from buffalo that had died long before the arrival of the hide hunters. Companies in the East offered an average of eight dollars a ton for bones they could grind into fertilizer or use in refining sugar. Buffalo horns were turned into buttons, combs, and knife handles. Hooves became glue.

Homesteaders in Nebraska and Kansas, desperate for cash because drought was withering their crops, turned to harvesting the skulls and skeletons littering the Plains. One entrepreneur in Texas stacked mounds of bones along the tracks of the Fort Worth and Denver Railway and made $25,000. "Buffalo bones," a Kansas newspaper reported, "are [now] legal tender in Dodge City." A company in St. Louis processed more than 1 million *tons* of bison bones; the Michigan Carbon Works became Detroit's largest industry. In the end, the bone trade would generate more profits—for the bone pickers, the railroads, and the industries—than the buffalo hides ever had.

"Even what remained of them was being taken away from their ground," N. Scott Momaday said. "It was like grave robbing, in a way." Dan O'Brien compared it to "a society trying to clean up a crime scene. This is the murder of buffalo, our brothers. Let's get rid of that. Let's hide it. Gone. *Pshhh!* Expunged."

"So, they took everything from us, and we understood that as a way of killing us off," Gerard Baker said. "They killed the spirit of the buffalo, in some cases, we thought. But that's why our prayers got stronger. That's why our people got stronger. They had to. If they didn't, we would have been killed off like the buffalo. Even though they kind of went away, we still had that connection, and that's what helped us survive as Indian people."

A species once numbering in the tens of millions had been reduced to fewer than a thousand—mostly small groups of a dozen or less, scattered in different corners across the West. Even those survivors were under assault from hunters looking for trophy heads to hang on someone's wall. "It's stunning how quickly we switched from having what we deemed to be a harvestable surplus of buffalo to none," Steven Rinella said, "but, it was just, '*Bam!*' They were gone."

For Rosalyn LaPier, the slaughter of the bison herds raises a bigger issue. "Why Americans are so destructive, I think, is an important question to ask," she said:

Why is that part of our story? Why is that part of our history? Why is that part of who we are as a people—that one of the things we have done is completely destroy the grasslands, completely destroy all of the animal species, including the bison, and think about these places, not as places that are important to who we are as a nation, but places we see as a resource to be exploited?

The hide hunters delivered the fatal coup de grâce to a species that had already been declining, but placing all the blame on them as "sort of the dregs of society" misses the larger point, according to Elliott West. "If you look more closely at these hide hunters, what you find is, they were just like everybody else, just a cross section of American life, ordinary folks. This was the American society of the Gilded Age that destroyed the bison, or nearly destroyed the bison. So, instead, all you've done mythically is to turn the hunters into these sort of stinking fly-blown outcasts—and then we can walk away from them."

Market forces were equally culpable, according to Sara Dant. "You have to look at the market as one of the primary culprits," she said:

We commodified nature, all of it. Land as a commodity; buffalo as a commodity; wolf pelts as commodity. All of these things become caught up in a market that has a value system outside of a healthy functioning ecosystem. And we like to think that we can blame some nameless entity—"the government did it," or whatever— but the truth is, *we* did it. We killed them. We killed them to the point where we almost lost them. And that was a loss that the bison could not recover from without artificial assistance.

"This is the largest land mammal in North America, in the biggest biome in North America, and it nearly goes extinct," said Andrew Isenberg. "When something like that happens, there's going to be more than one cause. It's got to be a lot of things that are contributing to it."

Whatever the cause—or combination of causes—the unsettling, uncomfortable, even unforgivable result was an ecological tragedy of monumental proportions. Dan Flores described its scale:

> All these rotting carcasses, the smell that emanated from them, it was the tangible sensory endgame of ten thousand years of North American ecology. Think about that for a second. Not very many places in the world can say that their landscape has a moment in time, where you could actually engage in a sensory apprehension of the end of ten thousand years. But that happened on the American Great Plains, on the southern Plains in the 1870s and on the northern Plains in the 1880s.
>
> There is no story anywhere in world history that involves as large a destruction of wild animals as happened in North America, in the western United States in particular, between 1800 and about 1890. It is the largest destruction of animal life discoverable in modern world history.
>
> This is one of the worst black marks, really, on the whole American historical story. It's a world that doesn't even last eight more decades after Lewis and Clark see it.

A Native American contemplates the railroad that would soon bring momentous changes to his homeland (opposite). The "Iron Horse" transported waves of Euro-American settlers to the Plains, who harvested "buffalo chips" for fuel (top) and built homesteads on the bison range (above).

THE KANSAS PACIFIC RAILWAY.
No. 2. Taxidermist's Department of the Kansas Pacific Railway.
Buffalo Heads used for advertising purposes.
PHOTO. BY R. BENECKE, ST. LOUIS, MO.

To promote its new railroad, the Kansas Pacific displayed bison heads (above) and ran excursion trains (right) for passengers to see—and shoot—at the herds. William F. Cody (opposite, top) was hired to supply meat to the construction crews, and earned the name "Buffalo Bill."

The Kiowa chief Satanta (top left) and the Comanche chief Ten Bears (top right) objected to the provisions of the Medicine Lodge Treaty in 1867 in Kansas (above). But the tribes agreed to move to reservations, after being promised that they would retain traditional hunting rights where the buffalo still roamed.

At the Fort Laramie Treaty conference in Wyoming Territory in 1868, one of the lead government negotiators was General William Tecumseh Sherman, now in command of the Army in the West (at top, sitting third from left; above, standing third from left).

NEBRASKA.—THE GRAND DUKE ALEXIS KILLING HIS FIRST BUFFALO, AT THE HUNT WITH THE INDIAN CHIEFS ON THE PLAINS.—FROM A SKETCH BY OUR SPECIAL ARTIST.

Russia's Grand Duke Alexis was hosted at an elaborate buffalo hunt that drew national attention. After he (top, center) and Lieutenant Colonel George Armstrong Custer (top, left) later posed for a studio photograph, Buffalo Bill superimposed his own image on some copies to share the limelight.

Young George Bird Grinnell (left) came west to dig for fossil bones, but returned to participate with Native people in a buffalo hunt (like the one above) and to learn the Indians' beliefs and traditional ways (below).

When tanners learned how to use buffalo hides for belts running industrial machinery (above), Dodge City, Kansas (top), became a boomtown.

Frank Mayer (left) joined thousands of other hide hunters (below) hoping to strike it rich. Rather than chasing bison on horseback, a new technique called "the stand" (bottom) made the killing more efficient and methodical.

Scenes of the slaughter: dead carcasses littered the Plains, but skinners usually took only the hides and tongues, leaving the rest to rot.

At camp (opposite, top) the hides were stretched for scraping, then taken by wagon to town (above) to be stacked for shipment east by railroad (opposite, bottom). After washing up and changing clothes, hide hunters proudly posed for photographs, sometimes using buffalo heads as props (top).

EVERY Evening.

VOL. III.—NO. 111.   WILMINGTON, DEL., MONDAY, JANUARY 12, 1874.   PRICE ON

VANDAL BISON HUNTERS.

Indiscriminate Slaughter of Buffaloes on the Plains—The Animals Will Soon Become Extinct—Skulls and Bones Bleaching Upon Every Acre of Their Range.

The Rocky Mountain (Denver) News says: The buffaloes of the plains have met their fate. Encroaching civilization has seal d their doom; and the inordinate greed of man has swept them from the face of the earth. Where years ago the mammoth herds of bison roamed the plains and were hunted only by the Indians as necessity demanded, now let the bleaching bones of millions of these noble animals sacrificed simply for their hides. For the past two years the work of destruction and annihilation has gone forward, and to-day there are not enough buffaloes to form what was at one time considered a moderate sized herd.

emotion except they follow ideas. They except inferentiated truths. Take John Calvin; he was a kind of christian Plato, without Plato's heart. For with John Calvin the great trouble was that he had no heart.

THE LAST BUFFALO.

"Don't shoot, my good fellow! Here, take my 'robe,' save your ammunition, and let me go in peace."

Newspaper headlines and magazine illustrations in the East (opposite and top) prompted a number of buffalo protection bills to be proposed in Congress. In 1874, one sponsored by Greenbury Lafayette Fort of Illinois (above, left) but opposed by Ohio's James Garfield (above, right) passed the House and Senate. It was "pocket vetoed" by President Ulysses S. Grant.

As a young warrior, Quanah of the Comanches (opposite) harbored an implacable hatred for Texans and hide hunters. His mother, Cynthia Ann Parker (above), had been taken captive by Comanches as a child, then married a prominent chief. But in 1860, Texas Rangers had raided their village and taken her and her baby daughter back against her will. They both died among the whites.

The cattleman and former Texas Ranger Charles Goodnight (above, left). The Comanche medicine man Isatai (above, right), who with Quanah led the attack on the hide hunters at Adobe Walls (below).

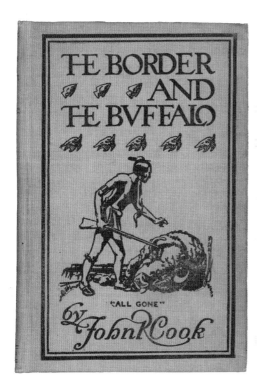

Years after their days as hide hunters, an aging John Cook (above) wrote a book about his exploits, and J. Wright Mooar (below, on right) displayed the hide of a white buffalo he said he had killed back in 1876.

To evade the Army's relentless retaliation for Custer's defeat
at the Little Bighorn in 1876, Sitting Bull (left) and his band of
Hunkpapa Lakotas had escaped to Canada. But when the buffalo
herds there dwindled, in 1881 he led his people back across the
border, and they were sent to the Standing Rock reservation
in what is now North Dakota (below), where Sitting Bull said,
"A warrior I have been; now it is all over."

Within just two years of the railroad's arrival in Montana Territory, the hide hunters had virtually eliminated the herds on the northern Plains. Tribes like the Blackfeet (top) grieved family members who starved to death; a Mandan man (opposite) offered prayers for the buffalo to return. Wolves and other scavengers feasting on bison carcasses, laced with strychnine, died in uncountable numbers (above).

Buffalo bones became the next
bonanza—gathered, transported,
and then ground up for fertilizer or
used in refining sugar. The Michigan
Carbon Works (right) became
Detroit's largest industry.

PART TWO

Back from
the Brink

SEVEN

Just in the Nick of Time

We are the most dangerous species of life on the planet, and every other species, even the Earth itself, has cause to fear our power to exterminate.

But we are also the only species which, when it chooses to do so, will go to great effort to save what it might destroy.

WALLACE STEGNER

Having survived the mass extinction of larger animals twelve thousand years earlier, by the mid-1880s the American buffalo now faced its own existential crisis. Most people believed that the continent's most magnificent creature was about to disappear forever.

"The first time I met a buffalo, I looked into his eyes, and it was like looking into the past and the future at the same time, because I really do think that they have seen the whole tragedy that has played out on the Great Plains," said Dan O'Brien:

And when you look in their eyes, there's an intelligence there that we recognize. And a sadness. And a lot of wisdom. I think that one of the ways they survive, and had survived for thousands of years, is they turn into the wind.

They move *through* the storm, rather than being chased by the storm. I've never lost one in a storm. When I ran cattle, we lost a lot of cattle in storms. Cattle go *with* the storm. The same storm can snow on them for three days because they keep moving away. A buffalo goes the other way, and the storm doesn't last as long because they go through it.

They are survivors. They've evolved, and their genes are telling them they're going to survive. They're tough as hell. And I think that that same thing that drives them to turn into a storm and to walk forward, is why we still have buffalo today.

They've gone through some terrible, terrible situations at the hands of man, but they keep facing into the wind, and they keep going.

At the same time that the American buffalo was facing extinction, Native Americans of the West had been dispossessed of most of their homelands, confined to reservations, and deprived of an animal that had fed their bodies and nourished their spirits for untold generations. Some thought the Indians, too, had become a "vanishing race." Growing up on the Fort Belknap reservation in north-central Montana, George Horse Capture Jr. said, he was taught a lesson his elders had learned from the bison. "'Turn and face the day' is something you hear when you're having a hard time," he remembered:

They say it's the way the buffalo is built—[in front] he's all shaggy, he's all "wooled up," and on the tail end, it's not the same kind of fur, not as thick, not as long. So, they say, in a bad storm, a buffalo has to turn and face that storm or else things won't be good for him. And I heard that saying, and as I started looking at them, it made sense to me. If you don't face the day, you don't face the storm, there could be problems.

As the nineteenth century ended, an unlikely group of Americans would begin to try, somehow, to pull the buffalo back from the brink of extinction. "The creature of the American West was the bison," said the historian Clay Jenkinson. "They're the symbol of America, with a capital 'A.' And to think that our Indian policy and our greed and our industrialization would just blink this thing out and we would just say, 'Well, that was then and this is now,' that

seems like a repudiation, somehow, of the very idea of America."
Dustin Tahmahkera, a Comanche cultural historian, linked the effort
to preserve the bison to the larger story of Native people's struggles
to survive during their darkest times: "Helping to bring these buffalo
back—I know there is such strength and resilience to where this is
not just a story of tragedy. This is a story of persevering and continuing on, forging new alliances, forging new partnerships, no matter
how tense they may be at times."

The road back would begin in different places, with different
people prompted by different, sometimes contradictory motiva-
tions. Unorganized at first, the individual efforts would slowly gain
momentum and then coalesce into a national effort to save the
national mammal from becoming just a memory.

"The early history of the modern conservation movement is full
of people who did the right thing for the wrong reasons, and the
wrong thing for the right reasons," said the writer Michelle Nijhuis.
"Many of the people who wanted to save the bison were motivated
by reasons that were all wrapped up with nationalism, in some cases
racism, and their own ideas about who they were and what the nation
should be. And then there were people who genuinely loved these
species and wanted to see them survive."

"There were a lot of things contributing to the near extinction of
that bison," according to the historian Andrew Isenberg:

> What that also means is that many things had to contribute to
> the preservation of the bison from extinction. The impulses of
> the people trying to preserve the bison from extinction are cer-
> tainly confused, [but] we can say that were it not for these people,
> with their particular motivations, the bison might well have gone
> extinct.

In the fall of 1883, a young New York assemblyman, the son of one
of Manhattan's most prominent families, became alarmed by reports
that the vast herds of buffalo were quickly disappearing from the
Great Plains. So he hurried west on the Northern Pacific Railway and

disembarked when he reached the Little Missouri River in the heart of the Badlands in what is now North Dakota. His name was Theodore Roosevelt. He was twenty-four years old—and he feared that the bison would all be gone before he had the chance to shoot one.

Six years earlier, in 1877, Roosevelt's younger brother Elliott (age seventeen at the time) had traveled to the Texas Panhandle during the massive slaughter on the southern Plains, simply for the adventure of hunting bison on horseback. Elliott's account—of riding up close enough to a bull to almost touch it with his hand; of killing five bison during a stampede that sounded like thunder; and of having most of his group's horses stolen by Comanches—had sparked tinges of jealousy in Theodore, who got off his train at two o'clock in the morning of September 8, determined to bring home his own buffalo head as a trophy. He tracked down a local guide named Joe Ferris, and they soon set off into the broken terrain.

Things did not go well. Rain fell for days, no bison was found, and "bad luck," Ferris recalled, "followed like a yellow dog follows a drunkard." The only game animal they saw was a mule deer, which Ferris brought down after Roosevelt's shot missed. Then they spied three old bulls in the distance, and decided to sneak up on them by crawling on the ground. "While doing this I blundered into a bed of cactus and filled my hands with the spines," Roosevelt wrote. He managed to get off a shot, and slightly wounded one of the bulls, but all three bison galloped off. Back on their horses, the two men rode eight miles in pursuit, before coming up on the buffalo at sunset. The wounded bull charged at them, and as Roosevelt took aim with his rifle, his horse's head moved and knocked the barrel into Theodore's forehead, opening a gash that poured blood into his eyes. The three buffalo disappeared. That night, a wolf spooked the men's horses from camp, and they spent hours tracking them down.

The next morning, they discovered another small group of bison. With a cold rain beating into his eyes, Roosevelt drew a bead on one of them. "I now made one of those misses which a man to his dying day always looks back upon with wonder and regret," he wrote. "I missed clean, and the whole band plunged into a hollow and were off before, with my stiffened and numbed fingers, I could get another shot." The mishaps kept piling up, one after another. Roosevelt's horse tripped in a hole and pitched him ten feet onto the ground; later, crossing what looked like a dry creek, it sank into a hidden mud hole and had to be dragged out with a rope. "Everything goes wrong that can," said Clay Jenkinson. "And Joe Ferris keeps saying, 'Maybe, we should go back. Come back next year.' And Roosevelt says, 'No, we're going to get a buffalo.'" They slept in wet blankets and, with no dry wood for a fire, lived on cold biscuits for meals. Ferris remembered Roosevelt one morning saying, "By Godfrey, but this is fun."

Finally, they encountered a big bull. This time, Roosevelt brought it down. He let out a whoop, did a dance around the carcass, and took out a hundred-dollar bill and presented it to Ferris as a bonus. They cut off some hump meat for a meal and then removed the bull's head, a "most tedious and tiresome work," Roosevelt wrote. But he was elated:

> The very toil I had been obliged to go through, in order to procure the head, made me feel all the prouder of it when it was at last in my possession.
>
> I felt the most exulting pride as I handled and examined him; for I had procured a trophy such as can fall henceforth to few hunters indeed.

Before heading home, Roosevelt impulsively invested some of his inheritance in one of the many cattle ranches spreading across the former buffalo range, during what was promoted as the "Beef Bonanza." He would return off and on for the next four years—to pursue what he called "the strenuous life" and to escape the grief he suffered when his wife and his mother died on the same day. "Black Care," he said, "rarely sits behind a rider whose pace is fast enough."

With Vic Smith, a former hide hunter, he went after other game, including grizzly bears, elk, antelope, mountain sheep, and moose—and another buffalo west of Yellowstone National Park—adding more trophies to the walls of his home at Sagamore Hill. His investment in ranching went bust during the fierce winter of 1886–87, remembered as the "Great Die-Up," in which hundreds of thousands of cattle drifted with repeated snow and ice storms, and froze to death. But Roosevelt had become, in his words, "at heart as much a Westerner as I am an Easterner." In a book he wrote about those times, *Hunting Trips of a Ranchman*, he bemoaned—and yet simultaneously justified—the wholesale slaughter that had befallen the buffalo, calling it "a veritable tragedy of the animal world . . . without parallel in historic times.

> While the slaughter of the buffalo has been in places needless and brutal, and while it is to be greatly regretted that the species is likely to become extinct, . . . it must be remembered that . . . its destruction was the condition [necessary for] the advance of white civilization in the West. . . .
>
> Above all, the extermination of the buffalo was the only way of solving the Indian question . . . and its disappearance was the only method of forcing them to at least partially abandon their savage mode of life.
>
> From the standpoint of humanity at large, the extermination of the buffalo has been a blessing . . . and I suppose the comparatively few of us who would have preferred the continuance of the old order of things, merely for the sake of our own selfish enjoyment, have no right to complain.

Shortly after the book's release, a review appeared in *Forest and Stream* magazine, written by George Bird Grinnell:

> Where Mr. Roosevelt details his own adventures he is accurate, and his story, in simple, pleasant fashion . . . at once brings us in sympathy with him.
>
> We are sorry to see that a number of hunting myths are given as fact, but it was after all scarcely to be expected that with the author's limited experience he could sift the wheat from the chaff and distinguish the true from the false.
>
> [His] experience of the Western country is quite limited, but this very fact in one way lends an added charm to his book.

Roosevelt took offense, and tracked Grinnell down at his office to complain. But the two men quickly realized they shared much in common: they both came from wealthy Manhattan families, and both had developed a love of the West and its big game animals. They turned the awkward moment into the beginning of a lasting friendship. "I think, between the two of them, that Grinnell is the conservationist who loves hunting," said Michael Punke. "I think Roosevelt is a little bit more of the hunter who comes to have an appreciation for conservationism." The difference was evident in another way. Roosevelt had two buffalo heads mounted on the wall of his home in Sagamore Hill; Grinnell kept two bleached buffalo skulls in his office—not as trophies, but as reminders of the bison's fate.

Together, they formed the Boone and Crockett Club to promote what they called "the manly sport" of hunting. At its first meeting, Roosevelt was elected president. "To these men—wealthy, exclusively white sport hunters—there was no contradiction between their concern for conservation and their love of hunting," Michelle Nijhuis said:

> They wanted to protect these species because they wanted to continue hunting them. I think their motivations were extremely complicated. Roosevelt's motivations were tied up with his own nationalism. He wanted to preserve what he saw as these American ideals. He wanted to preserve it in order to protect his own ideas about national progress, about white masculinity, about his own race.

Andrew Isenberg contended that in Roosevelt's promotion of "the strenuous life," "the manly sport" of hunting reflected a growing anxiety among certain men of the time:

> At the end of the nineteenth century, there are a lot of men who are terribly concerned that this increasingly urban and comfortable and cosmopolitan American society is pampering American men and making them too "soft," and so, what American men need

to do is, they need to experience the frontier, as these guys imagined their forefathers had, and this will toughen them up.

At the same time it promoted sports hunting, the Boone and Crockett Club also dedicated itself to "the preservation of the large game of this country" and called for strict regulations against the rampant market hunting that was destroying species of birds and animals across the nation. Through his friendship with Grinnell, Roosevelt was beginning to broaden his view about Americans' responsibilities toward wildlife—including the buffalo. "Those guys first started introducing the idea that we have to operate with restraint, and that was a revolutionary idea," said Steven Rinella, "this idea that we have wildlife that is owned by the public—the American people own wildlife. And the government, state and federal governments, will help regulate it on our behalf. We're going to make rules that we live by. We're going to identify those areas that are proven to be most catastrophic for wildlife populations, like unregulated market hunting, and do away with those things."

In early 1886, William T. Hornaday, the chief taxidermist of the Smithsonian Institution in Washington, was asked by the museum's director to make an inventory of the collection of bison skins and skeletons in storage. He quickly reported back that they didn't have much—and all of it was in poor condition. He started devising a plan to correct the problem.

At age thirty-two, Hornaday had already gained a reputation among his colleagues for impatience and arrogance, but he had also distinguished himself as someone who could hunt down exotic species and preserve them for display. He had grown up in Iowa, was orphaned at age fourteen, and studied taxidermy on a scholarship at Iowa State Agricultural College. He later landed a job with Ward's Natural Science Establishment in Rochester, New York, which specialized in providing museums with specimens from around the world. For nearly a decade, Hornaday led many of the company's most famous expeditions. In Florida, he became the first to confirm that crocodiles lived in North America, bringing back a fourteen-footer he had killed for display at the nation's centennial celebration. During two years in India, Malaysia, and Borneo, he skinned out a giant elephant, collected forty-three orangutans, and shot the biggest Bengal tiger ever killed at the time. Hornaday's account of his journey became a best-selling travel book. Now, he set his sights on the American buffalo. Michelle Nijhuis described the surprise that soon confronted him:

> He realized that the most well-appointed museum in the United States had very few specimens of one of the most iconic species on the continent, and he assumed, "Well, this is just an oversight, I'm going to get more of these." So, he wrote to people, all over the Plains, and said, "Where can I find bison hides? Bison skulls? Our collection needs them." And all of his contacts wrote back and said, "Good luck. There are no more bison; there are hardly any bison."
>
> And for Hornaday, who had spent his twenties hunting and killing animals all over the world, this came as a real shock. He described it as a "hammer blow to the head." A species that, to him and to many other people, defined the nation, was so rare that the Smithsonian Institution, the most prominent museum in the country, couldn't get hold of a skull or a hide at any price?

But one of his correspondents alerted Hornaday that a few bison had been spotted between the Yellowstone and Missouri Rivers in Montana Territory. He immediately took the train to Miles City, in hopes that he could kill some for the museum. With two assistants, a couple of hired cowboys, a Cheyenne Indian guide, and an escort of five soldiers, Hornaday was soon crossing the rugged landscape near the Missouri River Breaks, which was strewn with what he called "ghastly monuments of slaughter"—bones, sometimes entire skeletons and heads—that his group rode by in silence. "It was impossible to look at one without a sigh," he wrote, "and each group of skeletons brought back the old thoughts, 'What a pity! What a pity!'"

After two weeks of fruitless searching, they came upon a few surviving buffalo. They shot one old bull, but Hornaday considered it unsuitable for a museum display because most of its fur had already been shed in the late spring. They encountered three cows and a small calf; the cows got away, but one of the cowboys lassoed the calf. Hornaday named it "Sandy" and decided to bring it back with him, alive, on the train to Washington and the Smithsonian, where it quickly became a public attraction.

Hornaday was back in Montana in September, when whatever bison he could find would have full winter coats. After two months, he and his crew finally found and killed more than twenty specimens, including one gigantic bull. In its body he found four bullets from previous hunters. "He described shooting the bison, watching it struggle to keep its feet, and just glaring at him with rage," Michelle Nijhuis said. "And Hornaday was a man who had hunted animals all over the world. He enjoyed the hunt. But, as he remembered it, he truly felt regret at the death of this majestic bison." Like Roosevelt, Hornaday expressed mixed feelings about killing two dozen remaining members of a species that seemed to be headed for extinction, but rationalized what he had done:

> If [anyone] should feel doubtful about the ethical propriety of our last buffalo hunt, and the killing that we had to do in order that our National Museum might secure a few good wild skins out of the wreck of the millions, let him feel assured our task was no means a pleasant one.
>
> I am really ashamed to confess it, but we have been guilty of killing buffalo in the year of the Lord 1886. Under different circumstances, nothing could have induced me to engage in such a mean, cruel, and utterly heartless enterprise as the hunting down of the last representatives of a vanishing race. But there is no alternative.
>
> Between leaving them to be killed by the care-for-naught cowboys, who would leave them to decay, body and soul, where they fell, and killing them ourselves for the purpose of preserving their remains, there really was no choice.

Perhaps you think a wild animal has no soul, but let me tell you it has. Its skin is its soul, and when mounted by skillful hands, it becomes comparatively immortal.

Another bull was shot just before sunset, more than eight miles from their camp, and they decided to leave it for the night. When they returned the next day, they found that Indians had stripped the carcass, not only of its hide, but also of its flesh and tongue. The head was untouched, except that one side was painted yellow and the other painted red. "And Hornaday falls into a fit of anger—'They desecrated my buffalo; they've spoiled it!'—and he thinks it's vandalism," Clay Jenkinson said. "It's not vandalism. Natives have come and they have harvested the meat, which he wasn't going to do. They've taken the hide for their own uses. And then they have done the most important thing, which is to bow, in a sacred way, to this creature by painting it and positioning the skull. They're essentially saying, 'This is what you do when you kill this creature. You honor it. And you harvest it and use everything you can from it. And then, you find a sacred way of gratitude for the thing that it gave you.' And he misses the lesson. It's a sacred thing that they've done, and he's pissed off because they stole his specimen? But it's a great parable of the cultures."

"No one knows exactly what ceremony got performed around this particular buffalo," Dan Flores said, "but an animal whose head is painted like that, among some Native peoples, symbolizes an ending of things, a transition from one moment in time to another one. As the Crow leader, Plenty Coups, put it when he saw that the buffalo were gone, as far as he was concerned, nothing else happened in history. That was the end of history."

In 1805, in this same part of Montana, the Lewis and Clark expedition had encountered so many buffalo that the men had to throw sticks and stones at them, just to get them out of the way. Also in the same area, only six years before Hornaday's harvest of twenty-three specimens in the course of two months, a hide hunter could have killed more than that many bison in a morning's work. "We got in our expedition just in the nick of time," Hornaday proudly wrote to his superiors in Washington, estimating that perhaps only fifty free-ranging bison were left in all of Montana—and they would probably be gone by the end of winter. He was right. The next year, a collecting expedition from the American Museum of Natural History in New York City scoured the same region for three months. It did not find a single buffalo.

Back at the Smithsonian, Hornaday eagerly started work on a new way of displaying his specimens. He placed six of them in a group: the huge bull he had killed, a younger bull, a yearling, two cows—and Sandy, the little calf, which had died in captivity. All were positioned around a small alkaline watering hole near some clusters of sagebrush, buffalo grass, and prickly pear cactus brought back from Montana. They would be enclosed in the largest display case ever made for the museum: a glass cube sixteen feet wide, twelve feet deep, and ten feet high that would allow visitors to view the buffalo from all sides. As a taxidermist, he considered it his masterpiece.

"It was a revolutionary way of displaying quadrupeds," Clay Jenkinson said. "Hornaday was a little like Michelangelo with the Sistine Chapel. He was a bit of a prima donna. No one was to see it till he was finished." During his work on the display in the Hall of Mammals, he draped the enclosure with canvas to avoid distracting interruptions from onlookers. But in the spring of 1888, an impetuous stranger managed to get in and excitedly began peppering Hornaday with questions about the size of the big bull, what kind of rifle had been used to bring it down, and where the kill had taken place, guessing correctly that it had been on the Sunday Creek Trail on a ranch in eastern Montana. Annoyed but intrigued, Hornaday asked the man his name. The stranger stuck out his hand and introduced himself: "The name's Theodore—Theodore Roosevelt." With the handshake, another improbable fellowship of the bison began.

When it opened to the public, Hornaday's display became one of the museum's most popular displays. "It allowed people to get closer to a bison, or a replica of a bison, than certainly anyone should get to a bison in real life," said Michelle Nijhuis. "They were able to see how large these full-grown bison were in comparison to themselves. They were able to imagine what it might be like to have a bison's eyes on you, following you around as you moved. They were able to get a sense of these animals as living beings." (The so-called Hornaday Group would thrill the Smithsonian's visitors for nearly seventy years. As it was being taken down in 1957, the staff found a handwritten note from Hornaday, who had assumed that living bison might no longer exist in posterity. It said that he, personally, had killed them and apologized that future taxidermists might find his techniques crude. "When I am dust and ashes," he wrote, "I beg you to protect these specimens from deterioration and destruction as they are among the last of their kind." The collection was saved and ultimately restored and can still be seen at a small museum in Fort Benton, Montana, not all that far from where he shot them.)

At the start, Hornaday's intention had been scientific, but he began to see what he had done as more than a work of taxidermic excellence, according to Nijhuis:

> Hornaday thought, "This is my skillset. I am newly aware of this crisis. I'm going to use my skills to show people what's being lost. And, at the very least, I can preserve some specimens for science and I can show the public the dimensions of this tragedy." It was one of the only ways for people in the urban United States to get a sense of the majesty of this animal.

Hornaday hoped his display would help galvanize the public against the final extermination of bison in North America. He blamed the destruction on market forces and what he called "man's reckless greed," but he also believed that it had gone unchecked because of the apathy of average Americans. His new mission was to change that.

He was already writing a book, *The Extermination of the American Bison*, angrily chronicling the animal's demise and including a detailed map that showed how the buffalo's range—which once stretched from the East Coast to west of the Rockies, and from Mexico into Canada—had steadily collapsed since the 1700s. Based on his research, he estimated that there were now 541 bison in the United

States—256 living in a few zoos or privately owned herds, about 200 in Yellowstone National Park, and only 85 roaming free and unprotected on the Plains. Ironically, the Atchison, Topeka and Santa Fe Railway, which had once promoted excursions to shoot buffalo, now held 10 bison as a tourist attraction in Bismarck Grove, Kansas. Canada, Hornaday estimated, also had roughly 550 living bison in the Northwest Territories.

He was particularly incensed by the relentless work of the hide hunters over the previous fifteen years—and by the government's complete failure to do anything to save the species. It was all part, he said, of a larger "war on wildlife" that had reached a crescendo in the last decades:

> Here is an inexorable law of nature to which there are no exceptions: no wild species of bird, mammal, reptile, or fish can withstand exploitation for commercial purposes. Probably never before in the history of the world, until civilized man came in contact with the buffalo, did whole armies of men march out in true military style ... and make war on wild animals. No wonder the buffalo has been exterminated.
>
> Its record is a disgrace to the American people in general, and the territorial, state, and general government in particular. It will cause succeeding generations to regard us as being possessed of ... cruelty and greed.
>
> During the existence of the buffalo it was declared by many an impossibility to stop or prevent the slaughter. Such an accusation of weakness and imbecility on the part of the general government is an insult to our strength and resources. The protection of game is now and always has been simply a question of money.
>
> At last the game butchers of the great West have stopped killing buffalo. The buffalo are all dead!

He sarcastically noted that Montana had passed a law against killing bison—ten years after they had been slaughtered—and predicted that Texas might do likewise, now that the buffalo there had been eradicated. "With such a lesson before our eyes, confirmed in every detail by living testimony," he wrote, "who will dare to say that there will be an elk, moose, caribou, mountain sheep, mountain goat, antelope, or black-tail deer left alive in the United States in a wild state fifty years from this date, ay, or even twenty five?"

"Hornaday was not a shy man," Michelle Nijhuis said. "He was happy to trumpet the popularity and success of his display, and he started to think bigger. The next step, he thought, would be to begin to raise bison in captivity, so that the urban public could see real bison in real life." Hornaday had persuaded the Smithsonian to start a small zoo on its grounds on the National Mall. It included some deer, prairie dogs, bears—even a golden eagle donated by President Grover Cleveland—and four bison that had been captured in the Black Hills. People flocked to see them, making the site crowded with both animals and humans. Hornaday began pushing for a more spacious location. With congressional approval, he scouted the Rock Creek Park area of Washington and selected a site for a proper national zoo. Theodore Roosevelt, now the U.S. Civil Service commissioner in the capital and a rising political star, became an ally. "Whenever you really, really need me," he assured Hornaday, "call me."

EIGHT

CHANGES OF HEART

IN 1886, the same year as William T. Hornaday's expeditions to Montana, a former hide hunter named Charles Jesse Jones left his home near Garden City, Kansas, and headed southwest toward the Texas Panhandle, where ten years earlier he had taken part in the destruction of the buffalo herds on the southern Plains. The trip brought back painful memories:

> Often while hunting these animals as a business, I fully realized the cruelty of slaying the poor creatures. Many times did I "swear off," and would promise myself to break my gun over a wagon wheel when I got back to camp; yet always hesitated to do so until several hours had elapsed.
>
> The next morning, I would hear the guns of other hunters booming in all directions, and would say to myself that even if I did not kill any more, the buffalo would soon all be killed anyway. Again, I would shoulder my rifle, to repeat the previous day's murder.
>
> I am positive it was the wickedness committed in killing so many, that impelled me to take measures for perpetuating the race, which I had helped to almost destroy.

As a boy in Illinois, Jones had demonstrated a talent for capturing wild animals—squirrels, bullfrogs, even rattlesnakes—and taming them for resale. At twenty-one, he moved to eastern Kansas, where he tried to raise fruit trees; went farther west to homestead; and then, like thousands of other men struggling in the financial depression of the 1870s, became a buffalo hide hunter, at first making good money, often killing more than ten a day. There were other Joneses on the Plains at the time, and to keep them straight, the other hunters gave them nicknames: "Dirty Face" Jones, "Wrong Wheel" Jones. Charles Jesse Jones became, simply, "Buffalo" Jones, because he had achieved notoriety by capturing calves to sell for $7.50 each, or to bring them to county fairs and bet men that they couldn't be lassoed by anyone but himself.

When the once-massive herds began to dwindle, he sometimes argued with other hide hunters he met, including Frank Mayer, who recalled Jones lecturing them at their camp one morning: "'You and the other runners are a passel of damn fools, the way you are wiping out the buffalo. Don't you realize that in just a few years there won't be a damn buffalo left in the world?' No one would believe him. He was smarter than the rest of us. I admit it now. I wouldn't admit it on that Sunday in camp."

In 1879, the founders of Garden City, Kansas, recognized Jones's flair for promotion and hired him to help them persuade the Atchison, Topeka and Santa Fe to make it a depot stop on their railroad line. He laid out Jones Avenue (ten miles long); sold house lots; imported trees to add to the town's only existing tree; and in the town center constructed a series of limestone buildings he called the Buffalo Block, with a Buffalo Hotel.

After a fierce winter storm devastated the cattle herds on the southern Plains, he remembered seeing buffalo unfazed by similar weather. By his account, this gave him an idea:

> I thought to myself, "Why not domesticate this wonderful beast which can endure such a blizzard. . . . Why not infuse this hardy blood into our native cattle, and have a perfect animal?
>
> Where then is the animal that can compare with the buffalo? I will chain him and domesticate a race of cattle equal to, if not superior to, all ruminants heretofore known.

Dating back to the first Spanish conquistadors in the 1500s and some American colonists in the 1700s, others had previously considered the same possibility. But for Jones, the idea took on a new urgency. He believed that the bison might still have a future—if he could start a herd—and he was not shy about claiming the idea as his own. So he set off for the Texas Panhandle, where a few wild bands of buffalo were said to still be roaming. He managed to locate and lasso eighteen calves to bring back to Kansas, feeding them condensed milk on the route. Ten survived the trip.

He supplemented his herd by going to Canada and buying eighty-six bison, part of a private herd that had been started in the early 1870s by Charles Alloway and James McKay, both of Scots and Métis lineage. Traveling with a Métis hunting brigade, they had captured three calves, then three more, and started breeding them; in 1880, their herd was purchased by Colonel Samuel Bedson, the warden of the penitentiary in Stony Mountain, Manitoba, who grazed them on the prison grounds—and crossbred some of them with cattle. Jones made his purchase, loaded the buffalo into railroad stock cars, and headed back to Kansas with great fanfare. Crowds gathered at railroad depots to see his buffalo pass by. In Kansas City, where he invited a hundred members of the Kansas legislature to a private viewing, thirteen bison broke loose and stampeded down the streets before finally being recaptured. Jones didn't mind the trouble; he basked in the publicity it created.

He made even bigger news in 1889, when he mounted another foray into Texas, which he dubbed "The Last Buffalo Hunt." He sent regular dispatches by homing pigeons to Garden City, where they were telegraphed to the *Chicago Times*. During his three-month search, he located a small herd near Palo Duro Canyon and tried to drive it back to Kansas, though most turned back and he ultimately arrived home with only seven more calves. "He was kind of an adventurer figure from the nineteenth century," Dan Flores said, "and he would have translated well, I think, into reality TV. I do like the fact that he confronted his culpability and took on the responsibility of trying to save the animals that he had almost obliterated." Steven Rinella considers Jones a classic opportunist who "finds things to do to make a quick buck and pursues them. He becomes a collector of buffalo. He used to shoot them, now he collects them. Did he have a radical transformation? Maybe. I do believe he had a legitimate love for the animals, but he also had a love for the dollar."

Back at his ranch near Garden City, and at another he established near McCook, Nebraska, Jones experimented in crossing buffalo bulls with domestic cows—to create what he called "catalo." The results were mixed, at best. Too many cows died in calving, and too many calves were stillborn or sterile to make it as commercially profitable as he had hoped, though he continued promoting the idea and enjoyed newspaper accounts that called him "the owner of the only herd of domesticated buffalo in the world." Jones turned to trying to demonstrate that his buffalo could be useful. Milk from a domesticated bison cow, he claimed, was "the richest milk in the world," though the quantity was small (and probably not easy to obtain). He hooked two bulls to a cart he drove through Garden City and proposed that they be used to pull the town's streetcar. He claimed they could also be harnessed to a plow and a hay wagon, but they eventually proved too difficult to handle—stampeding for a nearby stream, taking everything, including Jones, with them.

Jones found better success in selling some of his bison to zoos and wealthy individuals interested in having their own herds. A dozen ended up in Utah, on Antelope Island in the Great Salt Lake, for a private hunting preserve. An English aristocrat bought ten bison for $1,000 each, creating a flurry of headlines when Jones arrived with them in Liverpool, where newspapers hailed him as the "Buffalo King." He later claimed that Britain's heir apparent, the Prince of Wales, invited him to a private meeting in Buckingham Palace, but he couldn't attend; instead, Jones said, he sent the future monarch a buffalo-hair rug and a picture of himself.

He would briefly go bankrupt in the 1890s—but he always found new ways to keep his name in the news. North of the Arctic Circle in Canada, he captured wild musk ox for American zoos; the Smithsonian sent him to Colorado to catch Rocky Mountain sheep; and, like Theodore Roosevelt, he wrote a popular book about his exploits, *Forty Years of Adventure*. But Buffalo Jones would always come back to the magnificent animal that had given him his nickname.

> I cannot think of much of anything but the possibility of doing something great with the buffaloes for humanity.
>
> My dream ... [is] a home for my little pets ... [to] let them roam at will with plenty of room for a long time.
>
> MOLLY GOODNIGHT

Molly Dyer had moved from Tennessee to Texas in 1854, at age fourteen. When both of her parents died, she took over caring for her five younger brothers and became a schoolteacher. In 1870, she married Charles Goodnight, who by that time was already a legend in Texas as an Indian fighter, Texas Ranger, cattle trail driver, and the first rancher in the Panhandle.

Being a cattleman, Goodnight had little sympathy for buffalo. On a trail drive in the 1860s, he had nearly lost his herd when a group of bison stampeded through them. At his ranch in the Palo Duro Canyon at the end of the Red River War, he had paid to have the buffalo in the canyon killed, so they wouldn't compete with his cattle for the grass. "Think of it in terms of what you might call the Great Ungulate Swap," Elliott West said. "Bison are subtracted; cattle are added. We're taking away the wild grazers, the wild ungulates, and replacing them with the ones that we own, the ones that we control. It's part of this larger process of a conquest of the West."

In 1878, Goodnight had sent some of his cowboys to drive the remaining bison out of the canyon and to shoot any stragglers. Molly, one of the cowboys remembered, "put a stop to the whole thing." She felt sorry for the buffalo, considered them worth preserving as part of the region's history, and asked her husband to find a few motherless calves she could nurture around the ranch house to keep her company. Her closest neighbor was seventy-five miles away. "[I was] not very enthusiastic over the suggestion," Charlie admitted, but he went out and roped a bull calf and a young female bison and brought them in for her. One of her brothers, working at the ranch, found a few more. When the calves matured, the bull impregnated two of the females, and a herd was started.

The bull, named Old Sikes, developed a penchant for making trouble around the cattle ranch. During feeding time at the horse corral, he stuck his head into the gate, lifted the whole thing up and off its hinges, then helped himself to the corn. He sometimes escaped his fenced pasture and wandered for months, only to show up during cattle roundups and disrupt everything. Once, when the bull got angry and chased a ranch hand back to the house, Charlie saddled up to set things straight. Old Sikes promptly chased him back, too.

In 1889, the Goodnights responded to William T. Hornaday's inquiries about private bison herds and wrote him that theirs now numbered thirteen. And Charlie—with Molly's encouragement—was trying to figure out how to make their herd grow and turn a profit. A buffalo, he said, has a brain a third larger than a domestic cow "and uses it." The best way to take care of them, he had learned, was "by just letting them alone. They won't live if they are penned up. They've got to have all the room they want."

Buffalo Bill was a good fellow, and while he was no great shakes as a scout as he made the eastern people believe, still we all liked him, and we had to hand it to him, because he was the only one that had brains enough to make that Wild West stuff pay money.

I remember one time he came into a saloon in North Platte, and he took off his hat and that long hair of his that he had rolled up under his hat fell down on his shoulders. It always bothered him, so he rolled it back under his hat again, and Brady the saloon man says: "Say, Bill, why the hell don't you cut the damn stuff off?"

And Cody says: "If I did, I'd starve to death."

TEDDY BLUE ABBOTT

By 1889, Buffalo Bill Cody was arguably the most famous American in the world. To millions of people he had become the dashing embodiment of a mythic West of bygone times. As a young man he had worked as a buffalo hunter for the railroads and as a scout for the Army during the Indian wars. His deeds were widely publicized—greatly exaggerated and sometimes created out of whole cloth—in scores of dime novels, some of which he turned into theatrical performances, always featuring Cody himself in the starring role. But the stage eventually proved too confining.

In 1883, he had launched "Buffalo Bill's Wild West," an outdoor show that promised "a year's visit West in three hours." It was, Cody said, "a noisy, rattling, gunpowder entertainment," featuring real cowboys and real Indians, Pony Express riders and Mexican vaqueros, and a series of vignettes supposedly demonstrating the history of the West—and Cody's glorified role in it. The authentic Deadwood Stagecoach was attacked—and saved by Buffalo Bill. A wagon train was raided—and saved by Buffalo Bill. A settler's cabin was surrounded by Indians and saved—by Buffalo Bill. A reenactment of the Battle of the Little Bighorn—"Custer's Last Stand"—ended with Buffalo Bill showing up while the words "TOO LATE" were displayed on a screen.

Each performance also included a stampede of buffalo and a mock hunt with Cody and his compatriots firing blank cartridges at the animals. The crowds couldn't get enough of it. "Everything that 'Buffalo Bill's Wild West' show was telling Americans is that this frontier experience is the quintessentially American experience; it's what makes Americans, Americans," said Andrew Isenberg. The nation's population was becoming increasingly urban and still concentrated principally in the East; for most Americans the West remained a place they had never seen in person. "What Cody did, brilliantly, is he said, 'I'll take the West to you,'" according to Elliott West. "'I'll carry it all out to New York City. I'll take it to Boston, or to Philadelphia. There, you can take part in it yourself, sit in the stands, and watch it all happen.'"

A million people attended his shows on Staten Island one summer. Another million paid to see him that winter at Madison Square Garden, where twenty of Cody's bison perished from pleuro-pneumonia. He managed to replenish them—from his ranch in Nebraska and, later, with seven he bought from Molly and Charles Goodnight's growing herd. Steven Rinella considers Cody a prime example of how the West had changed so dramatically:

> After killing four thousand of them, he became a guy that had this small collection of the animals and he's trying to prevent them from getting carried off by disease and coddling them, and wheeling and dealing in them, and paying far more money to maintain a herd than he ever made shooting the things in the first place.
>
> It's amazing how these transitions were so abrupt that a guy that kills four thousand then becomes a guy, within a decade or two, who's trying desperately to find a couple in order to take them on the road to teach people about what they lost—"they" being him, the other day. It's astounding.

Among the many spectators who flocked to Buffalo Bill's shows in New York City was the famous author Mark Twain, who sent him a letter suggesting that he consider an even larger audience. "Dear Mr. Cody," Twain wrote, "I have seen your Wild West show two days in succession, and have enjoyed it thoroughly. It is said on the other side of the water that none of the exhibitions which we send to England are purely and distinctively American. If you will take the Wild West show over there, you can remove that reproach."

In 1887, during his first stop for a triumphant tour of Europe, Cody arrived in England for the celebration of Queen Victoria's Golden Jubilee, bringing along ninety-seven Native Americans and eighteen buffalo. At one command performance, the Deadwood Stagecoach carried the kings of Denmark, Greece, Belgium, and Saxony, along with the Prince of Wales, while Cody himself drove the stage during a simulated Indian attack. "I've held four kings," Buffalo Bill told a reporter, "but four kings and the Prince of Wales makes a royal flush such as no man ever held before."

The *Birmingham Gazette* noted that "additional interest is attached to the buffaloes by the fact that they are almost the only survivors of what is nearly an extinct species. According to Colonel Cody there are not so many buffaloes on the whole American continent as there are in the exhibition." During the European tour, four more calves were born in London. Upon his return, Cody offered eighteen buffalo to the Smithsonian's small zoo, but William T. Hornaday regretfully declined, because there wasn't room for that many on the museum's grounds.

"Buffalo Bill Cody, of all people, played a role [in saving the bison] because he needed them for his show," said Clay Jenkinson:

> This is an age before television, an age before radio, but he was able to show the world what bison were like. Most Americans had never been to the Great Plains, and that's still true, but most Americans got their buffalo from Cody's "Wild West" or from Hornaday's glass box at the Smithsonian. So, these played an incalculably large media role, public relations role, in building a constituency in the country to do something to save this creature from extinction.

NINE

GHOSTS

The wild Indian exists no longer. The game on which he lived has been destroyed; the country over which he roamed has been taken up; and his tribes, one by one, have been compelled to abandon the old nomadic life, and to settle down within the narrow confines of reservations.

This change, by which an entire race has been called to give over the ways of wanderers, and to adapt itself to the life of a people of fixed abodes, is most momentous.

The magnitude of it is equaled only by the suddenness with which it has been wrought, and by its completeness.

GEORGE BIRD GRINNELL

As the nineteenth century entered its final decades, Native peoples of the Plains faced the most traumatic years of their history. The near extermination of the buffalo, devastating as it had been, was merely one part of the troubles engulfing them. The horse culture that had transformed their way of life had been stamped out. Indian nations that had gone to war against white encroachments had been defeated by the United States Army and placed on reservations. So were tribes that had always remained peaceful. Under law, Native Americans were not considered U.S. citizens, and to travel beyond a reservation boundary required government permission.

"A reservation was kind of a cultural laboratory in which these people were to be transformed into a new people, in terms of their culture, their family habits, their religion," according to Elliott West. "That was the purpose, that was the government's goal. The whole point of assimilating Indians, transforming Indians, was to open this area to settlement coming in."

Well-meaning reformers in the East, calling themselves "Friends of the Indians," pushed Congress to enact a number of provisions intended to hasten Native Americans' assimilation into the white culture now surrounding them. Children as young as five years old were taken from their families and sent to boarding schools, where they learned English and were severely punished if they spoke their native language. All vestiges of their traditional culture were to be removed. "Our belongings were taken from us," a boarding school student named Lone Wolf remembered. "Even the little medicine bags our mothers had given us to protect us from harm. Everything was placed in a heap and set afire."

"Education," said one reformer, "should seek the disintegration of the tribes.... They should be educated, not as Indians, but as Americans." The official slogan of the boarding school effort was "Kill the Indian, Save the Man." It was the equivalent of "saving" the bison by making them cattle. Both buffalo and Native people would be allowed to exist, so long as they didn't remain what they had always been and instead became what the prevailing society wanted them to be. Many people then (and now) considered it all "inevitable." Rosalyn LaPier disagrees. "There was a system in place in the nineteenth century that was both enslaving people and also taking Indigenous people's land and landscape to feed this capitalistic machine," she said. "It was not inevitable. It was planned."

In 1887, Congress passed the Dawes General Allotment Act. It gave each Indian family 160 acres of farming land and 320 acres of grazing land on the reservation. Then, all the remaining tribal land would be declared "surplus" and made available for white people to purchase. Tribal ownership—and the tribes themselves—were meant to simply disappear. "The Allotment Act was probably one of the most devastating acts for Indian people in the reservations," Marcia Pablo said. "They didn't understand private land ownership. You didn't own land. You were part of the land; you used the land for the resources as you needed them."

Before the Allotment Act, some 150 million acres remained in Native hands. Within twenty years, two-thirds of their land had been taken. The buffalo were gone, too. "Since the beginning, we and the buffalo have a long history together," George Horse Capture Jr. said. "Codependent, in a way. Just like my people, their people suffered from 'Manifest Destiny.' They were victims of genocide, ethnic cleansing, westward expansion. A shared history, all the way across." Gerard Baker agreed:

> We always say, "We're just like the buffalo." They almost exterminated us, too. What they'd do, they'd put buffalo in zoos. And the old people would say, "What did they do to us? They put us on reservations—and we couldn't get out of those reservations without a permit." The zoos kept the buffalo; the white people kept us on reservations. Same thing.
>
> There are stories about old men going to those zoos and seeing buffalo, and crying with their medicines. You can imagine the fence and this old man crying and praying. Pretty soon, those buffalo come over and look at him as he's praying and crying. And, then, he has to go. And the animals stay in the zoo.

In the buffalo's place, the government supplied cattle for the Indians to kill and eat. At one reservation, steers were released from a corral, one at a time, while mounted men chased after it and brought it down, just as they had brought buffalo down years earlier. Then its carcass would be stripped and carved up in the traditional way. At another Lakota reservation, the cattle were turned loose inside a large corral, and the same mock hunt took place. Eventually, the agent put an end to that and built a slaughterhouse to kill and butcher the cattle. The Lakotas burned the slaughterhouse down.

For Native people, the devastation of their surroundings wasn't limited to the disappearance of the bison, Rosalyn LaPier said:

We also have mining. We see the utter destruction of mountain landscapes—people using explosives to completely destroy places. This is shocking to Indigenous people. They had not seen that kind of destruction on the massive scale that they were seeing at that time, destruction after destruction after destruction that they were not just witnessing from afar, but witnessing up close and personal.

And there was mass slaughter of multiple animal species. It was not just the bison. What happened to the elk? What happened to the wolves? What happened to the grizzlies? Basically, all of the major mammals on the northern Great Plains were decimated. They saw, by that point, an almost total destruction of all of the animals that were sacred to them.

Whatever elk and grizzlies had survived could now be found only in the mountains. Bighorn sheep disappeared from the Dakota badlands. Market hunters killed millions of antelope. Herds of cattle and sheep now grazed where the buffalo had once roamed. With the bison gone, the prairie itself began changing. Millions of acres of soil were plowed for the first time. Wheat, corn, and other crops replaced native grasses. Buffalo wallows—where vital rainwater had once pooled—filled with sand.

On the southern Plains, in 1886, the Kiowa calendar showed a leafy tree above a lodge, signifying another summer without a Sun Dance, because no buffalo could be found to sacrifice for their ceremonies. But in 1887, the Kiowas were able to hold their sacred ritual—after they received the necessary buffalo bull from Charles and Molly Goodnight.

The next year's calendars used special drawings to commemorate the promise of a prophet named *Pá-iñgya*, who claimed that he had become invincible to bullets and that a whirlwind was coming that would blow all the Euro-Americans away, followed by a purifying prairie fire that would consume their buildings. Then, he predicted, the buffalo would return, and the Kiowas could resume their traditional way of life. Many Kiowas deserted their houses and crops, took their children out of the schools, and encamped on a nearby creek to await the fulfillment of *Pá-iñgya*'s prophecy. When it didn't come, they returned to their homes. (It was the second time such a prophecy had let the Kiowas down. Only six years earlier, in 1882, a different medicine man had promised that ceremonies he was holding in his tepee would bring back the buffalo.) Not far from the Kiowas, a Southern Cheyenne shaman named Buffalo Coming Out performed repeated ceremonies near the Wichita Mountains, directed at Mount Scott, asking the buffalo to reemerge. When they didn't, he finally gave up.

By 1890, North and South Dakota, Montana, Washington, Idaho, and Wyoming had become states, and the Census Bureau announced that the nation's population had reached 62,979,766. According to its count, of those nearly 63 million people, 248,253—about 0.4 percent—were Indians (not including those in Alaska Territory). Since the first census of 1790, the bureau had created a map with a "frontier line," proudly displaying the steady, westward march of settlement to document how much more land had been, in its terminology, "redeemed from wilderness by the hand of man." Now, the bureau's director said, such a line no longer made sense.

At the Standing Rock reservation in the Dakotas, the aging Hunkpapa leader Sitting Bull had returned from touring with "Buffalo Bill's Wild West" show, where he had been paid $50 a week—plus a $125 bonus—to ride around the arena once during each performance, promoted as "the slayer of General Custer." His contract also gave him the right to profit directly from the sale of autographs and pictures of himself to the awestruck visitors who came to his tepee. But after four months with Cody, Sitting Bull had seen enough of the white world. He could not understand why beggars were ignored on the streets of big cities, and he gave much of his pay away to newsboys and hoboes. Back at Standing Rock, he used his remaining money to provide feasts for his friends. And he tried to keep his people from participating in the Allotment Act. "[The white people] will try to gain possession of the last piece of ground we possessed," he warned them, adding, "Let us stand as one family as we did before the white people led us astray."

The summer of 1890 brought a drought that killed whatever crops the Lakotas were trying to raise. Because Congress had failed to appropriate adequate funding, the government had already cut rations at every reservation by more than 20 percent. Whooping cough and influenza spread among the hungry people, particularly the children. Across the West, the situation had become equally desperate on other reservations. "There'd be a certain amount of emptiness in a spot," George Horse Capture Jr. said. "Some of this is very hard to put into words. Sometimes, you can have this emptiness and you can't identify it. It's only an emptiness, you know? Maybe that would have been a part of it. But, also, we've got a lot of things that are gone."

Then word arrived that a new ceremony called the Ghost Dance was sweeping through many tribes of the West. Combining Christian and traditional Indian elements, and offering hope to dispirited Native Americans, it was preached by a Paiute medicine man named Wovoka:

> My brothers, I bring you word from your fathers the ghosts, that they are marching now to join you, led by the Messiah who came once to live on Earth with the white man but was killed by them.
>
> I bring to you the promise of a day in which there will be no white man to lay his hand on the bridle of the Indians' horse; when the red men of the prairie will rule the world.

Wovoka's prophecy required men and women to purify themselves, give up alcohol, and forswear violence. Then, they were to dance in a large circle, singing and calling upon the spirits of their ancestors. If they did, the Ghost Dancers believed, the whites would vanish and bison would cover the Plains again. "The buffalo are coming, the buffalo are coming," they sang as they danced. "Give me my arrows; Grandmother, give me back my bow. They say there is to be a buffalo hunt. Now we are about to chase the buffalo."

.   .   .

The average man seldom thinks about Indians, and when he does he thinks of them either with entire indifference or with contemptuous dislike.

He is moved in part by that narrowness which leads us to despise those who in appearance or by birth or tradition are different from ourselves—the feeling which leads many a white man to speak with contempt of Negroes or Chinamen. More weighty than this feeling, however, is the inherited one that the Indian is an enemy.   GEORGE BIRD GRINNELL

Though he lived in New York City, George Bird Grinnell spent parts of every year among the Pawnee, Blackfeet, and Cheyenne, listening to their stories, studying their religion, learning their history. In the fall of 1890, he watched the Cheyenne hold a Ghost Dance and understood the appeal of its message. "This is only what any of us will do," he wrote, "if we get hungry." But he also worried about where such desperation might lead: "It is quite possible that the Indians might be frightened into killing someone. . . . [More likely] some crazy-headed settler, or body of settlers, will attack the Indians and kill some, and if they do, they may start a war . . . and if a war is started now, it will be worse than the Custer massacre ever was."

In the Lakotas' adaptation of the ceremony, Ghost Dancers wore special shirts said to be impervious to the white man's bullets. Alarmed reservation agents feared that an uprising was imminent. Troops were called in. As a precautionary measure, the Standing Rock reservation's Indian police were ordered to arrest the most prominent Lakota chief—Sitting Bull. When some of his followers resisted, a fight broke out. Both sides began firing and a dozen people were killed. Sitting Bull was one of them.

Some of Sitting Bull's people fled south to the Cheyenne River reservation, where they joined another band of Lakotas, then headed farther west with them toward Pine Ridge, near the Black Hills. There, they planned to turn themselves over to General Nelson A.

Miles and his large Army force, and settle things peaceably before more blood was shed. But Miles misunderstood their intentions and sent the Seventh Cavalry—Custer's old command—to intercept them. The Lakotas were flying a white flag when they met the soldiers and settled down for the night at a creek called Wounded Knee.

The next morning, December 29, 1890, the troops began confiscating the Indians' weapons. Accounts vary as to what precisely happened next, but someone's gun went off. The soldiers immediately opened fire with rifles, revolvers, and four powerful Hotchkiss guns overlooking the camp. When the shooting stopped, more than 250 Lakotas—most of them women and children—were dead. So were 25 soldiers. The Indian corpses, strewn over the prairie in frozen postures of death, were eventually dumped into trenches serving as mass graves. "And what were they trying to do?" said George Horse Capture Jr. "They were praying. They tried to dance the buffalo back. And they paid with their lives." George Bird Grinnell placed the massacre in a larger context:

> The most shameful chapter of American history is that in which is recorded the account of our dealings with the Indians. The story of our government's [relations] with this race is an unbroken narrative of injustice, fraud, and robbery.
>
> Our people have disregarded honesty and truth whenever they have come in contact with the Indian, and he has had no rights because he has never had the power to enforce any.
>
> We are too apt to forget that these people are humans like ourselves, that they are fathers and mothers, husbands and wives, brothers and sisters; men and women with emotions and passions like our own.

That same year, the Kiowas became intrigued by Wovoka's preachings and sent a member of the tribe, Wooden Lance, to investigate. But when the prophet proved unable to help him communicate with his dead child, Wooden Lance returned to the Wichita Mountains to denounce the Ghost Dance as a fraud. Most of the Kiowas decided not to take it up.

Still, they hoped to celebrate a Sun Dance. Since a fresh buffalo head was not available, they planned to use an old buffalo robe as the centerpiece of the ritual. As they gathered to erect the center pole of the medicine lodge, a message arrived from their neighbor, Quanah of the Comanches, warning them that the reservation agent—worried about any large ceremonial gathering—had dispatched troops to stop them, by force if necessary. They abandoned the site and headed home, leaving the unfinished medicine lodge standing. The Kiowas would never hold another Sun Dance.

Theodore Roosevelt (left and below) went west to kill some buffalo, whose heads he displayed as trophies in his home (above). George Bird Grinnell (opposite, top) kept two buffalo skulls in his office (opposite, bottom) as reminders of the bison's slaughter.

When the taxidermist William T. Hornaday (above) created his display of bison he had killed in Montana for the Smithsonian (opposite) he tucked in a handwritten note to the future, worrying that they were the "last of their kind." The display included the remains of Sandy (left), the calf he had captured and brought back.

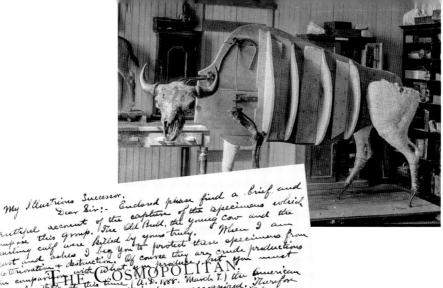

My Illustrious Successor.

Dear Sir:— Enclosed please find a brief and truthful account of the capture of the specimens which compose this group. The Old Bull, the young Cow and the yearling calf were killed by yours truly. When I am dust and ashes I beg you to protect these specimens from deterioration & destruction. Of course they are crude productions in comparison with what you produce, but you must remember that at this time (A.D. 1888. March 7.) the American school of Taxidermy has only just been recognized. Therefore give the devil his due, and revile not—

W. T. Hornaday.

THE COSMOPOLITAN

Vol. IV   OCTOBER, 1887.   No. 2.

THE PASSING OF THE BUFFALO.—I.

By William T. Hornaday.

Author of "Two Years in the Jungle."

Chief Taxidermist, U.S. National Museum.

AT last the game butchers of the great West have stopped killing buffalo are all dead! The time arrived for the Territories to enact laws against the killing of these and I am pleased to see that th Legislature has just rushed throu that effect—only ten years behin Next year, when the last buffalo o head still alive in the Panhandle hunted down and killed, it will the Lone Star State to frame a protection; but its final passage be expected until about 1897.

While the Territories are

Hornaday's zoo on the Smithsonian's lawn, including a few buffalo (above), would prove too small. In his angry book about the bison's systematic destruction, he included a map (opposite) showing how the species' range had shrunk over time. He estimated that fewer than 550 buffalo were now alive in the United States.

MAP
ILLUSTRATING
THE EXTERMINATION OF
THE AMERICAN BISON
PREPARED BY
W. T. HORNADAY.

EXPLANATION

Charles Jesse "Buffalo" Jones, a former
hide hunter (above), rescued some
calves in Texas (right) and started a
herd in Kansas, where he experimented
with cross-breeding them with cattle
to create what he called "catalo"
(opposite, top).

At the urging of his wife, Molly, the cattleman Charles Goodnight
spared a few buffalo calves from being killed, and the couple started
a small bison herd at their ranch in the Texas Panhandle.

THE BUFFALO BILL STORIES

A WEEKLY PUBLICATION   DEVOTED TO BORDER HISTORY

Issued Weekly. By subscription $2.50 per year. Entered at Second-class Matter at the N. Y. Post Office, by STREET & SMITH, 79-89 Seventh Ave., N. Y.

No. 245   NEW YORK, JANUARY 20, 1906.   Price, Five Cents

BUFFALO BILL'S LOST QUARRY

or FOLLOWING A COLD TRAIL

BY THE AUTHOR OF "BUFFALO BILL"

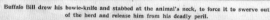

Buffalo Bill drew his bowie-knife and stabbed at the animal's neck, to force it to swerve out of the herd and release him from his deadly peril.

GRAND STAND AT LONDON SEATING 20,000 PEOPLE

Buffalo Bill Cody, already famous through dime novels, became an international celebrity with his extravagant "Wild West" show. Two of the highlights were a reenactment of "Custer's Last Stand" (opposite, bottom) and a mock buffalo hunt (below) using blank cartridges.

188

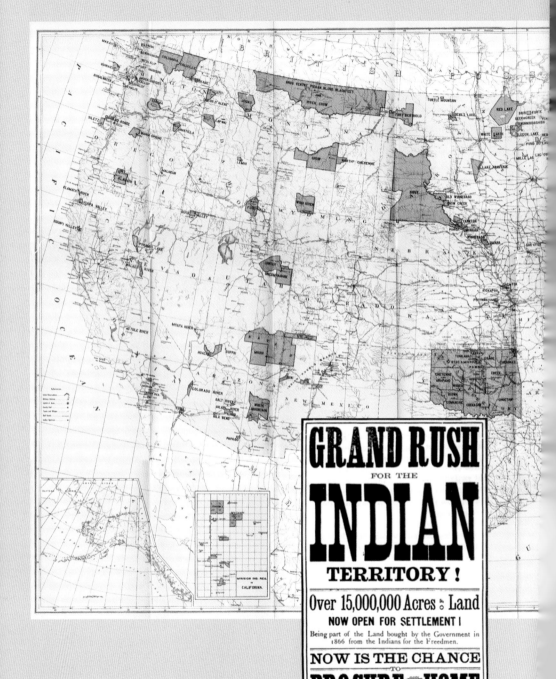

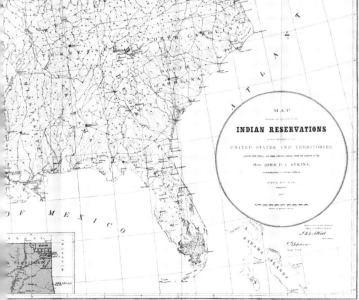

MAP
INDIAN RESERVATIONS
UNITED STATES AND TERRITORIES.
Hon. JOHN D. C. ATKINS,
PAUL BRODIE

By the last decades of the nineteenth century, Native Americans were confined to reservations, where the Dawes General Allotment Act further diminished their lands by declaring vast portions as "surplus" and open for white settlement. Under the slogan of "Kill the Indian, Save the Man," government boarding schools tried to strip Native students of all vestiges of tribal traditions.

With the bison gone, at some reservations men "hunted" corralled cattle (opposite, top) until the agent put an end to it; and the buffalo wallows on the Plains filled with sand (opposite, bottom). Sitting Bull (sitting, right) briefly joined Buffalo Bill (standing, center) for "Wild West" show performances, and sold autographed pictures of himself.

A hide painting (above) on a deerskin depicts a Ghost Dance, which promised to bring back the buffalo and return Native life to what it had once been. Some Lakota tribes also made special shirts (right) for the ceremonies. George Bird Grinnell (below, seated in center) spent his summers learning the stories of western tribes—and worried that an overreaction to the movement would lead to violence.

In December 1890, the government's effort to suppress the Ghost Dance resulted in Sitting Bull being killed by Indian police at the Standing Rock reservation. Two weeks later, at the Pine Ridge reservation, more than 250 Lakotas—most of them women and children—were killed by the Seventh Cavalry at Wounded Knee. Their frozen corpses (above) were eventually dumped into trenches (opposite) serving as mass graves.

TEN

THE LAST REFUGE

G ROWING UP in New York City, George Bird Grinnell had been a student of Lucy Audubon, the widow of the renowned ornithologist and painter. Among the things she taught the boy was how to observe and appreciate the natural world. "But even more significantly," Michael Punke said, "she teaches him about an ethic that was important to her that she called 'self-denial.' And what she really meant by self-denial was the notion that you would think about future generations, that you would not do things that you might want to do, in deference to thinking about how your children and grandchildren might live one day. And that ethic runs almost directly counter to the prevailing norms of the day."

As the editor of *Forest and Stream*, Grinnell put her lessons to work. He railed against the hat-making industry, which had created a fashion frenzy for the colorful plumes of birds in the Everglades, threatening the survival of egrets and ibises. And he decried the market hunters who were supplying restaurants with the meat of passenger pigeons, driving toward oblivion a bird that once existed in the billions and literally darkened the skies of North America. To help him carry on the fight against this commercial destruction of bird life, Grinnell founded the Audubon Society, named in honor of his mentor and her late husband. Five years later, he led a campaign to stop the wholesale deforestation of public lands and crucial watersheds by galvanizing hunters and fishermen to lobby Congress for the creation of the first national forests, using a simple message: "No woods, no game [and] no water; no water, no fish."

But for Grinnell, no issue loomed larger than the fate of Yellowstone National Park. Three years after the park's establishment, in 1875, working as a naturalist assigned to an Army reconnaissance, he had documented forty species of mammals and a hundred species of birds, immediately recognizing that the park was more than a collection of wondrous geysers and stunning waterfalls. It could serve, he thought, as a precious sanctuary for the wildlife that were under assault in the rest of the nation:

> We have seen … the Indian and the game retreat before the white man and the cattle, and beheld the tide of [settlement] … move forward, … which threatens before long to leave no portion of our vast territory unbroken by the farmer's plow or untrodden by his flocks.
>
> Of the millions of buffalo which even in our own time ranged the plains in freedom, none now remain. From the prairies which they used to darken, the wild herds, down to the last straggling bull, have disappeared.
>
> There is one spot left, a single rock about which this tide will break, and past which it will sweep, leaving it undefiled by the unsightly traces of civilization. In the Yellowstone National Park, protected from destruction by United States troops, are the only wild buffalo which exist within the borders of the United States.
>
> Here, in this Yellowstone Park, the large game of the West may be preserved from extermination … in this, their last refuge.

With Theodore Roosevelt, his friend and fellow officer in the Boone and Crockett Club, Grinnell had mobilized efforts to defend what he called "the people's park." Together they narrowly defeated repeated attempts in Congress to reduce Yellowstone's size, open it up to greater commercial exploitation and privatization, or even do away with it altogether. But their efforts to expand the park's boundaries and provide it with better protection were continually blocked.

At the time, there was no National Park Service. The Army was responsible for stopping poachers and for enforcing regulations against vandalizing the geyser formations. But Yellowstone existed in a legal no-man's-land, with no federal law giving the soldiers clear authority to prosecute offenders. Their only recourse was to issue a warning or, in the most serious cases, confiscate a poacher's equipment and temporarily expel him from the park.

In 1890, the park superintendent had estimated 200 buffalo still lived in Yellowstone. But by 1894, poachers had killed 114 of them—often removing just their heads, for which a Montana taxidermist offered $500 and then sold to people who wanted a trophy as decoration. "Every saloon in America wants to have a stuffed buffalo head to hang on the wall," Michael Punke said, "and the market for buffalo heads goes through the roof. What used to be a four-dollar shot, if you killed a buffalo and could sell its hide, becomes a five-hundred-dollar shot. And the response to that is poachers descend upon these few places where there still are buffalo remaining and try to kill them."

On March 13, 1894, two troopers out on patrol in a remote corner of Yellowstone heard shots in the distance. They hurried in that direction and soon came across several buffalo carcasses. A man stood hunched over one of them, so busily skinning it that he didn't realize anyone else was there until a trooper was beside him with a drawn gun. The poacher was Edgar Howell, who had been killing Yellowstone's bison for years. By one estimate he was personally responsible for the death of eighty of the park's bison.

As luck would have it, a reporter named Emerson Hough, on assignment for Grinnell's *Forest and Stream*, was also in the park—with a photographer—to write an article about Yellowstone in the winter. When Howell bragged that the worst punishment he could receive for his crime was expulsion from the park and the loss of only twenty-six dollars' worth of equipment, Hough realized he had stumbled onto a great story and quickly telegraphed it to Grinnell in New York City.

Grinnell knew just what to do. He began generating a public outcry for congressional action through a series of stories and editorials, along with photographs that included soldiers posing with the nine buffalo heads that Howell had not yet hauled out of the park.

"Grinnell popularizes the photographs, and it's a political lightning bolt in Washington," Michael Punke said. "Grinnell was very good at explaining that Yellowstone National Park belongs to all Americans. So that when a poacher is stealing from Yellowstone, he's stealing from you."

Roosevelt also sprang into action, promising, "I am going to use the recent unfortunate slaughter of buffaloes for all it is worth for trying to get legislation through." He stalked the corridors of the Capitol, lobbying for a bill that would institute fines of up to $1,000 and jail sentences of up to two years for offenders. Privately, Roosevelt told a friend, he wished the park's superintendent had found an excuse to "accidentally" shoot the poacher.

On May 7, 1894, less than two months after Howell's capture, President Grover Cleveland signed the bill into law, authorizing regulations that would protect the park, its geysers, and its wildlife—at least on paper.

Back in the East, William T. Hornaday's dream of a larger national zoo in Washington—which could provide space for more bison and other animals than the Smithsonian's lawn on the National Mall—had been approved by Congress in 1889, and he had been named to become its first superintendent. "Although the existence of a few widely-scattered individuals enables us to say that the bison is not yet absolutely extinct in a wild state," he wrote, "there is no reason to hope that a single wild and unprotected individual will remain alive ten years hence.

> The nearer the species approaches to complete extermination, the more eagerly are the wretched fugitives pursued to the death whenever found. Western hunters are striving for the [questionable] honor of killing the last buffalo.
>
> At least eight or ten buffaloes of pure breed should be secured very soon by the [National Zoo] ... and cared for with special reference in keeping the breed absolutely pure.

But in 1890, Hornaday abruptly resigned over continual disagreements with his superiors, who felt he was too controlling, too eager to claim public attention for himself, too quick to denounce anyone who disagreed with him, and not experienced enough to oversee such an undertaking. "He was quite notoriously temperamental, irritable, difficult to get along with," said Michelle Nijhuis, "but, at the same time, very charismatic, a great speaker, a great public advocate. He was genuinely passionate about the long-term survival of the bison."

When the National Zoo opened in 1891 on 166 acres in Rock Creek Park, Hornaday was living in Buffalo, New York, working for a real estate company. Then, in early 1896, the newly formed New York Zoological Society reached out, asking whether he would like to help them create what they envisioned as the world's largest zoo. Theodore Roosevelt was one of the moving forces behind the idea. He had once written that the "extermination of the bison" would be a "blessing" for the "advance of white civilization of the West." Now his view had changed. "When I hear of the destruction of a species," Roosevelt said, "I feel just as if all the works of some great writer had perished." The zoo, he hoped, might save many species—especially game animals like the buffalo—from total extinction.

Hornaday readily accepted the job to find the best location for the zoo, design it, and become its first director. In the Bronx, he was thrilled to come across a forested landscape he called "as wild and unkempt as the heart of the Adirondacks" and he felt a sense of "almost paralyzing astonishment and profound gratitude." The city government was persuaded to hand over 264 acres for the proposed zoo, and for the next three years Hornaday personally supervised every detail of the preparations—from deciding which trees could be cut down to what animals would be showcased.

When it opened in late 1899, the Bronx Zoo became an immediate success, soon attracting more than a million visitors a year. Many of them seemed particularly fascinated by the small buffalo herd, which in a few years would grow to twenty-six. Most of the bison were a gift from a well-to-do member of the Zoological Society's board, William C. Whitney, whose private game reserve in western Massachusetts included some bison that had originally been captured by Buffalo Jones. Molly and Charles Goodnight added three bulls and a cow from the Texas Panhandle.

Hornaday was proud that he could now display live buffalo—instead of dead ones, as he had at the Smithsonian Museum—to millions of Americans, who, he hoped, would join his crusade for wildlife. But he worried that a few bison preserved in zoos, or private ranches, or even in the small herd under the uncertain protection of Yellowstone National Park, were not enough:

> The buffaloes now in the [zoos] of the country are but few in number, and unless special pains be taken to prevent it, by means of judicious exchanges, from time to time, these will rapidly deteriorate in size, and within a comparatively short time run out entirely, through continued in-breeding.
>
> There is reason to fear that unless the United States Government takes the matter in hand and makes a special effort to prevent it, the pure-blood bison will be lost irretrievably through mixture with domestic breeds.
>
> There is no possible chance for the race to be perpetuated in a wild state, and in a few years more, hardly a bone will remain above ground to mark the existence of the most prolific mammalian species that ever existed, so far as we know. The only way to insure the perpetuation of the bison species permanently is to create large herds.

Hornaday's zeal for saving the buffalo stemmed from more than a sympathetic concern about the animal. "The decline of the bison affected his very strong sense of national pride," Michelle Nijhuis said. "In many ways, it was a symbol of the young United States. The idea that citizens of the United States had driven this species extinct was offensive to him." But, she added, "it was also tied up with his strong sense of racial superiority. He was stridently anti-Catholic; stridently anti-immigrant. He blamed Italian Americans and African Americans, without evidence, for the decline of songbirds in the American South." The problem of littering on the zoo grounds,

Hornaday complained, was the fault of immigrants who had arrived from southern and eastern Europe, "a vast horde of unapprecia- tive and ungrateful low-class aliens, that has now become a curse to this country." Native Americans, he wrote, were "lazy and shift- less." Hornaday, Nijhuis said, "was blind, quite willfully blind, to the enormous cultural and economic tragedy that the decline and near disappearance of the bison created for the Indigenous people of the Great Plains."

Hornaday's boss at the Bronx Zoo was Madison Grant, chairman of the New York Zoological Society and a widely admired conser- vationist who had led the effort to save the redwoods in California. Grant was also a leading proponent of a new pseudoscience called eugenics, which falsely claimed that human beings could be sepa- rated into a rigid, immutable hierarchy based not only on the color of their skin but also on the so-called "purity" of their ancestry. At the top were the "real" Americans—certain tall, blue-eyed white Protestants, like Grant and his friends—who, he thought, were the rightful inheritors and now stewards of the continent. Everyone else was cataloged in a descending order of genetic inferiority.

Grant would eventually put his racist theories in a book, *The Passing of the Great Race*, with a glowing preface by Henry Fairfield Osborn Sr., also a founder of the zoo. Theodore Roosevelt would praise it as "a capital book." With Grant's approval, Hornaday would put a five-foot-tall Central African named Ota Benga on display in the zoo's Monkey House, until a coalition of African American min- isters appealed to New York City's mayor to stop the "degrading exhibition." (More than century later, in 2020, the Wildlife Conser- vation Society, which now runs the zoo, officially condemned and apologized for the "bigoted actions and attitudes" of Grant, Osborn, and Hornaday. And in 2022, a statue of Roosevelt, mounted on a horse with two shirtless men—one a Native American, the other of African descent—trailing behind, was removed from the entrance of the American Museum of Natural History in New York City. The design, museum officials decided, "communicates a racial hier- archy that the museum and members of the public have long found disturbing.")

"They saw themselves as preservers of the essence of the American character," Elliott West said, "and they saw no contradiction whatsoever between those two things—between promoting eugenics, promoting the exclusion of some foreign types, or their disdain for Indian peoples, on the one hand, and the preserving of what they considered the best of the 'true' American 'Wild America.' These racists, these white supremacists, were only one group of those who were saving the bison. But they were sure there."

There were a lot of people who had different ideas about the buffalo. They came from different angles. But a lot of them came to the same conclusion, "Hey, we've got to do something here."

Some of these people took the hybridization with cattle route. Other people wanted to save them so they could shoot them. But there were some people who genuinely loved buffalo, maybe even had a spiritual connection to them, which drove, I think, most of the Native Americans that did this.

DAN O'BRIEN

More than fifteen hundred miles west of the Bronx Zoo, the two biggest herds in the nation were being managed by families on two Indian reservations on the northern Plains.

In South Dakota, Frederick Dupuis, a French Canadian fur trader, had married Good Elk Woman, a Minniconjou Lakota, and established a ranch on the Cheyenne River reservation. In the early 1880s, just as the hide hunters were finishing their slaughter on the northern Plains, the family had captured four bison calves, brought them back on a buckboard, and began raising them on the ranch. By 1898, Dupuis had died, and the family's buffalo herd numbered nearly eighty.

A Scottish immigrant rancher, James "Scotty" Philip—whose wife, Sarah, was an enrolled member of the reservation—bought the herd and later moved it to a fenced range of six thousand acres along the Missouri River, a few miles north of Fort Pierre. "Dupuis, Scotty Philip, those two guys, I think, were influenced by the Native

Americans," Dan O'Brien said. "These guys must have had either very tough wives, or they were really in love with them, because the women were the ones that drove these two hard-ass cowboys to go out and take care of these buffalo. These guys had the brains to listen to their wives. And we could all learn from that."

Though his main business was in cattle, Philip became fond of his bison. "If a man wants to get a fine lesson in the advantage of 'standing together,'" he said, "he need only watch a buffalo herd in stormy weather." As his herd grew, people often rode a steamboat up the Missouri from the state capital of Pierre, disembarked, and crowded the fences to watch it. Some Mexican officials visiting the ranch uttered condescending remarks about the buffalo bulls—saying they seemed lazy and nothing like the spirited Spanish fighting bulls that thrilled audiences south of the border. Philip offered to send two of his bison down to Juarez's Plaza de Toros and settle the matter in what became billed as the "Bullfight of the Century."

When it was released into the ring, Philip's eight-year-old bull, named Pierre, at first lay down in the warm sun, as if proving the skeptical Mexicans right. After the Mexican bull entered, Pierre slowly rose—but refused to move, even as the opponent charged his flank. At the last moment, Pierre turned quickly, and the two animals butted heads, bringing the Mexican bull to its knees. (Having been pursued by predators from behind for thousands of years, bison have developed not only uncommon speed but also the ability to pivot their massive frame on their front legs to defend themselves.) After several more attempts—each with the same knee-buckling result—the Mexican bull began circling the arena, looking for a gate to let him out.

In quick succession, three more bulls were sent to attack Pierre. Each time, he refused to move and knocked them down, one after the other. Then he stretched out on the ground and took another nap.

A week later, a younger bison bull, Pierre Jr., was scheduled to face a matador, but the provincial governor called off the spectacle. He had seen enough of the American buffalo's strength and speed, and was not willing to risk losing Juarez's best bullfighter.

By the early 1900s, the largest herd of buffalo in the United States—
more than three hundred bulls, cows, and calves—grazed on the
Flathead reservation in northwestern Montana, home of the Salish,
Kootenai, and Pend d'Oreille. Accounts of the herd's origins differ
in their details, but they all agree that sometime in the 1870s, one
of the Pend d'Oreille traveled out to the buffalo plains east of the
reservation and decided to bring four or six calves home with him—
back over the Rocky Mountains. According to tribal oral history, it
was a young man named Latatí—fulfilling a dream of his deceased
father that the bison might be saved from destruction by the hide
hunters. By the early 1880s, the calves had grown and the herd numbered thirteen, when two ranchers on the reservation, Charles Allard
and Michel Pablo, had bought them from Latatí's stepfather, Samuel
Walking Coyote.

Charles Allard was part Indian and married to a Pend d'Oreille
woman. He believed that the buffalo business could be "as good an
investment as real estate."

His partner, Michel Pablo, had been born on the Blackfeet reservation, the son of Otter Woman, a Piegan Blackfeet, and "Old
Man" Pablo, of Mexican heritage, who ran a freighting business out
of Fort Benton. After being orphaned as a boy, Michel ended up on
the Flathead reservation and became an interpreter. There, he married Agathe, a Pend d'Oreille woman. "She was a strong woman, as
I understand it, very strong," said Marcia Pablo, their great-great-
granddaughter. "She had lived through that devastation and loss for
Indian people that took away part of their heart, took away part of
their spirit, part of their soul. And to bring that back, I'm sure she
supported that. My great-great-grandfather had seen the buffalo in
their prime, when there were lots of them."

With twenty-six more bison purchased from Buffalo Jones, the
Pablo-Allard herd expanded on the reservation's lush pastures just
west of the Mission Mountains. Occasionally, the partners sold a few
bison to museums, zoos, and people hoping to start small herds of

their own—or to someone intending to resell a hide for $100 and a mounted head for $500. But, with fifty calves born each year, their herd kept growing. They briefly experimented with crossbreeding a few bison with cattle, but gave it up and got rid of all but the full-blooded buffalo.

When Allard died in 1896, his family began slowly selling off his bison to various buyers. With free grazing on tribal land, Pablo stayed put—and his herd increased. He often gave bison to his neighbors for food, celebrations, and ceremonies, which maintained their connection with the buffalo "and probably helped keep the songs and the ceremonies intact," Marcia Pablo said:

> It was much more than a business for him. It was like a destiny. He was a visionary.
>
> He knew we needed the buffalo on this Earth to survive as people. Not just Indians; we [all] need the buffalo to survive. We need that spirit, or our cosmology is not complete.

By 1902, Michel Pablo was now in charge of more buffalo than anyone else in the nation—including the federal government.

On July 5, 1902, George Bird Grinnell's *Forest and Stream* carried a front-page story about Pablo's growing herd of bison and devoted its back cover to a full-page photograph of some of them. Grinnell also noted, however, that despite the protection law passed back in 1894, poaching had not been completely stopped in Yellowstone National Park, and the number of wild buffalo there had dwindled to about two dozen. In private, he confided his fear that "buffalo in the United States are doomed."

A few days later, a handwritten letter arrived. It was from Buffalo Jones:

> My Dear Mr. Grinnell.
>
> The articles in your July 5th number about the buffalo on the Flathead reservation is to me of great interest. Your [photograph]

is of still greater interest, as I quickly recognize many of the older buffalo as those I caught by almost superhuman efforts.

The large cow with drooped horns was purchased from Mrs. Cole of Oxford, Nebraska, after her husband had been killed by a buffalo bull. The cow I mark #1. The bull that killed Mr. Cole [is marked #2].

Jones pointedly reminded Grinnell that in 1894, during the uproar over poaching in Yellowstone, he had offered to capture some of the park bison's calves and raise a new herd in a corral—and he mildly chastised Grinnell for not supporting the proposal. He noted that in the late 1890s, two different administrations had turned down similar offers. Then he wanted to make sure Grinnell heard something directly from him: with the help of the new president, Theodore Roosevelt, Jones had been chosen to be the park's game warden:

Well Bro[ther] Grinnell, I am to leave for the Yellowstone National Park tomorrow for the identical purpose to in a small way do [w]hat I advocated [many years] ago. Try and rescue the buffalo in the park, as well as to establish a herd of domesticated buffalo there.

And I feel equal to the occasion. Yet it is a pity I have had to wait so long, and until the herd has been reduced to such a few.

Well there is no use worrying over the unfortunate part of it, but hope and trust everything will work out to a satisfactory end. And a magnificent herd of America's greatest animal will be perpetuated forever.

Upon his arrival, Jones fenced in a big field near the park's headquarters and hotel at Mammoth Hot Springs and stocked it with twenty-one buffalo he purchased—eighteen from what had been Charles Allard's share of the Flathead reservation herd, and three bulls from Molly and Charles Goodnight. (Two of the Goodnights' bulls died the next winter, but some of their bison were already in the park. In 1896, they had sold two bulls and two females to an entrepreneur who placed them in a pen on Dot Island in Yellowstone Lake, where they served as an added attraction to patrons of his steamboat business, ferrying people from the Lake Yellowstone Hotel.) That winter, Jones tracked down Yellowstone's wild herd in a remote corner of the park, where he lassoed a few calves and brought them back on a toboggan to add to his collection.

In 1903, President Theodore Roosevelt showed up in Yellowstone, during a whirlwind national tour that covered a grueling fourteen thousand miles by train. After visiting the buffalo corral, he immediately set off on horseback with the park's superintendent and naturalist John Burroughs for a camping tour of the interior, leaving the rest of the presidential entourage behind. Uninvited, Jones tagged along with his dogs, intending to use them to tree a mountain lion for Roosevelt to shoot. Roosevelt told the superintendent to send Jones and the hounds home; he didn't intend to hunt in a national park, even though regulations at the time allowed killing predators.

Then the president spent two weeks watching elk herds and pronghorn antelope, mule deer and mountain lions through his binoculars—and he assured Burroughs that the game animals had by now become much more numerous than when he had last visited Yellowstone, twelve years earlier. The wildlife protection act he and Grinnell had fought to enact was beginning to work. And though Roosevelt did not encounter the park's wild bison during his visit, he was happy, he wrote, to learn that the buffalo in the fenced herd "are now breeding well."

Buffalo Jones's tenure as the park's game warden would last only a few years. The superintendent appreciated his efforts in establishing the new captive bison herd, but after that, he wrote, Jones's "usefulness in the park ended absolutely." He "had antagonized not only every individual whom he came in contact with," the superintendent added, but was also "generally prostituting himself" for commercial gain. "What Buffalo Jones does is, he just finds a new way to profit from the bison; he's going to profit from a tourist trade," Andrew Isenberg said, noting that the placement of Jones's buffalo was no accident—easily accessible to visitors, and far from the park's wild herd. "He invites tourists to stop by and see his small herd of bison. And he's selling souvenirs and he's selling mementos, and profiting, personally, from this, even though he's holding a government position there."

Concessionaires and tourists also objected to Jones's method of dealing with the bears that constantly begged for food and rummaged through garbage. Using a block and tackle and some rope arranged as a noose near a garbage heap, he would trap a bear's leg, then hoist it up—and publicly whip it with a willow switch. "I had the whole park up in arms against me," Jones wrote. The superintendent considered it "a disgusting spectacle" and ordered him to stop the practice—and sent a nine-page letter to Washington, hoping to be allowed to fire him. "In my opinion, Mr. Jones has never been honestly interested in the propagation of pure-blood buffalo...in the park," he wrote. "His sole idea in seeking the position of game warden...was to attain a little notoriety, and to use his position for the purpose of establishing a ranch where he could carry out his pet hobby of raising catalo."

Jones beat them to the punch and resigned, then went on a national speaking tour showing films of Yellowstone's wildlife and denouncing the Army's supervision of the park. A year later, he received permission to bring some bison to a national forest on the North Rim of the Grand Canyon, where he led hunting trips, captured mountain lions for zoos—and tried once more to breed catalo.

ELEVEN

BLOOD MEMORY

As I sit here in my home in the mountains of New Hampshire, I see through my study windows to the east the wondrous blue hills of the Croydon Range...clothed in all the beauty of New England autumn foliage.

Even as I write, I see the splendid herd of bison grazing on a hillside not far away, their dark brown bodies in strong relief against the light brown grass. For a month or more they have been wandering on the other side of the mountain, but now they are back again, and we shall enjoy the sight of them, perhaps for days to come.   ERNEST HAROLD BAYNES

O F ALL THE DIVERSE PLACES where a herd of buffalo could be found in 1904, none was more unlikely than the Blue Mountain Forest Reservation in western New Hampshire. Covering twenty-four thousand acres and enclosed within an eight-and-a-half-foot-high fence, it was the private retreat of Austin Corbin, a millionaire banker who owned the Long Island Rail Road and had developed Coney Island as a tourist resort. For years, he had stocked his New Hampshire estate with exotic game animals—elk and caribou, antelope and reindeer, Himalayan goats and wild boar from Germany's Black Forest—many of which, except the boar, did not survive for long in their new habitat. In 1892, Corbin had purchased 10 bison for $1,000 each from Buffalo Jones, and by 1904—eight years after Corbin died in a carriage accident—his heirs had a herd of 160.

That same year, after receiving a letter of recommendation from William T. Hornaday, the Corbin family agreed to provide an unoccupied house on the property to Ernest Harold Baynes, an eccentric nature writer from Boston. Baynes was scratching out a living by providing newspapers and magazines with stories—accompanied by photographs taken by his wife, Louise—about birds and snapping turtles, chipmunks and opossums. "He was a nature writer, a showman, a Doctor Dolittle–type character who trained animals and performed with them in order to inspire, among the public, the same affection he felt for these animals," according to Michelle Nijhuis.

At Blue Mountain, Baynes expanded his work, and Louise kept her camera ready to record it. They raised wolf pups they named Death and Dauntless; Romulus, the coyote; and Sprite, a little red fox. Baynes made friends with a newborn wild boar—then brought it with him on the lecture circuit until it grew to 250 pounds, with big tusks and a bad temperament. The couple adopted a bear cub, Jimmie, who ultimately grew into a rambunctious adult, breaking into the house in search of jam and sugar.

But what captivated Baynes the most was the buffalo herd roaming across the nearby pastures and forests. In his first encounter with them, they galloped away, except for an immense bull, who steadfastly refused to move. It was, he wrote, a profound moment:

Perhaps never did I feel so much ashamed in the presence of any animal as when, standing face to face with that magnificent creature, I thought of the wrongs his race had suffered at the hands of mine...the world's greatest massacre, the slaughter of the buffaloes.

"Here is this fellow who was born in India, born in Calcutta; he goes to English boarding schools; he's educated in the East," Elliott West said. "People would call him, today, an animal rights activist. With him, it's just sort of a personal fascination. Unlike someone like Goodnight, or someone like Hornaday, he has no personal acquaintance with the near destruction of the bison. He's simply fascinated with saving the wild world at this time that modern America, in general, is threatening so much of it."

Baynes began spending time observing the bison herd—hiding behind stone walls or trees, or peeping from the foundations of abandoned farmhouses. When he stood in the open to take a picture of one bull, he wrote, it "positively refused to 'look pleasant,' chased me up a tree, and made matchwood of my camera." "I still maintain," he added, "that there is no subject more worthy of the photographer."

With the help of the preserve's gamekeeper, he captured three bison calves only a few weeks old—two young bulls he named War Whoop and Tomahawk, and a female he called Sacajawea—and brought them back to his barnyard. At first he fed them cow's milk from a baby bottle, Baynes said:

> They began to treat me with the respect due the head of the commissary department, [although] when they had finished they had no use for me and if I attempted to keep on caressing them, one of them would butt me vigorously.
>
> [Though they] made me black and blue and very sore, through [those calves] a dying race sent its message to the American people. It spoke of strength and vigor and courage, of a natural fitness to live.
>
> As I thought about [them], I felt sure that if the American people would but give the buffalo a chance, every bull, every cow, every tawny calf would do its best to carry on.
>
> I decided that the time had come to teach them what they could do for man in order that he in turn might learn what he could do with them.

Baynes began training War Whoop and Tomahawk individually to accept a rope halter and amble down a farm road. "Every day," he wrote, "there was a tussle to get them [going] and another to keep them from getting back too fast." Then he put a yoke on the pair and introduced them to a bit and harness to pull a cart. In the first attempt, they galloped off, careening down the road until the cart hit a clump of bushes and turned over, breaking its shafts and splitting in two. He kept at it, sometimes attaching them to a stone sled to slow the young bulls down, until, he said, "I had the thing I had been working for—a team of buffalo calves really under control, a convincing bit of evidence that the buffalo can be domesticated and added to our list of [draft] animals."

When the calves were five months old, he took them to the Sullivan County Fair, about ten miles from Blue Mountain, where they created a sensation pulling a stone sled that carried a barrel of apples, then a wagon with a load of hay. For a grand finale, they pulled him and a small cart around the fair's racetrack at full speed. "I did not see the crowd, for my eyes were on the buffaloes," he wrote, "but plainly did I hear the quick, rushing sound, as with one move ten thousand people rose to their feet before breaking into a cheer for my youngsters who were so nobly, if unconsciously, proving to the American people the value of their race, and who were making a splendid appeal for the preservation of the last few hundreds of the North American bison, one of the very grandest animals the world ever produced."

Spurred by his success at getting people's attention, Baynes took War Whoop and Tomahawk on the road. At a sportsmen's show in Boston, President Roosevelt's son, Theodore Jr., was allowed to drive the buffalo cart. At the New England Fair in Worcester, Massachusetts, Baynes challenged anyone to match their domestic steers of the same age as his bison bulls to "contests of speed and strength." According to Baynes, there were no takers:

> These exhibitions had two effects on the farmers: one, the swift conviction that the calves were as speedy and strong as I said they were; the other, that while they were docile now, there was no telling how long they would be.
> "Baynes hitches 'em up," one local farmer said, "and they take him where they damn please."
> I didn't blame the farmers for being skeptical.

By the time War Whoop and Tomahawk were two and a half years old, they were famous. Baynes brought them to the Central Maine

Fair, where a young farmer accepted his challenge for a race, but only had a single steer. Baynes selected War Whoop to answer. "The result," Baynes wrote, "was not in doubt for a moment. This was the last appearance of my calves. They were trained to awaken interest in the American bison . . . and they had done their share. I took them back to [Sacajawea]. Then I brought all three of them back to the Corbin herd. Their work was over."

Because of the costs involved, the Corbin family began talking about getting rid of their buffalo herd. To save the bison as a species, Baynes now believed that a national organization should be created, and the federal government needed to establish several more protected herds, besides the one in Yellowstone National Park. Relying on private ownership, he thought, was not enough. "An individual owns a small herd; that individual dies," Steven Rinella explained. "It's up to that individual's heirs: Do they sell them off for slaughter? There was a real vulnerability."

In Walpole, New Hampshire, Baynes discussed his ideas with Professor Franklin W. Hooper, director of the Brooklyn Institute of Arts and Sciences. Hooper encouraged him to write to a number of prominent Americans, including President Roosevelt. "He wrote to all the bigwigs and wealthy people he could think of," Dan O'Brien said, "and when that letter crossed Roosevelt's desk—probably one of a hundred letters that day—he saw 'buffalo' on it and he read it carefully. And he goes, 'You know, this Baynes guy has got a good idea; we should do something about this.'" The president responded enthusiastically and promised to address the issue in his upcoming annual message to Congress:

> To the Senate and House of Representatives,
>
>   I desire . . . to urge upon the Congress the importance of authorizing the President to set aside certain portions of the [forest] reserves, or other public lands, as game refuges for the preservation of the bison . . . and other large beasts once so abundant in our woods and mountains, and on our great plains, and now tending toward extinction.

We owe it to future generations to keep alive the noble and beautiful creatures, which by their presence add such distinctive character to the American wilderness.

To enlist public support for the president's proposal, Baynes launched a speaking tour and dispatched a flurry of articles to newspapers and magazines. One, entitled "Help Save the Buffalo," for the Nature-Study Club of *Woman's Home Companion*, proposed a letter-writing campaign to bolster the cause:

> We can save the buffalo if we all work together. Let each one make a point of getting a letter (addressed to me) from some prominent man or woman, stating that he or she is in favor of the government taking immediate steps to preserve the few remaining buffaloes. In leading this movement I need all the letters of this kind I can get, and I want one from every part of the country. Don't fail to get me at least one, and I know that you will be glad to have had a hand in saving for America the grandest of all her native animals.

Baynes had also been corresponding with William T. Hornaday, who shared his belief that multiple federal herds were crucial. The confines of zoos and the uncertainties of private herds provided no guarantee that buffalo would exist in another generation. Hornaday also worried about crossbreeding with cattle—and about a "genetic bottleneck" developing because most of the existing collections of bison were so small. "In some of the surviving bison herds that make it into the twentieth century, there are a dozen, or fewer, animals," Andrew Isenberg said. "And there's one dominant bull who may be siring all of the animals. So, it's a problem with inbreeding. What happens is a lack of genetic diversity. There are too few breeding pairs that are put together. Genetic anomalies start emerging within these small bison herds because there's just not enough genetic diversity among them." There were other threats as well, according to Steven Rinella: "When we got to the era when you could just count them up, there were so few here and there, and they were concentrated in certain little pockets, it was alarming to people. It was perfectly plausible that you could have a disease break out and it would kill half of the animals left in the country. A lightning strike could have walked away with 10 percent."

Still, few people at the time envisioned turning buffalo loose on the kind of expansive ranges they had once inhabited, Rosalyn LaPier said:

> Part of the motivation for the Americans who were interested in preserving bison at the turn of the last century, was not to return them to the wild. It was actually to preserve them so that people could see them, almost as a zoo-type species.
>
> There was no interest, at that time, in creating large landscapes where bison could be a wild species. There was an interest in creating small landscapes, where bison could be preserved, where people could go see them.

Only a mere handful of existing herds at the time numbered more than fifty: the Corbin herd in New Hampshire, the Pablo-Allard bison in Montana, the Goodnights' in Texas, Philip's herd in South Dakota, and the combination of captive and wild buffalo in Yellowstone National Park. Much more common were those found in what were referred to as "zoological gardens" or "menageries"—city zoos that often kept only one to four bison as part of their collection of other animals and birds.

Keokuk, Iowa, had four buffalo in its Rand Park zoo and had sold some to the Page Woven Wire Fence Company in Michigan, which the company took to state and county fairs in the Midwest to promote its product with the slogan "A fence that would hold a buffalo would hold any farm animal." Hornaday used Page fencing at the Bronx Zoo, but he was already looking into places where a new herd could be started—and be expected to thrive. "The work wasn't done," Steven Rinella said. "There had to be a place for them to go. People that were focused on this problem recognized a couple of things. They needed more buffalo; they needed to create dedicated space for them; and they needed to have concerted efforts to breed them and create more, just to fight the genetic extinction."

By 1904, the most imposing house on the Comanche reservation in Oklahoma Territory, called the Star House, was a two-story structure with spacious wraparound porches. Inside, the home boasted ten-foot ceilings, a large dining room with formal wallpaper and a wood-burning stove, and plenty of bedrooms for a big family. Its proud owner was Quanah Parker, the leader of the Quahada band of Comanches. "The story goes that Quanah had met a military general who had three stars on his uniform," said Dustin Tahmahkera, his great-great-grandson, "and Quanah said, 'I deserve more than that,' and more than doubled that with the stars on the roof of the Star House."

No tribe on the southern Plains had been more feared than the Comanches, and none had fought longer against white settlers, ranchers, railroad builders, buffalo hunters, and the United States Army. Quanah and his Quahadas had held out the longest, the last to surrender and settle on a reservation in 1875. But now, no Comanche was more committed to helping his people adapt to reservation life than Quanah—who had added his deceased mother's last name to his own as a sign of respect for her memory.

"He was a natural leader," his great-grandson Ron Parker said. "In one century, he was a warrior; in the other century, he led us into the new world. He was preparing us for that." N. Scott Momaday, whose Kiowa ancestors shared the reservation with the Comanches prior to its division by the Allotment Act and the sale of "surplus" lands, said that the early twentieth century presented a challenge to all Indians:

> Trying to live in two worlds is a very common thing among Native American people. Quanah must have been struggling within himself to live in those two worlds. He was rather successful at it, I think. He had many white friends; he was regarded with great respect by his own people. But he must have lived in turmoil some

of the time, wondering which way to go, which direction to take at this fork in the road that he had been given.

The adjustments were difficult, Dustin Tahmahkera added, but necessary: "He would adapt and adapt, time and again, to do what was best for his people. He saw that certain eras were fading, but he never stopped being Comanche."

Quanah applied the same traits that had made him a successful warrior and tribal leader—confidence, courage, cunning, and the ability to persuade people to follow him—to his dealings with white officials and businessmen. He negotiated an arrangement that permitted cattle drives across reservation lands in exchange for taxes on each wagon and each cow; and he brokered an agreement to lease grazing rights to white ranchers on prairie land that had once teemed with buffalo, after they agreed to pay a proper fee and hire more than fifty Indians as cowboys. With a Durham bull he received from Charles Goodnight, he eventually built his own cattle herd of five hundred head on what was called the "Quanah Pasture," and he ran a 150-acre farm with crops and two hundred hogs, tended by a hired white man. He created stationery with a printed letterhead announcing "Quanah Parker: Principal Chief of the Comanches" and traveled to Washington, D.C., a number of times to meet with politicians and government bureaucrats about Indian issues. At his big house, he hosted a constant stream of prominent visitors, from the commissioner of Indian affairs to the British ambassador. With them, he never talked about his time as a warrior, focusing instead on winning them over with his easy manner and ready sense of humor.

On some things, Quanah Parker never compromised. He always wore his hair long and in braids, even when wearing a business suit. He openly advocated the use of peyote in religious ceremonies, though it was banned by law and the rituals had to be conducted in secret. "The white man goes into his church house and talks *about* Jesus," he explained about the use of the hallucinogen, "but the Indian goes into his tepee and talks *to* Jesus." And despite strict government rules outlawing polygamy on reservations and constant pressure from the superintendent, he had eight wives, with whom he fathered twenty-four children. He and his family also adopted two non-Indian boys, one of whom Quanah had met at a circus in San Antonio. Dustin Tahmahkera described Quanah's response to officials who insisted he change:

> It's said that, during one of his trips to Washington, D.C., Quanah was talking to some of the politicians, and they're trying to explain to Quanah, "You can't have all these wives." And he says, "If I can't have all these wives, *you* go tell them." Time and again, it was that kind of wit and that kind of rhetorical maneuvering that Quanah was known for, being able to get things done the way he wanted to have them done for the people.

On March 4, 1905, Theodore Roosevelt was inaugurated for his first full term as president of the United States. Riding in the parade were six Native American leaders from different western tribes, including Geronimo of the Apache and Quanah Parker of the Comanche. Invited to a reception in the White House, Quanah learned that the president was planning a hunting trip to Oklahoma in April and he offered to return Roosevelt's hospitality. When the president's train arrived in Frederick, Oklahoma, Quanah was among the three thousand people gathered to welcome him. After Roosevelt spoke, he invited Quanah to say a few words, and the two leaders shook hands. "I got more cheers than Teddy," he said later.

Then, with a small group, the two men spent several days camping, hunting coyotes, and getting to know one another better. "We know that Roosevelt does not have a favorable impression of Indigenous people anywhere on the planet," Dan Flores said:

> He has the idea that Indigenous people represent an earlier form of humans. Quanah is a charismatic figure. He's highly intelligent. I think what draws Roosevelt to Quanah, is that Quanah seems to bridge the worlds, and Roosevelt, he knows he's not going to bridge the world to Native people.

After the hunt, Quanah hosted the president for lunch at his Star House, instructing his wives to make sure the large table was set with big goblets next to each plate. The goblets at the White House had been small, he told them, and he wanted to be more generous. "Quanah is a true host to Roosevelt," Dustin Tahmahkera said:

> He's not a tour guide who has just arrived on the job. Quanah intimately knows these lands. He was born there. He grew up there. So, I can imagine him having an intimate knowledge that he perhaps was willing to share. It's during this time, where Quanah can talk, one on one with Roosevelt, to be able to help further instill these ideas about the importance of the land, the importance of, not just preserving the relatively few buffalo left, but being able to revitalize herds.

The president spent the night sleeping on one of the porches. Before he left the next morning, he presented Quanah with a small porcelain cup—and some news. Congress, he said, had given him the authority to create a preserve for large game animals, especially buffalo, and his trip to Oklahoma had convinced him that the Wichita Mountains would be a perfect location. Back east, reporters referred to Roosevelt as the "cowboy president." To Quanah Parker, he was now the "buffalo president."

The cause for creating a federal bison preserve took on added urgency shortly after Roosevelt's visit, when the Miller brothers in north-central Oklahoma staged a highly publicized extravaganza at their ranch near the Ponca reservation to inaugurate a new Wild West show of their own. More than fifty thousand people showed up to fill the arena, drawn to the event by the promise that the grand finale would be a buffalo hunt featuring the eighty-year-old Apache chief Geronimo.

It turned out to be some cowboys and Indians on horseback chasing a single bull—and a man, being driven in an automobile, firing the shot that brought the buffalo down. Geronimo finished it off and posed for photographs that were turned into postcards. The American Society for the Prevention of Cruelty to Animals, joined by groups of sports hunters, raised a public outcry about the event that reached all the way to the White House.

On June 2, 1905, President Roosevelt signed an executive order designating sixty thousand acres of national forest as the Wichita Forest and Game Preserve—the first of its kind. It was land that had been taken from the Comanches during Allotment. In New York, William T. Hornaday began poring over maps and reading reports from a biologist he sent to Oklahoma to select a portion of the new preserve that would be best suited for starting a bison herd.

And on December 8, in the reception room of the Bronx Zoo's Lion House, the first meeting was convened of a new organization, the American Bison Society—the fruit of an idea Ernest Harold Baynes had been promoting for more than a year. "The objects of this Society," the group declared, "shall be the permanent preservation and increase of the American bison."

Hornaday was elected as its president, Baynes to serve as its secretary. Theodore Roosevelt had agreed to lend his name as honorary president. It was in keeping with Roosevelt's *real* presidency—of the United States—which became dedicated to his belief that a vigorous federal government was essential, the only force capable of combating the immense and destructive power of the robber barons, monopolies, and trusts that controlled the nation's railroad, banking, oil, timber, and mining interests. He also championed the cause of conservation as no president had ever done: creating national parks, national forests, national monuments, national bird sanctuaries, and national wildlife refuges.

With the creation of the American Bison Society, Baynes immediately went to work publicizing it and soliciting donations and memberships. He persuaded the publishers of *Field and Stream* to join the cause and offer to pay the first-year dues for any new subscribers. He embarked on a lecture tour, and in every town gained editorial support from local newspapers. After a presentation in Worcester, Massachusetts, Baynes enrolled fifty new members and raised $670. With President Roosevelt's support, Hornaday began lobbying Congress to put up $15,000 for fencing and buildings at the preserve. To sweeten the bargain, he promised that the Bronx Zoo would donate fifteen of their purebred buffalo to provide the seed stock. Some of them, descendants of bison that had originated from the herds of Buffalo Jones and the Goodnights, would be returning to the land of their ancestors. "We're relatively familiar with the idea of species reintroductions now, but no one had ever attempted anything like this before," Michelle Nijhuis said. "I think it really speaks to Hornaday's ambition. And, as blinkered as he was in so many respects, he had great foresight and imagination when it came to the American bison and what it was possible to do to protect them."

On October 11, 1907, everything was ready. Hornaday had personally designed special crates for each animal—nine cows and six bulls—for their 1,500-mile journey to Oklahoma. At the Fordham railroad station in the Bronx, they were loaded onto two freight cars usually reserved for transporting expensive thoroughbreds—with collapsible stalls, large water tanks, and plenty of hay. Then began one of the most unlikely buffalo migrations in history. "They have to move them, not from the last wild bastions, the last canyon, or hideouts of the animals in the American West; they have to move them from the Bronx Zoo back to the American West," Steven Rinella said:

> Not only that, but by *rail*. All this time we've been taking hides and tongues, and shipping them in trains to be consumed in the East. People in the East had been taking trains out to shoot the animals out the windows and just leave them to rot on the prairie. But all of a sudden, now, we're at this point where we have a small herd of them in the biggest city on the continent. And they put fifteen on a train and drive them back out West.

Their destination was the Wichita Mountains, the place where some Native people believed the bison had first emerged onto the surface of the Earth, and where they had gone to hide until people had learned to provide them with the honor and respect they deserved.

Seven days after their departure, the buffalo arrived at the train station in Cache, Oklahoma, and were taken twelve miles by wagon to a holding corral, before their release into the preserve. Among the spectators awaiting the bison was Quanah Parker—along with other Comanches and Kiowas, some of them old enough to remember the days when buffalo covered the prairie, and some of them children who had only heard about buffalo in stories. "I'd like to imagine that Comanches were calling out *tasiwóo, tasiwóo* [the Comanche word for buffalo]," Dustin Tahmahkera said, "calling out to those buffalo and being able to reestablish some kind of relationship between Comanches and those who had, for generations, provided so much for us." N. Scott Momaday also tried to re-create what the moment was like:

> What must have gone on in their minds, in their blood memory? They had to be amazed and probably joyful. Also, a kind of remorse, a kind of sadness. Quanah Parker cried when he saw the buffalo return. I can imagine that. I think that could very well be true, not only of him, but of many other people who witnessed this miracle of return.

For nearly two generations, following the destruction wrought by the hide hunters in the early 1870s, the Kiowa had passed along a legend told by Old Lady Horse about the last buffalo herd. That herd had walked, she said, into Mount Scott, "where the world was green and fresh, as it had been when she was a small girl," where "the rivers ran clear, not red, [and] the wild plums were in blossom, chasing the red buds up the inside slopes. Into this world of beauty the buffalo walked." After some time in the holding corral, the fifteen buffalo from the Bronx Zoo were let loose, free to wander on their new—and old—home, within sight of Mount Scott. For Momaday, the completeness of the circle seemed transcendent:

> Old Lady Horse, I like to think of her there. If you think of the interior of the mountain as being green and lush, maybe the last buffalo range of all, you can imagine them coming back at some point. This mountain will open up again and they will come back and it will be as it was. We will be alive again in our souls.

If you're going to have a return of the buffalo, it should be there, where they disappeared. That's somehow fitting and as it should be.

If she had seen their return, I think she would have dropped to her knees and wept in thanksgiving. Her sense of the sacred would have been realized at that moment as a high point in her life. That makes the story whole.

Less than a month after the buffalo's arrival, two calves were born. Within six years, the herd had doubled in size.

TWELVE

Big Medicine

To Mr. W. T. Hornaday. My dear sir:

Buffalo will never be preserved through private individuals, no longer than the present owners live.... We have no children, and when we die the estate will go to relatives, and I know the first hard work they will do will be to squander this herd as they believe it to be an expensive and foolish thing.

It is to be hoped...the government or some state would take the matter up on a perpetual way. I would have more confidence in the general government than any state.

CHARLES GOODNIGHT

A S PLANS WERE BEING made for the Wichita Mountains refuge, William T. Hornaday had already begun looking for a location for another federal buffalo range. He ignored Molly and Charles Goodnight's offer of theirs, possibly because of its proximity to the new preserve in Oklahoma, possibly because of his worries that some of the Goodnight herd might be the product of crossbreeding. He and the New York Zoological Society considered the Corbins' private reserve in New Hampshire and one in Illinois; nothing came of it. They supported a bill in the New York legislature for a state-owned herd to be established in the Adirondack Mountains. The bill passed, but the governor vetoed it.

Then, because of the Allotment Act, much of the Flathead res-ervation in Montana had been declared "surplus" and was about to be opened to homesteaders. Michel Pablo realized that his grazing lands would be divided up and sold in the impending land rush. Marcia Pablo recounted her great-grandfather's bleak view of what would happen next:

> He raised my grandfather, Lawrence Pablo. He took Lawrence to the top of this hill, and he said, "I want you to look out over this landscape, Lawrence." He said, "In your lifetime, you're going to see all this marked up in fences and squares." You can't run six hundred head of buffalo on a hundred and sixty acres, so Michel saw the finger of doom for his buffalo.

"The American Bison Society, and associated groups, were not at all interested in preserving bison on behalf of Indigenous people in the Great Plains," Andrew Isenberg said. "In fact, in many ways, the preservation of the bison comes at the expense of Indigenous people. These [early preserves] are created when what had been very large reservations were diminished in size through Allotment. So, ironically, the killing of the bison by hide hunters, in the 1880s, had come at the expense of Native people; and, the preservation of the bison, in the early twentieth century, also comes at the expense of Native people."

Pablo offered to sell his buffalo to the United States for $250 each. President Roosevelt favored the proposal; George Bird Grinnell and others endorsed it. The conservationist John Muir had once written, "I suppose we need not go mourning the buffaloes. In the nature of things they had to give way to better cattle." Now, he added his name to the list of supporters, saying, "I heartily accept a place on the committee for saving the Pablo-Allard herd of buffalo, or any other of the pitiful remnants of the noble species now on the verge of extinction." But Congress refused to appropriate any money.

When Pablo learned of the decision, his son-in-law recalled, "he was moved to manly tears." "He was so hopeful that the buffalo would stay in the United States," according to Marcia Pablo. "He was devastated. I know Michel loved his buffalo. When he had to sell them, his spirit was broken. He was crushed, because every time he went out among them and every time he saw them, he felt that connection and that relationship, almost a kinship."

The Canadian government, looking to create a new Buffalo National Park in Alberta, however, jumped at the opportunity. They signed a contract to pay Pablo $245 per head for his whole herd. With Joe Allard, son of his former partner, Pablo recruited seventy-five local cowboys—many of them Native, some of them white and mixed-blood—and began rounding up the buffalo in the summer of 1907. Pablo had estimated that it would take them two years to gather his herd into corrals and get them onto freight trains for shipment to Canada. It took more than five. Instead of 350 bison, to his surprise it turned out he had nearly twice as many—and they often proved unwilling to leave their home range.

"Have you ever tried to herd buffalo?" Germaine White said. "It's not easy. They are the most astonishingly agile, athletic animals. They can stop on a dime. They can turn on a dime. But, one thing they don't do well is take orders. You don't mess with a two-thousand-pound animal too much—and survive." It was "chaos," Marcia Pablo added. "I remember my grandpa saying, you had to be able to read the buffalo and read what their action was going to be. He said, 'You always watch their tail and their head. If that tail went up, look out.' You were going to get run over."

As it was being driven into the shipping corral, one buffalo turned and sank its horns into a horse, lifted it *and* the cowboy riding it into the air, and carried them a hundred yards before dumping them on the ground. The cowboy survived, but the horse was gored to death—one of five horses that died during the roundups. Emily Irvine, part Indian and the only woman wrangler during the buffalo roundups, was credited with single-handedly diverting a herd to prevent a disastrous stampede. Pablo felt so grateful, he gave her his best buffalo cow as a reward.

One of the other participants at two of the roundups was the painter Charles M. Russell. In 1880, at age sixteen, he had left his home in St. Louis for Montana, where he became a cowboy for eleven years, before deciding to support himself as an artist. By now, Russell was world-famous for creating works that portrayed a West

that seemed to be a fading memory, symbolized by the image he
attached to every painting, next to his initials: a buffalo skull. For
Russell, the chance to take part in another roundup—this time of
living buffalo—proved irresistible. He rode with the cowboys, told
stories of the old days around the campfire, and sketched watercolors
to his heart's content, sometimes adding them to illustrate letters he
sent to friends. In one, he described a close call with an enraged bull,
which was driven away at the last minute by shots from Pablo's son.
"I don't think the lead hurt the bull any," Russell recalled, "but I tell
you for a second or two my hair didn't lay good." One day, part of
the herd unexpectedly crossed the Pend d'Oreille River, scattering
everyone in camp:

> I wish you could have seen [the buffalo] take the river. They hit
> the water on a dead run [and] they left her at the same gait.
>   A photographer from Butte come near [to] cashing in.... We all
> said good-bye to him and figured on a funeral, but lucky for him
> there was some cedar [trees] there and he clawed up one, coming
> out shy a camera, hat, and most of his pants.
>   Barring th[o]se trimmings, he was all right.

Ultimately, Michel Pablo would deliver more than 670 bison to
Canada for its national park. Meanwhile, in the United States, news
of the sale had created a national furor. A Denver newspaper report
was typical of the coverage:

> President Roosevelt may easily be imagined stamping his feet and
> grinding his teeth when he hears that his cherished ambition to
> secure for American national parks the famous herd belonging to
> Michel Pablo...has been defeated by...energetic officials of the
> Canadian government.

The *New York Herald* ran a story under the headline "Roosevelt's
Buffalo Herd Captured by Canada."
Officially, the American Bison Society praised Canada for step-
ping in to save the largest buffalo herd in the world, but privately,

William T. Hornaday was seething. When Ernest Harold Baynes offered to go to Montana to observe the transfer on behalf of the organization, Hornaday shot down the suggestion. He wrote Baynes that he did not want an officer of the Bison Society to "witness the triumph of Canada [and] see the Pablo herd taken from us." Instead, Hornaday used the negative publicity to push Congress into appropriating $40,000 to purchase and fence twenty-nine square miles of land in the Flathead reservation for a new buffalo preserve—not far from where Pablo's herd had been grazing. "How dumb can this be?" Marcia Pablo said. "What an insult. You had the chance to buy this premier herd, and you make a bison range right in the midst of where they were? It doesn't make any sense." A member of the Bison Society's advisory board, Dr. Morton Elrod at the University of Montana in nearby Missoula, had recommended the site. Among its attributes, he argued—besides being in an area already proved to be conducive to successful buffalo propagation—was that it was closer to a railroad than Pablo's grazing lands, and "a visitor may step off the train and in five minutes be in the range."

The Bison Society then launched a private campaign to raise $10,000 to buy the seed stock. Baynes threw himself into the fund drive, spending much of 1908 on the road giving 113 lectures, and producing reams of copy for any publication that would run it. Calling the bison "our national animal" and arguing that "the breeding of catalos is not really saving the buffalo," he pressed the cause with urgency:

> According to a proverb, there are three things which, once gone, never return to a man—the spoken word, the sped arrow and the lost opportunity. Our opportunity to prevent the massacre of the buffaloes has gone, but our opportunity to save the survivors, and thus to pay in part the debt we owe the race, is here, and we must take it now, if ever.

Most of the donations came from people in the East, many of them women, including twenty-one from Boston who got together and chipped in $500—twice the amount donated by Andrew Carnegie, and more than the $366 that came from Montana donors. Kansas, Texas, and the Dakotas—the other states where the hide hunters had done the most damage—contributed nothing, though Nebraskans provided $100. An Indianapolis newspaper also voiced skepticism of the plan. "Why Boston people," it editorialized, "should take an interest in the buffalo and why any intelligent person should care for the preservation of these moth-eaten, ungainly beasts...are conundrums no one answered." Still, Baynes's fund drive raised $10,565.50, exceeding its goal.

By this point, Baynes's relationship with Hornaday had deteriorated even further. Part of his travels had brought him to the West, where he met with Pablo and other bison ranchers in Montana, the Goodnights in Texas, and the owner of the bison herd on Antelope Island in the Great Salt Lake. Hornaday told some Bison Society members he thought Baynes was profiting from his lecture tour more than he was raising in donations, and complained about "the way he goes around saying how he saved the bison...nobody else is on the map. [But] I don't mind his saying he started the Bison Society." "Hornaday considered almost everyone to be a rival," Michelle Nijhuis said. "Baynes was no exception. He considered Baynes to be a bit of a dilettante, not a serious conservationist."

Since some of Pablo's herd had not yet been rounded up for shipment to Canada, Baynes hoped the Bison Society could still buy some of them. But no deal could be arranged. Pablo said he wouldn't break his agreement with the Canadians, which infuriated Hornaday. He would never, Hornaday wrote a colleague, "ask favors of a half-breed Mexican-Flathead." The reservation agent told George Bird Grinnell that the problem was Hornaday's "unpardonable sin" of racial hostility. Like Baynes, Grinnell was also at odds with Hornaday. He was a "crank" who "delights in a row," Grinnell told a friend, and he had given up dealing with Hornaday except through intermediaries. The two would later exchange bitter letters. On one, Grinnell was particularly frank:

> I appreciate more fully than most people the vast amount of effective work for protection which your great energy has enabled you

to accomplish, [but] I think that your combative attitude—and as I see them—exaggerated methods injure the cause of game protection by alienating the sympathies of people who, by different handling, might become its friends and partisans.

Grinnell also told a friend he didn't agree with the "scientific racism" promoted by Madison Grant, Henry Fairfield Sr., and Hornaday. "Races of men have been mixing up ever since bipeds without feathers began to travel the earth," he said. For his own part, Hornaday saw no reason to change his beliefs or moderate his tactics in his single-minded pursuit of his goals. "I am," he proclaimed, "positively the most defiant devil that ever came to town."

In the end, the Bison Society purchased thirty-four buffalo from Alicia Conrad of Kalispell, Montana, whose family had bought part of Charles Allard's herd back in 1902. Thanks to Baynes's visit, she also donated a prized bull and cow. The Goodnights in Texas donated two of their buffalo. The Corbin family in New Hampshire gave three from their herd.

By October 17, 1909, the fencing was complete, and the animals were released to graze on the new National Bison Range. The United States now had three federal herds under protection—in Yellowstone, the Wichita Mountains, and western Montana.

Seventy-five of Michel Pablo's buffalo had eluded capture for Canada, and for a while they grazed outside the new preserve's fences, sometimes creating problems for the new homesteaders in the region. The state of Montana claimed jurisdiction over what came to be called the "outlaw herd" and declined any suggestions to try to move them inside the new federal bison range. Poachers went to work and eventually killed them all.

Within the next six years, more protected herds were established. Wind Cave National Park, in South Dakota's Black Hills, started one with fourteen bison from the Bronx Zoo; nearby Custer State Park began with thirty-six buffalo purchased from Scotty Philip's estate. At Fort Niobrara in Nebraska, six bison were donated by a local rancher, who had purchased them from Buffalo Jones, and two more came from Yellowstone's herd. Though it eventually didn't do well enough to continue, a federal herd was even established in a national forest near Asheville, North Carolina, stocked by six buffalo from the Corbin family in New Hampshire.

In the Texas Panhandle, Molly and Charles Goodnight had not stopped hoping that their buffalo herd could also be permanently preserved for the future. The couple organized a coalition calling for a Palo Duro Canyon National Forest Reserve and Park. Legislation to create it was introduced in Congress three times. Each time, the bill was turned down because the land was not federally owned and purchasing it was considered too expensive. (Part of the original ranch became Caprock Canyons State Park in 1982, and a herd, descended in part from the Goodnights' buffalo and now called the Texas State Bison Herd, was moved there in 1997.)

Goodnight never stopped trying to come up with ideas to make the buffalo business profitable. He sent a pair of socks made from buffalo hair to General John J. Pershing, saying the Army should try them to keep soldiers' feet warm. He and Molly developed what they called "Buffalo Balm," made from bison tallow, which a Dallas physician claimed was effective against everything from rheumatism to pneumonia, tuberculosis to cancer. Goodnight said it was also good for cleaning oil paintings and silverware. "It stands a fair chance to become the discovery of the age," he wrote to the American Bison Society when he sent them samples. The society passed them on to some New York doctors, who reported back that they could not find any medicinal uses for it, but one thought it might work better to grease automobile gears.

Like Buffalo Jones, Goodnight had experimented in developing a hybrid breed of catalo—Goodnight used Angus cattle; Jones preferred Galloways. And, like some others in the small but far-flung community of crusaders for the bison's preservation, the two men became antagonists. Goodnight considered Jones an egotistical publicity hound who overly embroidered everything about his career. He scoffed at Jones's claim to have taken part in the capture of Billy the Kid; as a leader of the Panhandle Stock Association, Goodnight had hired a man to help Sheriff Pat Garrett with the task in 1881, and from him knew differently. He ridiculed an anecdote in Jones's book about riding with two bison calves tucked in his arms while being surrounded by a pack of wolves, which Goodnight considered an impossibility. And, when the American Bison Society invited him to join the organization, he told an official that Jones had actually acquired much of his knowledge about buffalo ranching, including crossbreeding, from Goodnight, who had been doing it longer. "While I do not pose as [a] great authority upon buffalo," he said, "it is a fact I've done more with them and learned more about them than any other man, and do not enjoy having this information used in a selfish way." He and Jones exchanged contentious letters, though their dispute was never a public one.

But the old Indian fighter had, over time, become friendly with a number of Native tribes. He provided the Taos Pueblo with the seed stock for their own herd so they would have a source for the hides and tallow they needed for their traditional ceremonies. And he helped Quanah Parker's efforts to have the chief's mother and little sister reburied on the Comanche reservation in Oklahoma, not far from where the Wichita Mountains herd now grazed. In thanks, Quanah presented Goodnight with a lance he had used in the raid against the hide hunters at Adobe Walls in 1874.

Quanah had become more prominent than ever. He had one of the first residential telephones in the area, owned a car, and had appeared in the silent motion picture *The Bank Robbery*, filmed near his home in Cache. A town in Texas and a railroad to it had been named for him. At an event promoting the new railroad line at the Texas State Fair, he spoke briefly, saying, "We are the same people now." In 1911, he wrote to Goodnight saying he planned to bring fifty other Comanches with him to the ranch in Palo Duro Canyon to "see your buffalo and make these old Indians glad." But he never made it. Quanah Parker died within a month and was buried next to his mother and sister, as he had wanted.

Five years later, Goodnight invited some Kiowas to his ranch.

They came to help him make a film that would capture scenes from the West the eighty-year-old Goodnight still remembered—more authentic, he hoped, than the romanticized Westerns filling movie theaters across the nation. The highlight was a buffalo hunt. Real Indians rode after a real buffalo herd, and finally brought one down with bows and arrows. At a barbecue the next day, a Kiowa named Horse rose to speak. "All Kiowas always remember Mr. Goodnight... the best white man," he said, mentioning the time back in 1887 when the big herds seemed to be gone forever from the southern Plains, and Goodnight had supplied them with a bull for the Kiowa's last Sun Dance.

In 1913, the United States came out with a new design for the nickel. It was designed by the sculptor James Earle Fraser, who said he wanted a coin "that could not be mistaken for any other country's coin." On one side, the new nickel showed the profile of an American Indian. On the other was an American buffalo, modeled after a bison Fraser had seen in New York City's Central Park Menagerie.

"We know its name, it was called Black Diamond and it lived in a cage," said Steven Rinella:

> This confined creature, eventually, had nowhere to go, no one that wanted to take care of it. It was sold to a butcher. And the model for the buffalo head nickel was processed and parted out, and sold as meat, in the Meatpacking District in Manhattan. That was the animal's fate.
>
> But it stands to us now like this distinctly American, enduring symbol, and it opens up this idea of just how conflicted the symbol is. We look at it and we see a symbol of wilderness and a symbol of the wanton destruction of wilderness. We look at it and see freedom and American prosperity. And we look at it and see the ravages of capitalism. Whether he knew it or not, he hit the nail on the head in terms of a long-term, lasting idea that we would look at and be puzzled by it.

The symbolism also puzzled George Horse Capture Jr.:

You look at that old nickel, there's a buffalo. At one time, they almost wiped them to extinction. Why did the Euro-Americans put that buffalo on that nickel? Was it just a curiosity, or was it something that kind of meant something to them in an odd way? So, in my confusion, and my need to understand, is: Do you have to destroy the things you love?

In 1917, the Department of the Interior joined the effort to honor the animal that the nation had nearly exterminated. Forty-three years earlier, in his annual report, Secretary Columbus Delano had written, "I would not seriously regret the total disappearance of the buffalo from the western prairies." Now, the department decided that its official seal should prominently feature the image of a buffalo bull, with a bright sun rising behind it.

By 1933, the American Bison Society reported that 4,404 buffalo existed in 121 herds in forty-one different states. More than half of those buffalo were grazing in nine government-protected herds. Compared to the millions of buffalo that had once covered the Plains, those were tiny numbers, but enough—and in enough different places—that the society began making plans to disband, declaring the American buffalo finally safe from extinction.

That same spring, seventy-five calves were born on the National Bison Range in Montana. One of them, a little bull, had blue eyes and white hair—an extremely rare occurrence. The staff at the Bison Range called the little bull "Whitey" at first, and its presence turned the preserve into a tourist attraction for a while. But to the Salish, Kootenai, and Pend d'Oreille on the Flathead reservation—and to virtually all other Native tribes—a white buffalo represented more than a statistical oddity. It held special spiritual power and sacred meaning. "A white buffalo is so sacred and so full of hope and goodwill for the tribes," Marcia Pablo said. "It is just a huge blessing to

the tribes, just a tremendous gift from Creator." It was considered
"big medicine"—and that became its name. Marcia Pablo was three
years old when she met her first buffalo, which turned out to be Big
Medicine:

> My grandpa and my dad took me to the Bison Range and wanted
> me to touch him. He was so old. He stood inside this fence and
> he didn't move. So, they got me over the fence, somehow; it was
> illegal, I know.
>
> But, I touched him, and I thought he would be soft, his head,
> like my teddy bear. It was bristly. And that was my first impression:
> He's big and I love his eyes. And he's *bristly*.

Big Medicine would live to the age of twenty-six—longer than
most bison bulls. He would father many calves and become the most
famous buffalo bull of all time. After he died in 1959, his body was
preserved and prominently displayed at the Montana State Historical Society museum in Helena. He was a symbol of hope. And, just
like his ancestors, he was bristly.

The American buffalo had been brought back from the brink of
disappearing forever. Their salvation was never inevitable—in the
same way that their near extinction was not inevitable. Both were
the result of individual choices and, ultimately, national decisions.
"In the context of everything else that was going on in the nineteenth century," Michael Punke said, "what was amazing was not the
destruction of the buffalo; what's amazing is that the buffalo managed
to be saved."

The trail away from the edge had begun, nearly fifty years earlier,
with what Michelle Nijhuis called "disparate do-it-yourself bison
protection efforts." A young Pend d'Oreille walks some calves from
the Montana plains over the mountains to his reservation in the Flathead Valley. A family on the Cheyenne reservation in South Dakota
brings a few home in their buckboard. A wife on an isolated ranch
in the Texas Panhandle persuades her cattleman husband, who had
just cleared the area of any remaining bison, to take mercy on at

least four calves. In Canada, two men traveling with a Métis hunting brigade capture three calves and start a herd they sell to a prison warden. A former hide hunter from Kansas, gripped by regret over his part in the great slaughter, decides to lasso some calves for breeding purposes. A gaudy showman, who had also once made a living killing buffalo, decides to make them part of a show that would thrill millions of people around the world. A taxidermist, intent on at least preserving stuffed specimens of a dying species, turns to starting two zoos to display living ones. A nature writer, living on the New Hampshire estate of a millionaire who liked stocking it with exotic animals, becomes fascinated by the buffalo there, then obsessed about their future. An Ivy League scion of a Wall Street banker, trained in paleontology and ancient extinctions, becomes interested in the West, its Indigenous people, and its animals, especially the buffalo, and decides to devote himself to saving them from the same fate. He convinces another young man from an elite Manhattan family, whose primal impulse was to gun down large beasts for wall trophies, to think more broadly; and that man goes on to become the greatest conservationist president in United States history.

All of these buffalo saviors were prompted by their own motives, some of them noble and idealistic, some of them crass and even distasteful. Some didn't know any of the others; and some that did, didn't like each other. But together, this American amalgam somehow managed to change the "drive lanes" of history and eventually lead the bison's trail away from what otherwise would have been a colossal *pishkun*—a buffalo jump of an entire species over the cliff of extinction.

Some species were not offered such a reprieve. Carolina parakeets, heath hens, ivory-billed woodpeckers, the Labrador duck, the great auk, Audubon bighorns—all disappeared. By 1910, only two passenger pigeons had survived from the market-hunting onslaught against the billions that had existed only fifty years earlier. Both lived in the Cincinnati Zoo: Martha, a female, and George, a male (named after the nation's original First Couple). George died that year, leaving Martha as the only passenger pigeon left in the world—until she died on September 1, 1914. It was as if, in some alternate, yet not in the least implausible historical universe, Black Diamond or Big Medicine had been the final, sad representatives of the continent's most magnificent mammal—well known but remembered only on a coin or as a taxidermy display of a species that once existed. Thanks to the efforts of many individuals and organizations—and then action by a federal government that had once refused to act—for the bison, at least, the precipice of extinction was no longer at hand.

Being saved from extinction, however, is not the same as being wild and free again. At the time the American Bison Society disbanded in 1935, they had succeeded in their stated mission, Dan O'Brien said, "but their understanding of the problem was shortsighted. They didn't know about ecosystems. They thought, if you got a buffalo, you've saved him. That's not it. You've got to save their habitat." Michelle Nijhuis agreed:

> They were not thinking about the importance of protecting habitat; they were not thinking about the relationships among species that were so important to protect, and also protecting relationships between humans and other species. Protecting iconic species is just the beginning of conservation.

If the story of the American buffalo is a cautionary tale, it should have lessons to teach. This one has several, starting with the story of how, in its heedless rush to conquer a continent, a young nation proved itself fully capable of inflicting incalculable damage on the bountiful natural world it encountered, and equally capable of ignoring what that destruction meant to the continent's original inhabitants. The near demise of the buffalo is simply Exhibit A in that much larger tragedy. "It seems to me, if it has one lesson for us today, that lesson would be: Be careful, be careful," Elliott West said. "Human beings think they know everything that they're doing; they think they're in control. But they don't; and they aren't. And the result can be catastrophe on a scale that we cannot possibly predict." Marcia Pablo worried that, all around the globe, the lesson remains unlearned:

We're still destroying species. Why is it so important to devastate the environment and the habitat these creatures need? It's usually because a dollar is more important than the life of a species. She's all we have, is this Earth, and we destroy that, we're destroying ourselves.

The buffalo should have given us a lesson. We're supposed to make decisions that go seven generations beyond you. So, if you're making a decision today, like the tribes do, you're supposed to be looking at what's that impact going to be seven generations from today.

Well, Michel Pablo's seven generations are my grandchildren. And we can see what impact his decisions made in what's happening. But we aren't doing that with everything else. We just don't get it. We aren't looking at the future. We're looking at right now. And that's not far enough.

But, as the writer and historian Wallace Stegner suggested, there is another lesson on the other side of the coin: "We are also the only species which, when it chooses to do so, will go to great effort to save what it might destroy." Such was the case for Americans and what became their national mammal. They *chose* to change course before it was too late. They would then make the same choice with another national symbol, the bald eagle. Eagles had been systematically killed as a predator and then nearly eradicated by the ravages of DDT, before a national effort in the late twentieth century—which also included the passage of landmark legislation like the Clean Water Act, the Clean Air Act, and the Endangered Species Act—revived them.

Yellowstone, the world's first national park, is a part of that same lesson. It began, in 1872, as an attempt to save a scenic wonderland from the destruction befalling most of the other landscapes of the West, and though it, too, required saviors in its early years, it launched a movement that eventually resulted in more than four hundred national park sites, covering more than 84 million acres. The initial impetus for setting Yellowstone aside had nothing to do with wildlife protection; tourism and nationalism lay behind the park's establishment. As an unintended consequence, however, it also provided the bison with a "last refuge" when the species needed it the most. It all could have turned out differently.

The story of the American buffalo is unfinished and still being written, taking new turns, facing new challenges, and offering more lessons yet to be fully learned. "It's a lesson in how to live sustainably with nature," Sara Dant said:

> It's going to take the environment that bison lived in, for bison to get to be bison. Until you have those big prairies, across which buffalo can roam, you're not going to get buffalo the way buffalo once lived.
>
>   We didn't do a very good job. We almost screwed it up. But we didn't. And so, there's hope. To me, that is what this animal represents, as well. It's a possibility of what could come. And, who knows? We might even still yet get wild bison.

For Dan Flores, what the future holds is a question of what's been learned from the past. "You don't get a lot of chances to correct history's mistakes," he said. "You get a few. And when you get them, you damn sure better take advantage of them. I think we've got an opportunity to do this with buffalo. And, if we do, I think America can look back on its history and say, 'We got wise.' After all, we're Americans and buffalo are Americans, too."

Today, the United States is home to more than 350,000 bison. Native peoples oversee 20,000 of them; roughly 20,000 more are protected in federal and state preserves in what are called conservation herds. The rest exist in zoos or in private herds, where many of them are confined like cattle, fattened in feed lots, raised for slaughter. But some ranchers and nonprofit organizations—like the Nature Conservancy, the Wildlife Conservation Society, the World Wildlife Fund, the National Wildlife Federation, and American Prairie—have committed themselves to providing their buffalo with more room to roam and native grasses to eat—something closer to the habitats they once knew. In 2006, after seventy-one years of dormancy, the American Bison Society was reconstituted, with a broader goal of helping restore wild bison to large North American landscapes.

"It's going to be a big job," Dan O'Brien said, "but if human beings think they're the best animal in the world, now is our chance to prove it." Clay Jenkinson is cautiously optimistic:

> This is about experimenting in ways to recover the health of the continent. It's a kind of an indicator species; it tells you who you are. If no buffalo? That's one America. Buffalo in something like a wild state, that's a different America. Until buffalo can move, more or less at will, over vast grasslands, we haven't restored them at all. But to turn them loose in the way that they were meant to be, the way they were when Lewis and Clark came through, when Plains Americans were flourishing, it's a dream that I thought would never happen. And it's probably going to happen.

The most important work of restoring bison to their homelands is being done in concert with the people whose lives have been intertwined with the buffalo for more than ten thousand years. In 1991, representatives from nineteen tribes gathered in the Black Hills to consider forming the InterTribal Buffalo Council and organize attempts to bring some of the bison from Yellowstone and other federal preserves back to Native reservations—as an act of healing that would reestablish a sacred connection that had been broken for more than a century. An elderly Lakota woman took one of the founders, Fred Dubray, aside. "It's best you ask the buffalo if they *want* to come back," she said. So the group held a ceremony to do what she suggested. "They said they wanted to come back," he remembered, "but they said they didn't want to come back as cows. They wanted to be *buffalo.* They wanted to be wild again." By 2022, more than eighty tribes in twenty states controlled their own herds—more than twenty thousand buffalo grazing on nearly a million acres of tribal land. And on the Flathead reservation, where the Confederated

Salish and Kootenai tribes had taken over management of the National Bison Range, plans were being made to repatriate Big Medicine and display him at the place where he was born.

"There have been a lot of challenges for both bison and Indigenous people," said Germaine White, of the Confederated Salish and Kootenai. "Bison were nearly exterminated, and we had a similar experience. But bison are resilient; they have adapted. And they have taught us how to be resilient and adapt. They've survived; we've survived. They're here; we're here. We both persist."

Gerard Baker, who once managed the buffalo herd at Theodore Roosevelt National Park and has helped his Mandan-Hidatsa people start one on their reservation at Fort Berthold in North Dakota, also sees lessons in the long, still-evolving story of the American buffalo:

> There's a story of greed. And, unfortunately, that's a human factor, a human emotion that we still have—the greed in trying to take the environment away to make more money. There's a lesson to be learned in that we cannot, as human beings, afford to do that to our relatives, the animals. Those are our relatives. They are part of us. And when you look at a buffalo, you just don't see a big shaggy beast standing there. You see life. You see existence. You see hope. You see prayer. And you see the future for your young ones, the future for those not yet born.

At the Fort Belknap reservation in Montana, George Horse Capture Jr. is director of Aaniiih Nakoda Tours, where visitors can view the tribes' herd of more than five hundred bison roaming on a twenty-two-thousand-acre grassland—as well as a smaller herd, more genetically "pure" from cattle genes, that came from Yellowstone National Park as part of a program that still generates controversy and resistance among some Montana ranchers. "It's nothing to be alarmed about, you don't have to worry about your world collapsing," Horse Capture said:

> Seeing them coming back, seeing them in places where their ancestors were, seeing them in their ancestral regions, that's a

good thing. My people lived with them for thousands upon thousands of years, and the modern-day people can, too.

With this adventure, endeavor, that's going on with the buffalo, what I want for my people, I want for your people. I'm not stingy. I want your grandchildren to see them. I want your boy to tell stories, when you ain't here anymore. He can tell your grandchildren, "I was with my dad, your grandpa, to go see them. And it was good."

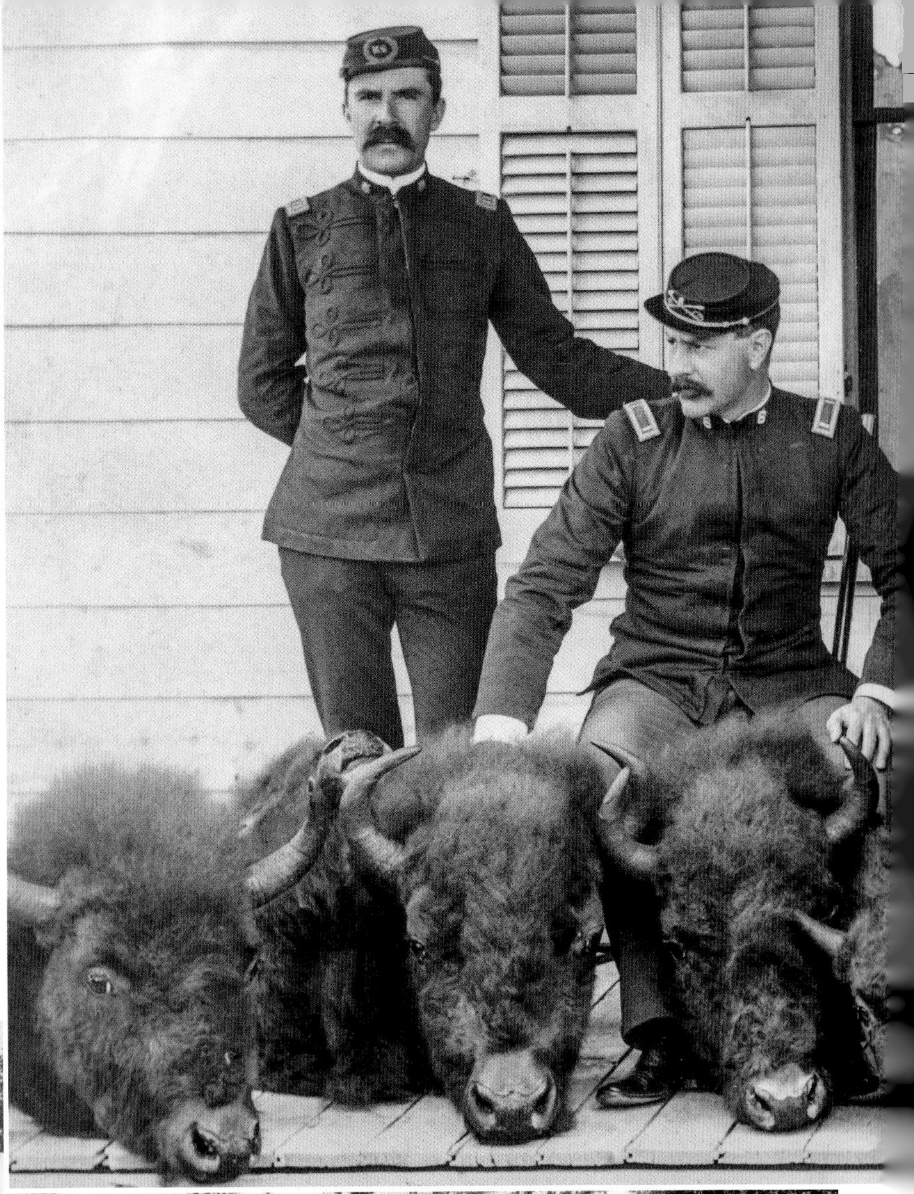

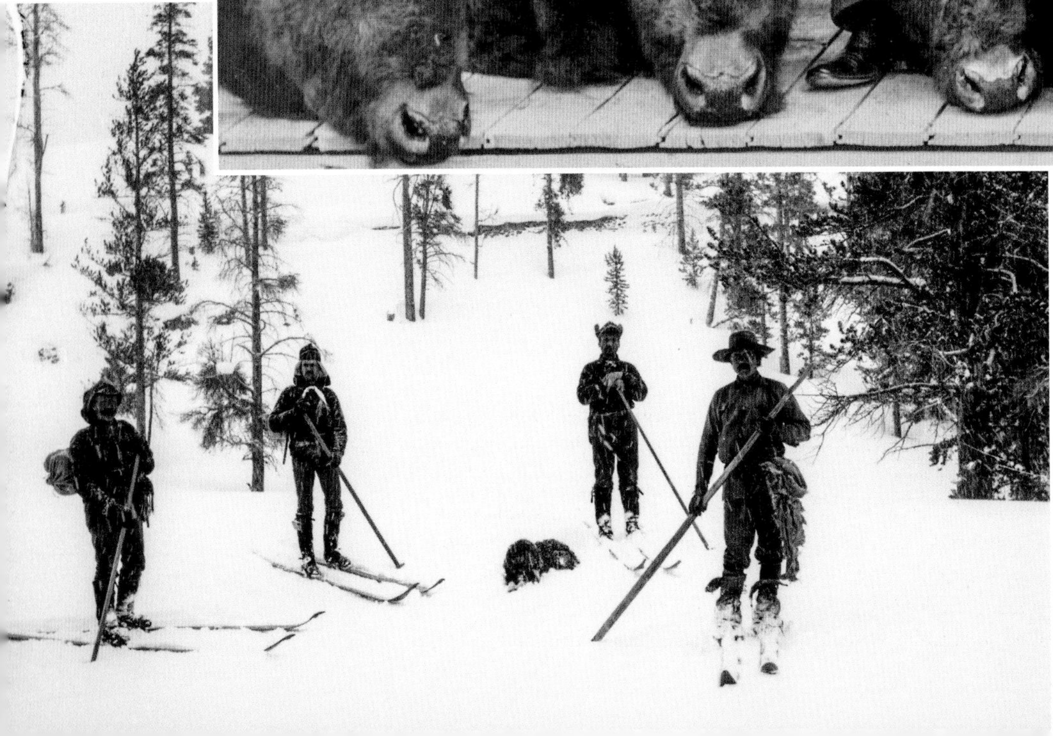

Poachers like Edgar Howell (opposite, on right) routinely killed bison in Yellowstone National Park's dwindling herd, knowing that the maximum punishment was temporary expulsion from the park and confiscation of his supplies. In March 1894, when Howell was captured once again, George Bird Grinnell's *Forest and Stream* magazine publicized the problem with a gruesome photograph of his slaughter (above). The public outcry prompted Congress to finally take action and pass a law with strict penalties.

William T. Hornaday (right) designed the National Zoo in Washington, D.C. (below), and then did the same for the Bronx Zoo in New York (opposite, top), which he ran for thirty years.

Frederick Dupuis and his wife Good Elk Woman (left) rescued some bison calves and started a herd in South Dakota, before selling it to Scotty Philip (below, sitting second from left) and his Lakota wife Sarah (standing, center).

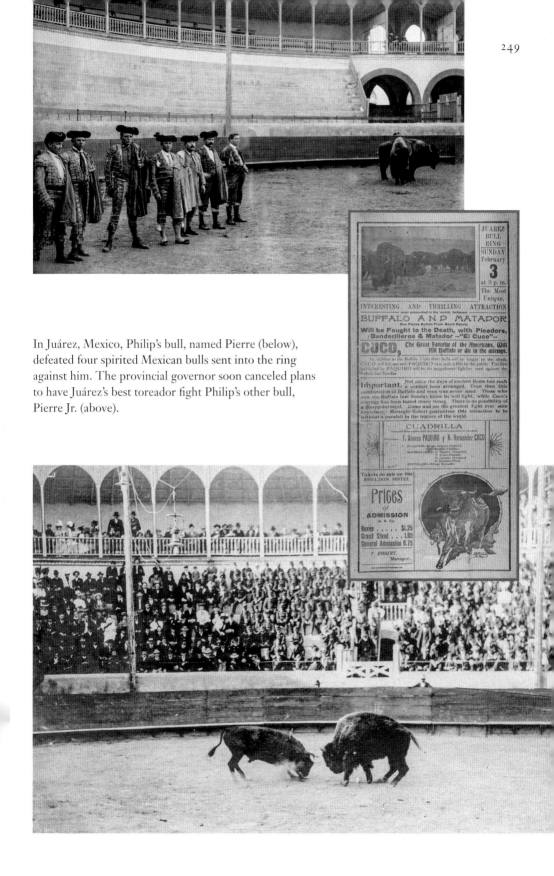

In Juárez, Mexico, Philip's bull, named Pierre (below), defeated four spirited Mexican bulls sent into the ring against him. The provincial governor soon canceled plans to have Juárez's best toreador fight Philip's other bull, Pierre Jr. (above).

On the Flathead reservation in Montana, Michel Pablo (above) and Charles Allard (below) raised a successful buffalo herd. After Allard's death, Pablo continued in the business (opposite), and it became the largest herd in the world.

St. Charles, ✠ ✠

EUROPEAN.

No. 495 PENNSYLVANIA AVENUE N. W.

Opp. B. & P. Depot.

WM. KALETSKI, Prop'r.

Washington, D. C., July 8 1902

My Dear Mr Grinnell: The Articals in your July 5th Number about the buffalo on the Flat Head reservation is to me of greate intrust. Your Supplement is of still Greater intrust; as I quickly recognize many of the older buffalo, as those on

Buffalo Jones wrote George Bird Grinnell (opposite, top) that he had been appointed game warden at the Yellowstone National Park. But he was less interested in the wild herd (left) than in raising a domesticated one that was fenced in (above). When Jones publicly whipped "problem" bears (top) and profited from the sale of souvenirs (right), the park threatened to fire him, and he resigned.

BUFFALO AND HALF-BREEDS

OWNED BY

C. J. (BUFFALO) JONES,

OF GARDEN CITY, KANSAS.

No 11. Group of Buffalo.
          S 1 year old ¾ Buffalo
          B 7   "   "   male   "   wt. 3,000 lbs.
No. 12.   5   "   "   cow ½   "
No. 13.   3   "   "   male ¾ "
No. 14. 1and2 "   "   ¾ "
No. 15. 1and2 "   "   ¾ "
No. 16.   3   "   "   cow ¾   "   Seal
No. 17.   6   "   "   male   "   wt. 2,600 lbs.
No. 18. D 5   "   "   cow ½   "   wt. 1,350 lbs.
          E 2   "   "   "
          F 3   "   "   ¾ "   Seal
No. 19. A 1   "   "   ¾ "
          B 7   "   "   male   "   wt. 3,000 lbs.
          C 3   "   "   ¾ "

C. J. Jones himself appears in Nos. 14, 15 and 19.
    Boudoir size, price 25 cents each.
    Cabinet size, price 20 cents each.
☞ Nos. 11, 14, 18 and 19 are Boudoir; the others are Cabinet Size.
    Mailed to any address on receipt of price.
        Address **H. L. WOLF,**
        Box 38, Garden City, Kansas

The nature writer Ernest Harold Baynes and some of his animal friends (above) at the millionaire Austin Corbin's exotic game preserve in New Hampshire (opposite, top). Baynes soon became most fascinated by the Corbin family's buffalo herd and began championing the species' revival.

To create public interest in the bison's fate, Baynes adopted three calves and trained two of them to pull a cart. He took them to fairs and exhibitions around New England before returning them to their herd.

Charlestown, N. H

1905 EIGHTH ANNUAL EXHIBITION AND FAIR

of the Sullivan County Fair Association
will be held at Highland View Park

OCTOBER 3, 4 and 5, 1905

AT CLAREMONT, N. H.

KEEP THE DATES IN MIND   **A HUMMER IN COMPARISON WITH OTHERS GONE BEFORE**

CAVALRY DRILL EACH DAY OF THE FAIR

In addition to the regular program, there will be every afternoon, an exhibition drill by the famous Troop G, 15th U. S. cavalry. This is captain Dodd's old troop, which won such fame at Madison Square, New York city. The troop also gave a very satisfactory drill on Barnes flat, Claremont, not many years ago, well remembered by many.

$2050 - IN PURSES FOR THE RACES - $2050

TUESDAY, OCT. 3	WEDNESDAY. OCT. 4	THURSDAY, OCT. 4
2:25, ... $250	2:14 Pace, . . . $300	Free-for-all, Trot and Pace, $300
Local Race, Trot or Pace 50	2:24 Trot, . . . 250	2:18 Trot, . . . 300
	2:22 Pace, . . . 300	2:17 Pace, . . . 300

Music by the American Band

WAR WHOOP, TOMAHAWK

only team of buffalo calves in existence.

Driven by

ERNEST HAROLD BAYERS

each day of the Claremont Fair

October 3, 4 and 5

UNIQUE

Vaudeville Entertainment

Japanese Day Fireworks

afternoon of Oct. 4 and 5

EXCURSIONS ON ALL RAILROADS AT SPECIAL RATES

Train will leave Claremont for Newport at 6 p. m., October 4 and 5.

ADMISSION, 35c   **Children Under 12, 25c**   **CARRIAGES FREE**

At Quanah Parker's
"Star House"
(above) he kept
a portrait of his
mother (left).
He had multiple
wives and kept his
long hair in braids
(opposite, top),
and when he went
coyote hunting with
President Roosevelt
(opposite, bottom),
he used the occasion
to talk about
restoring buffalo
to his homeland in
Oklahoma.

In 1905, an extravaganza billed as "the last buffalo hunt" drew a huge crowd to a ranch in Oklahoma, where the Apache chief Geronimo (above) ceremonially carved the bull that had been shot by a man in an automobile.

    That same year, President Roosevelt (opposite) signed an executive order creating the first federal bison preserve in the Wichita Mountains. Six months later, the American Bison Society was founded (opposite, top), with Hornaday (front, center) as its president and Baynes (front, right) as secretary.

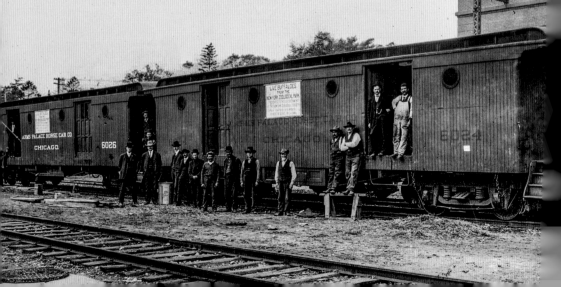

In 1907, Hornaday donated fifteen buffalo from the Bronx Zoo, which were shipped by rail to the new preserve in Oklahoma and then taken by wagon to a holding corral. Kiowas and Comanches gathered to see them before they were released near the sacred Wichita Mountains.

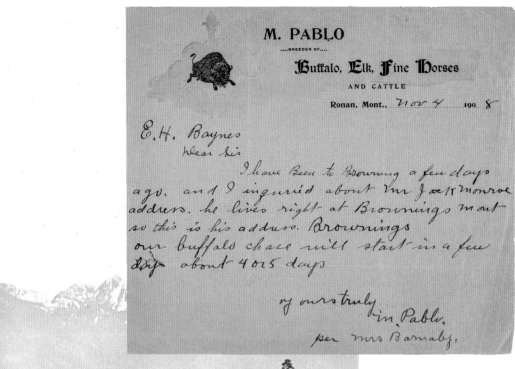

M. PABLO

....BREEDER OF....

Buffalo, Elk, Fine Horses

AND CATTLE

Ronan, Mont., Nov 4 190 8

E. H. Baynes
Dear Sir

I have Been to Browning a few days ago. and I inquired about Mr Jack monroe addres. he lives right at Brownings mont so this is his addres. Brownings

our buffalo chase will start in a few days about 4 or 5 days

yours truly
M. Pablo.
per Mrs Barnaby.

Because of the Allotment Act, much of the Flathead reservation was to be opened to white settlement, and Michel Pablo would lose the grazing land for his big herd. When Congress refused to buy it, he signed a deal with Canada. He and Ernest Harold Baynes exchanged letters, and Baynes photographed him when they met in Montana.

Pablo's buffalo roundups took more than five years of hard and sometimes dangerous work. Cowboys had to herd the bison into a series of corrals, take them by special wagons to the railroad line, then urge them up the chutes to freight cars for shipment to Canada.

The famous cowboy artist
Charles M. Russell took part in
two of Pablo's buffalo roundups—
and illustrated some of his letters
to friends with watercolors of what
he experienced.

Great Falls, Mont.
MAR 1 3 PM 1922

LONG BOY
Dept Cree Indian
HAYRE
Mont

Friend Young
the shield
they wer
thank you
well
picture

Oct 27 1921

a long time answering
letter you   Your daughter came
and I want to thank her for
one of you and a bull that
compared to the one you droped
If I rember right he got one
leg in front of his humpe
on and Banky wasent eaven
looked like he didnt mean to make
it want to go that far so you
kids a present of your raw hide
kids then the buffalo wint
bosses have joined them and
we have crossed the big devide
that has made us strangers
the cream let these combat
on down on your range I'll
do the same
wher to you and your
is me and my small of
friend C M Russell

Co
I think
seven
range

Jan 12
1910

Frend Fiddel back
    I got that skucum
hat band, an if it wasent
for savying your history
ya think you'd spent som of
your time at one of those
rest resorts where cow punchers
go for the helth of other people,
you savy.   I did[e]nt need to put
this sketch   in for you. its for
people   that cant read.

CANADA BUYS BUFFALO HERD

Largest Herd in the World About to Be Sold to a Foreign Government.

News of Canada's purchase of Pablo's herd created a national furor and prompted Congress to create a second bison preserve in Montana. The Bison Society launched a campaign (opposite) that raised money to buy more than thirty buffalo from a private ranch, which were herded (below) to the National Bison Range, not far from where Pablo's herd had recently grazed.

ROOSEVELT'S BUFFALO HERD CAPTURED BY CANADA

STRENUOUS EFFORT FOR THE DOMINION'S BIG WILD GAME RESERVATION WINS IN AN EFFORT TO GET THE LAST GREAT HERD OF BISON IN THE UNITED STATES

HELP

SAVE THE BUFFALO

Only prompt and concerted action of the American people can save the Buffalo from extermination. The American Bison Society, of which President Roosevelt is the Honorary President, is the only existing agency which can combine the strength of the many friends of the Buffalo the country over, and bring the resultant force to bear at the right time and place. It needs you as one of its members; as such you can do a great deal of good.

FIELD AND STREAM will pay your first year's membership. All we ask is that you either extend your subscription to FIELD AND STREAM two years or send us two new subscriptions.

Fill out the blank form at the bottom of this page, send it to us, together with three dollars, and we will enter your two subscriptions on our subscription list and send one-third of the money to the Secretary of the American Bison Society, together with your name and address, so that you will be duly enrolled as a member of the Society and receive your membership ticket, entitling you to all of the Society's privileges, literature, etc. We are not reducing the price of FIELD AND STREAM, but we are willing to give a third of your two subscriptions toward Saving the Buffalo. We want you to be a member of the Society and to follow the instructions you will receive from the Society's Secretary from time to time. We put up the money and you get the credit. Do not delay, but send your subscriptions at once. Much depends upon the Society's work with the Congress now in session. Money is needed, and names of members.

The American Bison Society

gratefully acknowledges   Dollar   from

as a contribution to the founding of the

Montana National Bison Herd

for the

Perpetual Preservation of the Species

1908   President

Some of the herd Molly and Charles
Goodnight (opposite) had started were
given to Native tribes so they could
continue their bison ceremonies. An aging
Quanah Parker (right and above) gave
Goodnight the lance he had used in the
attack on the hide hunters at Adobe Walls
back in 1874.

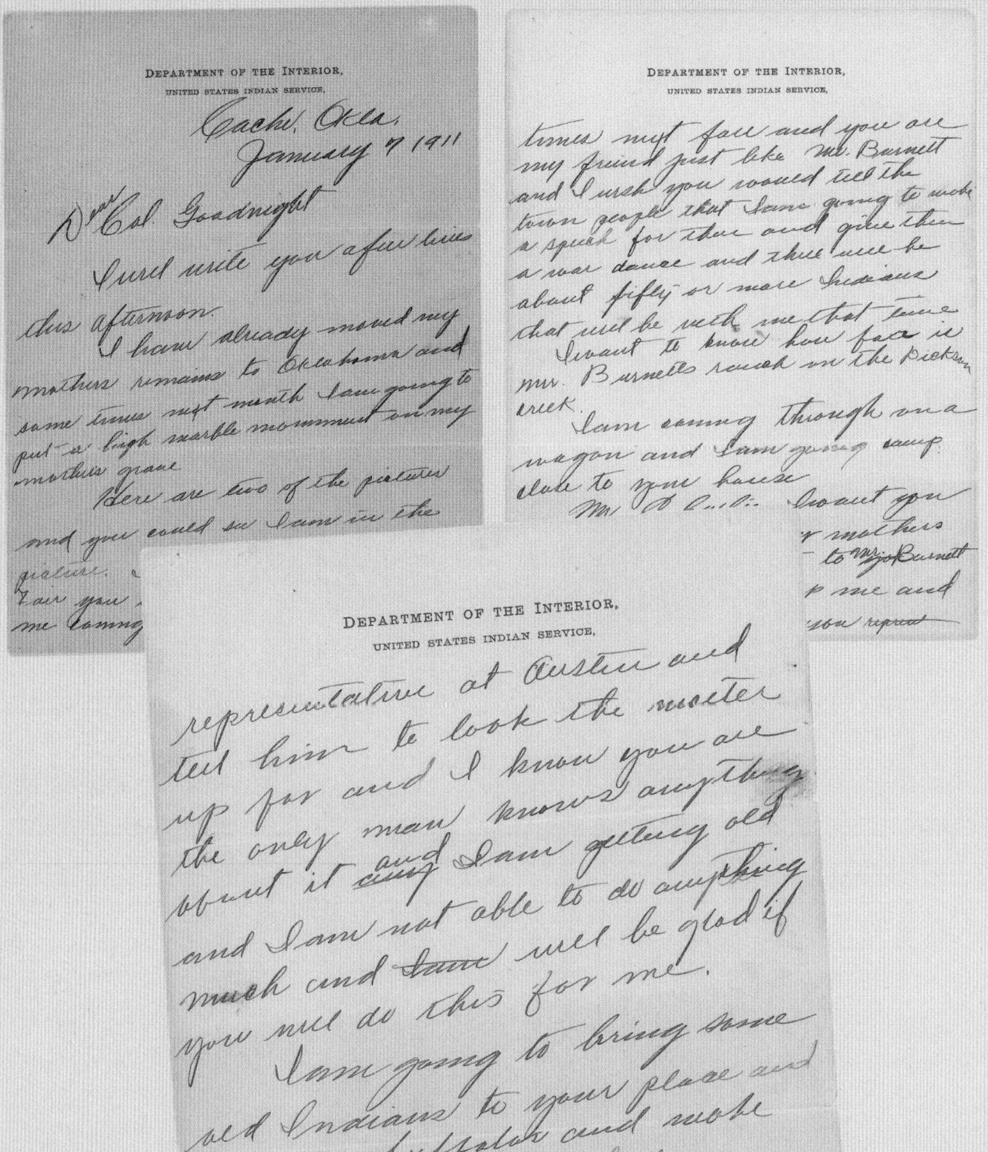

Cache, Okla.,
January 7 1911

Dr Col. Goodnight

Yours truly
Quanah Parker

Shortly before he died in 1911, Quanah Parker wrote Goodnight, saying he hoped to bring some Comanches to "see your buffalo and make these old Indians glad."

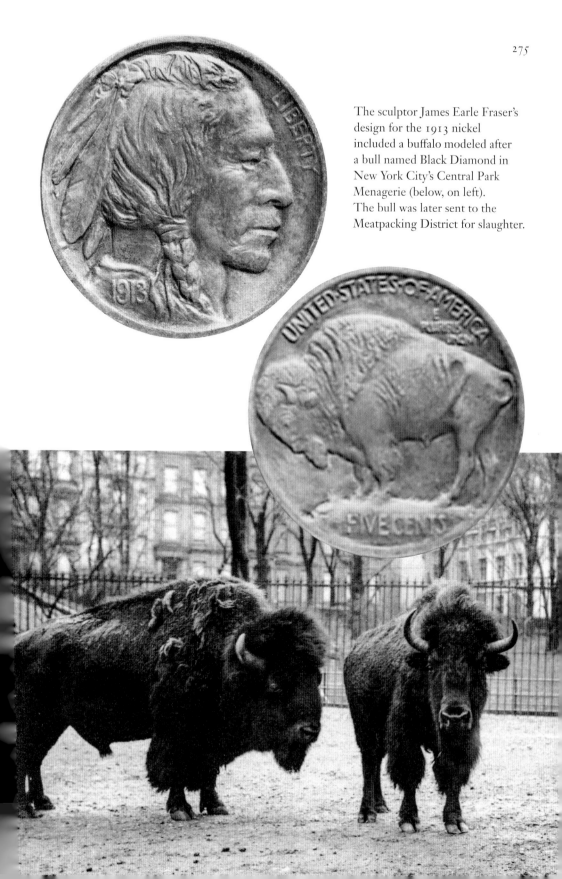

The sculptor James Earle Fraser's design for the 1913 nickel included a buffalo modeled after a bull named Black Diamond in New York City's Central Park Menagerie (below, on left). The bull was later sent to the Meatpacking District for slaughter.

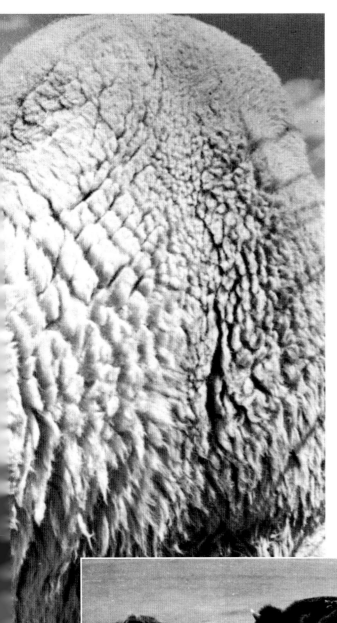

The white buffalo born on the National Bison Range in 1933 was seen as a symbol of hope and special spiritual power to Native people, who named it "Big Medicine." He lived for twenty-six years. His preserved body, displayed for more than fifty years at the Montana State Historical Society, is scheduled to be returned to the Flathead reservation, where the Confederated Salish and Kootenai tribes have taken over management of the Bison Range.

The American buffalo
was saved from
extinction, but still
faces challenges to its
long-term future.

Four buffalo bulls—and a friendly
cowbird—greet the rising sun of a
new day.

AFTERWORD:
BUFFALO BROTHERS

My fascination with the American buffalo and its history began in the early 1980s, as I researched a magazine article and then a book about retracing the route of the Lewis and Clark expedition of 1804–1806. Theirs was the United States' first official venture into the West, and I wanted to learn what had changed between the time of their journey and mine, nearly two centuries later—to see what we, as a nation, had made of the vast and bounteous land they had been the first white Americans to experience and record in their journals.

Like them, I spent most of my time on the Great Plains, the second-largest grassland in the world. The landscape itself in many respects seemed as stupefying to me as it did to the Corps of Discovery—undulating, virtually treeless, humbling in its immensity under a horizon-to-horizon bowl of sky. But equally astonishing to them was the profusion of wildlife they began encountering: prairie dogs, wolves, pronghorn antelope, grizzly bears, elk, and buffalo. So many buffalo. The Great Plains I was crossing had become a wildlife desert, dominated now by domestic cattle and cultivated wheat fields. I came across a number of prairie dog villages and occasionally saw a few antelope, but wolves, elk, and grizzlies were no longer Plains animals.

To see any bison took some work, but with help I located two herds. North of Fort Pierre, South Dakota, I visited Roy Houck at his Triple U ranch. At the time, his herd was the second-biggest in the United States (after Yellowstone National Park's) and numbered three thousand—the same size as one Lewis had noticed in the same vicinity in 1804. The difference was that Lewis would see even larger herds throughout the Great Plains, and for months his expedition was never out of sight of the animals; they were everywhere. I only caught a fleeting glimpse of Houck's bison, far off across rolling humps of prairie. Years later I saw them on a movie screen, after the producers of *Dances with Wolves* used the ranch as its prime location; and later still, when Ken Burns and I filmed there for our documentary film about the Corps of Discovery.

It was Gerard Baker who really introduced me to the national mammal of the United States. Gerard is a Mandan-Hidatsa, the tribes that befriended Lewis and Clark during the long, cold winter of 1804–1805 in what is now North Dakota, offering the strangers friendship and food, sharing stories about their customs, and providing advice about the trail ahead. Gerard and his wife, Mary Kay, showed me the same hospitality—one thing that hadn't changed over the years—and over time, he made it clear that understanding the story of the American buffalo required understanding the history and beliefs of the American Indians. The two are intertwined and inseparable.

Gerard took me to his mother's house on the Fort Berthold reservation, where he had used willow saplings and a tarp to construct a small sweat lodge. After shoveling some red-hot stones from a nearby fire into a pit in its center, we crawled inside, closed the cover, and began to perspire—especially so after he dipped a buffalo tail into water and sprinkled the rocks to raise clouds of steam. It was cleansing "bad spirits" from our body, he explained, so he could properly relate tales of Lone Man, the principal culture-hero in his tribe's stories of their creation. This kind of oral transmission of knowledge, history, ritual, and belief had been going on for thousands of years among his people, as with so many other tribes who, without written words, relied on person-to-person storytelling from one generation to the next in order for their culture to survive. Over the centuries, it became their blood memory.

Gerard and I also spent a frigid winter night in a replica of an earth lodge he had built at the Knife River Indian Villages National Historic Site, where the Hidatsas had lived during Lewis and Clark's visit. As the temperature dropped to 30 or more degrees below zero outside, the fire inside the earth lodge kept us warm. Gerard lit and then extinguished a small rope of sweetgrass, and with the smoke smudged the lodge in each of the four directions. He sang a Hidatsa song. We boiled a supper of potatoes, onions, and buffalo tripe (the membrane lining a bison's stomach). To his people, buffalo tripe had been a delicacy—"Hidatsa lobster," he joked. Saying he knew I wanted an authentic experience, he gave me five big buffalo robes: one to sleep on, and four to sleep under. Then he unrolled a down-filled sleeping bag for his own use, and announced it was a "tradition" that whoever has the most buffalo robes in an earth lodge is responsible for keeping the fire going through the long night. His gentle teasing—something used by many Indian uncles and aunts to instruct younger members of an extended family—was his way of simultaneously testing me and demonstrating that I might be accepted into his.

Gerard was near the start of a long career in the National Park Service, and as district ranger at the Theodore Roosevelt National Park's north unit, part of his duties included supervising 150 bison in the surrounding Badlands along the Little Missouri River. During a summer visit, when I stayed at his and Mary Kay's house, he learned that two buffalo bulls had escaped from the park's reinforced-fence boundaries. His job that day was to track them down. If they were still close enough to the park, he would try to herd them back; if not, and they strayed too far onto nearby private ranchland and farms, park regulations meant he would have to shoot them. We set off in a pickup to find them as quickly as possible.

The search lasted more than half the day—sometimes on gravel roads, then, after we sighted them in the distance, several hours over broken, sagebrush-covered ground until we rounded a small butte and there they were, standing on a gravel road near an untended oil well, as if waiting for us. Gerard checked the landmarks and his map. The bulls were twenty miles from the nearest park boundary. Trying to herd them back would be impossible.

Gerard reluctantly removed his 30.06 rifle from its rack, loaded it with 150-grain shells, and took aim at the bigger bull. I heard him whisper something in Hidatsa before the rifle shot rang out. Then he said something again, and brought down the other one. He took out some big hunting knives, and as we walked toward their lifeless bodies, I asked about what he had said before each shot. "Hidatsa prayer," he answered. "The buffalo's got a powerful spirit. I don't want him to suffer. I was asking for a clean, quick kill that will release the spirit without too much pain. They're our relatives."

The rest of the afternoon was devoted to dealing with the carcasses. By long-standing park policy, the meat would be offered to area nonprofit groups and the Fort Berthold reservation; the hides and heads would go to the Fort Union National Historic Site, a former trading post near the confluence of the Yellowstone and Missouri Rivers. But first, we had to skin the hides and sever the heads. Gerard had radioed for assistance, we went to work, and I learned firsthand just what a hard, messy job it all is—and has always been. Skinning a hide requires a combination of both cutting and pulling the bison's thick coat from the fatty tissue that holds it to the meat. Our hands and arms became caked with dark, dry blood, and we had to stop occasionally to sharpen the knives on whetstones and to flex our cramped fingers. The day was hot; pesky flies buzzed all around, and swiping them and our own sweat away smeared our foreheads with more blood.

As part of the process, the buffalo's belly had to be slit open—carefully, very carefully, so its bladder didn't rupture and spray urine everywhere. (I witnessed what can go wrong when we dealt with the second carcass. Our arms were tired, we were in a hurry to finish before evening, and . . . well, you can imagine the result.) With the belly opened, the bison's four stomachs ballooned out, as if someone had pulled the cord on an inflatable life raft. Its lungs and coils of intestines spilled onto the ground.

The liver and kidneys and heart were now exposed, and after wiping his knife blade clean, Gerard reached down and sliced off a chunk of the purplish-brown liver. He offered it around to our small crew. All of them declined, and one, a new park employee on her first day of work, turned a pale green. Then he reached over to me, the piece of raw liver glistening on his knife blade. Gerard is an imposing figure: six feet five inches tall, with his long hair in braids dangling to his shoulders. He loomed over me, with that big knife and a hunk of raw liver. "It's something we do," he said, looking me square in the eye in a way I understood was not teasing. "It'll give you some of the buffalo's strength." I took the piece and began chewing. It was warm, slightly crunchy, surprisingly sweet, and strong-tasting. He smiled, cut off another chunk, and ate it. We did the same thing with slivers of raw kidney. He nodded—and we went back to finish our work.

Looking back forty years to that moment, I consider it a ritual of sorts: two then-young men from widely different American cultures sharing the sacraments from a fallen buffalo to forge a friendship that has lasted the rest of our lives. More than a friendship, actually—a *brotherhood*, after his family later adopted me into their clan. The two buffalo bulls had brought us together. And since my brother Gerard Baker feels a kinship with the bison, the buffalo are now my brothers, too.

My journey along Lewis and Clark's trail changed my life. It led to many other explorations of our nation's complicated past, particularly in the West, and turned into a continuous search to understand Americans' conflicted relationship to the land and the natural world. The buffalo, I eventually learned, were not only the keystone species of the Plains, holding everything together; their story also provides a keystone for coming to grips with our shared human history. They provide the critical link connecting two opposing sides of an arch to one another. What different cultures thought about the bison and what they did with those animals reveals the gap between those cultures, the Natives' and the newcomers', as starkly as any American story I know.

At the heart of that story lies a profound tragedy. No retelling of American history can be considered complete without recognizing and recounting it. Our nation's own blood memory requires remembering our shameful, bloody moments. At the same time, following the buffalo trail offers the hopeful evidence that nothing in history is inevitable. People—nations—can make grievous mistakes. They're also capable of learning from those mistakes, of acknowledging them and then deciding to go in a different direction. At this moment in history when the poaching and slaughter of exotic animals for trophies, the continuing degradation and destruction of habitats, and a warming global climate threaten the existence of thousands of species—and possibly human existence itself—the story of the American buffalo's near extinction and subsequent resurrection reminds us of both points. We are fully capable of wreaking incalculable damage on the natural world *and* we have the capacity to stop and take corrective action.

In the steam of a sweat lodge, the fire's glow of an earth lodge, and the taste of raw liver on a hot summer day in North Dakota, Gerard began my tutorial in a fuller understanding of the people who had been inhabiting the continent alongside the buffalo for thousands of years by the time Lewis and Clark showed up in their homeland. "We believe that, when the Creator made everything, he put a spirit into everything, made them alive," he told me. "Even the trees and the grass and the rocks and the rivers—everything, including the animals. And he gave them the ability to talk. We still believe they have spirits. The animals can still talk to us through prayer. And through vision. And through sacrifice."

My readings and research and interviews with other Indigenous people, always supplemented by visits with Gerard, have deepened my appreciation of that perspective. In *Sacred Nature: Restoring Our Ancient Bond with the Natural World*, Karen Armstrong, a former nun who became an authority on comparative religion, points out that many tribal people across many continents shared it: "a continuum of time and space, where animals, plants, and humans are all permeated by an immanent sacred force that draws them into a synthesized whole" and "a sense [of] reciprocity between themselves and the natural environment, where we moderns see it as a mere backdrop to human affairs."

Black Elk, a Lakota medicine man, once described it to the poet John G. Neihardt, when he recounted a vision he had as a young boy on a mountaintop in the Black Hills:

> And round about beneath me was the whole hoop of the world. And while I stood there I saw more than I can tell and I understood more than I saw; for I was seeing in a sacred manner the

shapes of all things in the spirit, and the shape of all shapes as they must live together like one being.

And I saw that the sacred hoop of my people was one of many hoops that made one circle, wide as daylight and as starlight, and in the center grew one mighty flowering tree to shelter all the children of one mother and one father. And I saw that it was holy.

In 1876, Black Elk, a second cousin of Crazy Horse, had killed and scalped one of Custer's soldiers at the Battle of the Little Bighorn. After joining "Buffalo Bill's Wild West" show and touring Europe, he came home to the Dakotas, where he was injured during the Wounded Knee massacre of 1890. In 1904, he converted to Catholicism and began baptizing hundreds of Indians—though some of his people still considered him a Lakota holy man—combining what he thought were the best parts of Christianity and traditional beliefs. In 2016, the U.S. Board on Geographic Names unanimously changed the name of the highest peak in the Black Hills, where he had experienced his vision, from Harney Peak (named for an Army general whose men had killed Lakota women and children in a punitive expedition in 1855) to Black Elk Peak. A year later, the bishops of the U.S. Catholic Church unanimously voted to recommend him for sainthood.

Those touch points, encapsulated in one man's life, illuminate just how entangled and nuanced America's history can be. The same can be said of Quanah Parker, whose life's journey took him from an implacable hatred of whites, especially Texans, and a lethal war to rid the southern Plains of hide hunters, to a man of peace who would live to see the buffalo return to the sacred Wichita Mountains. "We are the same people now," he said at an event commemorating a new railroad line in Texas named in his honor.

So, too, with Charles Goodnight. He had fought Indians as a Texas Ranger, blazed cattle trails across Native homelands, and established a ranch in the Palo Duro Canyon, once his men had cleared out the remaining bison. But then, at his wife Mary's urging, he started a buffalo herd that helped save the species from extinction, provided a bull for the Kiowas' last Sun Dance, and, though having

taken part in the capture of Quanah Parker's mother and little sister
fifty years earlier, helped arrange for their reburial back among the
Comanches. The lance Quanah gave him in appreciation—which
he had used in the fight against the hide hunters at Adobe Walls,
and which Goodnight later gave to the American Bison Society—
symbolizes the larger story of the American buffalo. It has its own
blood memory, representing the violent clash between two cultures,
one of them fighting against both brutal subjugation and the wanton
slaughter of the animal central to a way of life. But the lance's story
didn't end there. It later became a gift from one proud old warrior
to another, after two fierce antagonists somehow became friends and
fellow advocates for the buffalo's resurrection. Now more than a historical artifact, Quanah's lance represents not only resistance, but
resilience, and the possibility of reconciliation.

"We always say, 'We're just like the buffalo,'" my brother Gerard
explained to me many times. All the other Native people we interviewed reiterated that notion. To an expanding nation in the nineteenth century, intent upon not just claiming the West but controlling
it, the bison and the Indigenous people who populated the Plains
were both in the way. Both witnessed the loss of the land that had
sustained them—one ending up behind fences in zoos, the other confined to reservations. Both were deemed to be inevitably vanishing.

  Even on the surface, the parallels are clear. But comprehending
the scale of the devastation—cultural, psychological, spiritual—
requires an understanding of the deep history of the people and the
buffalo, as they evolved together over the course of more than ten
thousand years. In 1890, when the Ghost Dancers tried to bring the
buffalo back with their ceremonies and ended up dead and buried
in a mass grave at Wounded Knee, "something else died," Black Elk
said. "A people's dream died there. The nation's hoop [was] broken
and scattered. There is no center any longer, and the sacred tree is
dead." The next census, in 1900, counted a Native American population of 237,200—the lowest point in American history.

But the buffalo didn't disappear and Indians were not a vanishing race. "Our prayers got stronger," Gerard told me. "They had to. That's why our people got stronger. The buffalo is still here, and we're still here." To him—and others we interviewed—the story of Native perseverance is as important as the story of their systematic dispossession and the concerted attempts to strip them of their culture. Having felt such a profound connection with the buffalo for millennia, it should not be surprising that Plains people continue to identify the bison's story with their own.

"Bison were nearly exterminated, and we had a similar experience," Germaine White, of the Confederated Salish and Kootenai, told us. "But bison are resilient; they have adapted. And they have taught us how to be resilient and adapt. They've survived; we've survived. We both persist."

Even at the existential nadir that coincided with the Ghost Dance, the dramatic loss of tribal land through the Allotment Act, and the efforts, principally through boarding schools, to strip Indian children of their people's traditions—"Kill the Indian, Save the Man"— Native people were already demonstrating the adamant resolve to resist and survive. They turned *into* the storm and pushed forward. As Justin Gage explains in a recent book, *We Do Not Want the Gates Closed Between Us: Native Networks and the Spread of the Ghost Dance*, they turned the tools of oppression on their head. They used the railroad networks—which had once ushered in such dramatic changes on their homelands—to visit one another (often in defiance of regulations about travel outside their reservation). The newfound literacy they had acquired in government schools allowed them to communicate with each other across great distances through letters and telegrams—now using the common language of English between tribes who spoke a profusion of different tongues—to discuss the daunting obstacles they were facing and to share strategies for overcoming them. They also sent letters directly to officials in Washington to lodge complaints about the abuses of their reservation agents.

It became an act of cultural jiu-jitsu against the effort to atomize any sense of "Indian-ness," and instead created a pan-Indian con-

sciousness that had not previously existed and continues to these
days. To be sure, the challenges confronting Native people—from
poverty to poor health care to persistent discrimination—remain
substantial. But progress against them has a better chance through
collective action. The expanding success of the InterTribal Buffalo
Council, which now includes more than eighty tribes in twenty different states restoring bison herds to their reservations, is simply one
example of such efforts. By 2021, the population estimate for American Indians and Alaska Natives in the United States reached 7.2 million (4.4 million of whom identified solely as Indigenous, the rest as
mixed-blood), and a Native American was serving as secretary of the
Department of the Interior.

Gerard's life story, I think, exemplifies this larger trend. His parents insisted that he get a good education, yet also steeped him in the
traditions of his ancestors. After graduating from college, he joined
the National Park Service and steadily rose in its ranks. Every step
along the way, he demonstrated the same desire to share a broader
story of American history that had led him to take a young reporter
from New Hampshire into an earth lodge and to track down two
wandering bison. As superintendent of the Little Bighorn National
Battlefield, he worked to make sure that what was once called the
Custer Battlefield honored *both* of the American forces that fought
there, the Seventh Cavalry and the Native tribes defending their
way of life. He invited tribal representatives to participate in the
battle's annual commemoration ceremonies and oversaw the addition of a metal sculpture, the Spirit Warrior Memorial, that now
stands on the other side of the crest of Last Stand Hill. In 1998, amid
death threats he and his family received over such an expanded
(and honest) view of what happened there, he moved on to other
assignments.

He became superintendent of the Lewis and Clark National Historic Trail and, during the three-year national commemoration of
the expedition's bicentennial, persuaded the multiple tribes along
the route, many of them initially reluctant to participate, to use it as
an opportunity to tell their stories of that time and remind people
that they still existed. Later, as the first Native American superinten-

dent of the Mount Rushmore National Memorial, he asked nearby tribes to establish a small cluster of tepees underneath the escarpment carved with the faces of four presidents, where Native interpreters could recount what the Black Hills have always meant to them.

When he retired, Gerard was an assistant director of the Park Service, at the time the highest position ever held by a Native American in NPS history. His ambition now is to make sure his grandchildren get educated and learn to succeed in the modern world, as his children have done, yet also make sure they understand the traditional ways of their people. An accident demonstrating how to erect a tepee required him to be airlifted to a hospital, but he recovered and keeps at it in good spirits. He plans to add some buffalo on the ranch he and Mary Kay have in Montana, and he is working with his tribe to start a larger herd on the Fort Berthold reservation. "The buffalo are so important to us, as a symbol of our existence, and the symbol of our difficulties," he told me:

> A lot of Plains tribes now have their own herds of buffalo. They still use them as a food source; they still use them as a ceremonial source. We're coming back strong, like the buffalo are again.
>
> I'm hoping people will take a look at the buffalo in a new way. Not as an animal, but as a living being. I'm hoping people can know that buffalo can coexist with everybody. They can coexist with our cows. They can coexist with people. And if we give them a chance, like I think we should, it will strengthen us as not only human beings, but as Americans.

Since I'm a few years older, in one sense Gerard is my little brother. But he's six inches taller, and I've learned much more from him than the other way around. He was my first teacher about the buffalo. Through his playful teasing, his stories, and our shared experiences he taught me to open my eyes and see them in a new light: as magnificent representatives of the interconnection between people and the natural world, as well as a portal for understanding the complicated human history that unfolded in the nation he and I both consider our own. In doing so, he also opened my heart, which I hope is now as big as his.

During the project that created this book and the documentary film it draws from, I was in Fort Benton, Montana, where we conducted some interviews and filmed the display of William T. Hornaday's buffalo group, which once enthralled millions of people in the Smithsonian. Now the display is back in north-central Montana, much closer to the place where Hornaday collected the buffalo almost 150 years ago.

As we prepared for some close-up shots, I took out a tissue to wipe the dust off their glass eyes, and realized I knew their personal story. There was little Sandy, the calf Hornaday had captured and brought back to Washington, where it died in captivity so far from home and its mother. And there was the giant bull Hornaday had shot, watching the rage in its eyes, as he remembered, while it struggled to its feet before dying. In its body, he found four bullets from other hunters who had tried to bring it down. With those stories flooding my emotions, I needed a tissue for myself.

But then I remembered that Hornaday believed he was preserving something important for future generations. He envisioned a time when his exhibit would likely be the *only* way Americans could see what this species once was—an imposing time capsule wrapped in fur. "When I am dust and ashes," he wrote in the note that he hid in the display case, "I beg you to protect these specimens from deterioration and destruction as they are among the last of their kind." I felt grateful that those specimens had indeed been protected from "deterioration and destruction," and were still on display for public viewing. Grateful even more that they were not "among the last of their kind."

That night, we traveled to the Upper Missouri River Breaks, where live buffalo can still be found roaming on the land of American Prairie, one of the nonprofit groups dedicated to restoring bison and the grasslands that sustain them in an environment closer to what was once their domain. An hour before the sun came up, we located a small group of bulls grazing on a gentle slope. Like the hide hunters, we kept our distance and established our "stand," this time to shoot buffalo with a camera instead of a Sharp's rifle.

Buddy Squires, our longtime cinematographer, worried that they would wander off in the wrong direction and ruin the shots he hoped to take of them with a rising sun behind them. I separated from the crew and walked slowly up the slope, keeping my distance from the bulls but flanking them. They noticed me in the predawn light, but were undisturbed and kept on grazing, moving incrementally toward the crest.

Then something came over me and I began talking to the buffalo. I pointed toward the reddening sky in the east, and told them I now considered them as the representation of the sun on Earth, a majestic manifestation of the interconnection between all living things and the *Wakan Tanka* permeating the universe. I apologized for what my people had nearly done to them and said how happy I was that they still existed and that together we could greet the sun of a new day.

The first sliver of radiant gold emerged on the horizon and I found myself singing. It was a feeble attempt to imitate one of the songs Gerard had sung to me, hobbled by the fact that I only know a few words of Hidatsa, but heartfelt. A few prairie dogs popped out of their burrow holes, either because the day was breaking or because they wanted to find out who was making this noise so early in the morning. Some cowbirds began trilling their own, more beautiful songs that sounded like clear water running in a babbling brook. The buffalo bulls kept grazing contentedly as the golden sliver became a glowing ball, illuminating the entire prairie landscape that seemed to stretch out forever in every direction. And I saw that it was holy.

Now I found myself dancing as I sang, suspended in a transcendent euphoria, plugged into everything that surrounded me. Buddy shouted that the shooting moment was over; he had the footage he had hoped for, and the whole crew was ecstatic. I came back to earth and joined them to celebrate. I remember thinking, "I only wish my brother Gerard had been here." Then again, I think he was.

Dayton Duncan
Rindge, New Hampshire

INTERVIEWEES

GERARD BAKER, a Mandan-Hidatsa from North Dakota, had a long and distinguished career in the National Park Service, from starting as a seasonal worker at the Theodore Roosevelt National Park to being the first Native American superintendent of the Mount Rushmore National Memorial and later the first NPS assistant director for American Indian relations.

SARA DANT, the author of *Losing Eden: An Environmental History of the American West*, is the Brady Presidential Distinguished Professor and Chair of History at Weber State University.

DAN FLORES retired in 2014 as the A. B. Hammond Chair in Western History at the University of Montana. His books include *Wild New World: The Epic Story of Animals and People in America* and *American Serengeti: The Last Big Animals of the Great Plains*.

GEORGE HORSE CAPTURE JR., Aaniiih (Gros Ventre), is the director of Aaniiih Nakoda Tours at the Fort Belknap reservation in Montana.

ANDREW ISENBERG, the Hall Distinguished Professor of American History at the University of Kansas, is the author of *The Destruction of the Bison: An Environmental History 1750–1920*.

CLAY JENKINSON is an author, historian, and public humanities scholar. In 1989, he received the National Humanities Medal, the highest honor bestowed by the National Endowment for the Humanities. Among his books is *A Free and Hardy Life: Theodore Roosevelt's Sojourn in the American West.*

ROSALYN LAPIER, an enrolled member of the Blackfeet of Montana and Métis, is an environmental historian and ethnobotanist. She is the author of *Invisible Reality: Storytellers, Storytakers and the Supernatural World of the Blackfeet* and is a professor at the University of Illinois, Urbana-Champaign.

N. SCOTT MOMADAY is a Kiowa novelist, essayist, and poet. His novel *House Made of Dawn* was awarded the Pulitzer Prize for Fiction in 1969. He was named the Oklahoma Centennial Poet Laureate, and in 2007 was awarded the National Medal of Arts at the White House.

MICHELLE NIJHUIS has written about science and the environment for many magazines, including *Smithsonian, National Geographic,* and *The New York Times Magazine.* She is the author of *Beloved Beasts: Fighting for Life in an Age of Extinction.*

DAN O'BRIEN has been an endangered-species biologist, falconer, rancher, and writer. Among his books are *Great Plains Bison* and a memoir, *Buffalo for the Broken Heart.* In the 1990s, he founded the Wild Idea Buffalo Company and began converting his cattle ranch in South Dakota to raising sustainable buffalo meat and restoring the prairie grasslands.

MARCIA PABLO is the tribal coordinator/program analyst for the Bureau of Land Management in Billings, Montana. She grew up on the Confederated Salish and Kootenai reservation, where her great-great-grandfather, Michel Pablo, raised what at the time was the world's largest bison herd.

RON PARKER, a great-grandson of Quanah Parker, was a Vietnam War veteran and former Army captain, and a founder of the Quanah

Parker Society and Center, in Quanah, Texas. He died on December 12, 2022.

MICHAEL PUNKE is a novelist, biographer, and former government official. He was the U.S. ambassador to the World Trade Organization. His novel *The Revenant*, about the fur trapper Hugh Glass, was adapted into a feature film. He wrote *Last Stand: George Bird Grinnell, the Battle to Save the Buffalo, and the Birth of the New West*.

STEVEN RINELLA is an outdoorsman, conservationist, and host of the television series and podcast *MeatEater*. Among his books is *American Buffalo: In Search of a Lost Icon*.

DUSTIN TAHMAHKERA, a Comanche, is an associate professor and Wick Cary Endowed Chair in Native American Cultural Studies at the University of Oklahoma. He has written extensively about Native American portrayals in the media, and is working on a digital exhibit, "Cinematic Comanches," which includes the role his great-great-great-grandfather, Quanah Parker, played in the 1908 silent film *The Bank Robbery*.

ELLIOTT WEST retired in 2022 from the University of Arkansas, where he was Alumni Distinguished Professor of History. He is a past president of the Western History Association. Among his many books are *Contested Plains: Indians, Goldseekers, and the Rush to Colorado*, which won the 1999 Francis Parkman Prize from the Society of American Historians.

GERMAINE WHITE is an educator and conservationist. As the information and education specialist for the Natural Resources Department of the Confederated Salish and Kootenai in Montana, she took part in her tribes' successful effort to take over the management of the National Bison Range from the federal government.

ACKNOWLEDGMENTS

We have been planning to tell the "biography" of the American buffalo for nearly four decades, and even drew up a proposal and lengthy outline for it in the late 1990s in anticipation of a PBS broadcast at the turn of the new century. But other projects always seemed to intervene. Looking back now, we believe the delay made our film and this book better, despite our occasional impatience to get more fully engaged and remove them years ago from the "to-do" list we keep in our desks.

One of the many unintended, but beneficial, consequences of waiting so long was that Julie Dunfey could be the lead producer of the film. It's hard to imagine completing the project without her. Faced with innumerable obstacles and complications caused by the COVID-19 pandemic, she somehow kept things moving forward and on schedule. We thank her for her steady stewardship, as well as her heartfelt devotion to telling this story as best as we know how.

During the long gestation of this project, and particularly over the course of the last several years, we've been blessed by the encouragement and help many people have graciously provided—far too many to name in this space, though we hope all of them understand our gratitude.

Our Florentine Films "buffalo team" did extraordinary work (most of them remotely during the pandemic), and their dedication to every detail deserves special recognition. Julianna Brannum, the consulting producer, and coproducer Susan Shumaker took on innumerable tasks with equal amounts of enthusiasm and professionalism. Craig Mellish, the editor, turned a script on paper into a visually stunning film, ably assisted by J. Alex Cucchi. (Craig also served as a field producer on some of the filming shoots and scouted locations in advance, adding some wonderful photographs that ended up in the film.) Emily Mosher, associate producer, led the effort to amass more than six thousand still images for the editors to choose from. Buddy Squires, who has been part of Florentine Films from its founding in the 1970s, served as the principal cinematographer, compiling stunning footage of bison around the country; Jared Ames assisted him at every shoot. (We also thank the other cinematographers, named in the film credits, for adding additional, equally memorable footage.) Other members of the core team were Nora Colgan, Will Duncan, Charlie Graham, Loren Howard, Dave Mast, and Daniel J. White. Paul Barnes, though retired, came through in a pinch to help with the interview of N. Scott Momaday. The Florentine Films family in Walpole also includes Elle Carrière, Jennifer Fabis, Chris Darling, Jillian Hempstead, Stephanie Greene, Kathleen Ohlson, and Karen Domina; without them, nothing gets done.

We thank Peter Coyote for once again narrating our film, and also the many talented actors, listed in the credits, for bringing historical quotes to life. Many talented musicians and composers contributed to our soundtrack, but we especially want to acknowledge the work of Bobby Horton, whose work has graced our films since *The Civil War*.

We also thank the many places—national and state parks, Native reservations, and private ranches and sites overseen by nonprofit organizations—that allowed us to film their bison herds, whose presence onscreen provided not only such vivid visual material for our storytelling, but also incontrovertible proof that the national mammal was saved from extinction.

Early in our project, a group of historians and bison experts kindly read the rough draft of the script (which was twice as long as the final one) to provide helpful comments and important corrections; later they viewed a rough assembly of the film and did the same. We were extremely fortunate that W. Richard West Jr., the founding director and now director emeritus of the Smithsonian Institution's

National Museum of the American Indian, agreed to serve as our senior advisor; we benefited greatly from his patient guidance. The other advisors were Keith Aune, Jason Baldes, Gerard Baker, Colin Calloway, Sara Dant, Dan Flores, Andrew Isenberg, Rosalyn LaPier, Dan O'Brien, Michael Punke, Elliott West, and Geoffrey C. Ward. We also thank those who agreed to be interviewed on camera for our film, whose comments in the film and this book added so much depth to our storytelling and whose short biographical information appears elsewhere in these pages.

Our film could not have been made without the financial support of our funders: Bank of America; the Corporation for Public Broadcasting; the Better Angels Society, and its members; the Margaret A. Cargill Foundation fund at the Saint Paul & Minnesota Foundation; Diane and Hal Brierley; the Keith Campbell Foundation for the Environment; John and Catherine Debs; the Kissick Family Foundation; Fred and Donna Seigel; Jacqueline Mars; John and Leslie McQuown; Mr. and Mrs. Paul Tudor Jones; the Volgenau Foundation; the Evelyn and Walter Haas Jr. Fund; and the Marilynn and John Hill Foundation. For nearly fifty years, PBS has been the home for our films, and we urge anyone who believes, as we do, in its mission of presenting the nation with quality, educational programming to donate to their local PBS station. Special thanks to Paula Kerger for her leadership in that mission. Thanks, too, to our long-standing producing partner WETA-TV in Washington, including Sharon Percy Rockefeller and John Wilson. Joe DePlasco and his team at DKC Public Relations help us alert millions of Americans about our upcoming films. Drew Patrick serves as our legal counsel.

Since the start of our project, two people involved in the film have passed away: Ron Parker, one of our interviewees; and Tim Clark, our dear friend who for many years came to our studio in Walpole to read historical voices for several of our films and also sat in to view works-in-progress to offer insightful comments. Like their families, we mourn their loss.

For this book, we thank our agent, Jay Mandel of William Morris Endeavor Entertainment; our editor, Andrew Miller; his assistant, Tiara Sharma; and our designer, Maggie Hinders. Dayton also thanks Dianne and Will Duncan for being his first-line readers of the initial manuscript, and Will for his invaluable help in the research.

Nothing we do is conceivable without the support and love of our families: Sarah, Lilly, Olivia, and Willa Burns; and Dianne, Emme, and Will Duncan. They are the essence of our blood memory.

Ken Burns
Dayton Duncan
Walpole, New Hampshire

Selected Bibliography

For our PBS documentary, we conducted eighteen extended on-camera interviews, totaling more than thirty hours, only portions of which could be fit into our four-hour film. This book allowed us to include much more of what we were told, and we are grateful to be able to share those additional insights. Many of our interviewees have written important books about the American buffalo and its history, and we heartily recommend them to anyone seeking to dive deeper into the subject, since those works were equally crucial to us in our research.

Likewise, while this book contains more information—and more stories and historical characters—than the film, we do not consider it in any way a comprehensive history. Rather, it attempts through narrative storytelling to introduce readers to the topic; to *invite* them into what we consider a significant saga in the larger sweep of American history and prompt them to learn more from sources that can provide even more detail and historical context. What follows is a selected bibliography of the principal written sources we relied on.

Armstrong, Karen. *Sacred Nature: How We Can Recover Our Bond With the Natural World.* London: Bodley Head, 2022.

Aune, Keith, and Glenn Plumb. *Theodore Roosevelt & Bison Restoration on the Great Plains.* Charleston: History Press, 2019.

Barsness, Barry. *Heads, Hides & Horns: The Compleat Buffalo Book.* Fort Worth: Texas Christian University Press, 1985.

Baynes, Ernest Harold. *Wild Life in the Blue Mountain Forest.* New York: Macmillan Company, 1931.

Baynes, Ernest Harold, and Louise Birt Baynes. *War Whoop and Tomahawk: The Story of Two Buffalo Calves.* New York: Macmillan Company, 1929.

Bechtel, Stefan. *Mr. Hornaday's War: How a Peculiar Victorian Zookeeper Waged a Lonely Crusade for Wildlife That Changed the World.* Boston: Beacon Press, 2012.

Bridges, William. *Gathering Animals: An Unconventional History of the New York Zoological Society.* New York: Harper & Row, 1974.

Brinkley, Douglas. *The Wilderness Warrior: Theodore Roosevelt and the Crusade for America.* New York: HarperCollins, 2009.

Calloway, Colin G. *One Vast Winter Count: The Native American West Before Lewis and Clark.* Lincoln: University of Nebraska Press, 2003.

———. *Our Hearts Fell to the Ground: Plains Indian Views of How the West Was Lost.* Boston: Bedford/St. Martin's, 2018.

Catlin, George. *Letters and Notes on the Manners, Customs, and Condition of the North American Indians.* New York: Wiley and Putnam, 1841.

Cook, John R. *The Border and the Buffalo: An Untold Story of the Southwest Plains.* New York: Citadel Press, 1967.

Cunfer, Geoff, and Bill Waiser, eds. *Bison and People on the North American Plains: A Deep Environmental History.* College Station: Texas A&M University Press, 2016.

Dant, Sara. *Losing Eden: An Environmental History of the American West.* 2nd ed. Lincoln: University of Nebraska Press, 2022.

Dary, David A. *The Buffalo Book: The Full Saga of the American Animal.* Chicago: Swallow Press, 1974.

Davies, Henry E. *Ten Days on the Plains.* Ed. Paul Andrew Hutton. Dallas: DeGolyer Library, Southern Methodist University Press, 1985.

Davis, Jack E. *The Bald Eagle: The Improbable Journey of America's Bird.* New York: Liveright Publishing, 2022.

Dehler, Gregory J. *The Most Defiant Devil: William Temple Hornaday & His Controversial Crusade to Save American Wildlife.* Charlottesville: University of Virginia Press, 2013.

Dippie, Brian W. *The 100 Best Illustrated Letters of Charles M. Russell.* Fort Worth: Amon Carter Museum, 2008.

Dixon, Olive K. *Life of "Billy" Dixon: Plainsman, Scout, and Pioneer.* Austin, TX: State House Press, 1987.

Duncan, Dayton. *Out West: An American Journey.* New York: Viking Penguin, 1987.

———. *Scenes of Visionary Enchantment: Reflections on Lewis and Clark.* Lincoln: University of Nebraska Press, 2004.

Duncan, Dayton, with Ken Burns. *The National Parks: America's Best Idea.* New York: Alfred A. Knopf, 2009.

Easton, Robert, and Mackenzie Brown. *Lord of Beasts: The Saga of Buffalo Jones.* Tucson: University of Arizona Press, 1961.

Flores, Dan. *American Serengeti: The Last Big Animals of the Great Plains.* Lawrence: University of Kansas Press, 2016.

———. *Wild New World: The Epic Story of Animals and People in America.* New York: W. W. Norton & Company, 2022.

Gage, Justin. *We Do Not Want the Gates Closed Between Us.* Norman: University of Oklahoma Press, 2020.

Gard, Wayne. *The Great Buffalo Hunt.* Lincoln: University of Nebraska Press, 1959.

Garretson, Martin S. *The American Bison: The Story of Its Extermination as a Wild Species and Its Restoration Under Federal Protection.* New York: New York Zoological Society, 1938.

Gorges, Raymond. *Ernest Harold Baynes: Naturalist and Crusader.* Boston: Houghton Mifflin, 1928.

Greene, Candace S., and Russell Thornton. *The Year the Stars Fell: Lakota Winter Counts at the Smithsonian.* Washington, DC: Smithsonian Institution Press, 2007.

Gwynne, S. C. *Empire of the Summer Moon: Quanah Parker and the Rise and Fall of the Comanches, the Most Powerful Indian Tribe in American History.* New York: Scribner, 2010.

Hagan, William T. *Charles Goodnight: Father of the Texas Panhandle.* Norman: University of Oklahoma Press, 2007.

Haley, J. Evetts. *Charles Goodnight: Cowman and Plainsman.* New York: Houghton Mifflin, 1936.

Hämäläinen, Pekka. *The Comanche Empire.* New Haven: Yale University Press, 2008.

———. *Lakota America: A New History of Indigenous Power.* New Haven: Yale University Press, 2019.

Harrigan, Stephen. *Big Wonderful Thing: A History of Texas.* Austin: University of Texas Press, 2019.

Harrod, Howard L. *The Animals Came Dancing: Native American Sacred Ecology and Animal Kinship.* Tucson: University of Arizona Press, 2000.

Hornaday, William Temple. *The Extermination of the American Bison.* Washington, DC: Smithsonian Institution Press, 2002.

Hunt, Alex. "Hunting Charles Goodnight's Buffalo: Texas Fiction, Panhandle Folklore, and Kiowa History." *Panhandle-Plains Historical Review,* LXXVII, 2004.

Inman, Colonel Henry. *Buffalo Jones' Adventures on the Plains.* Lincoln: University of Nebraska Press, 1970.

Isenberg, Andrew C. *The Destruction of the Bison.* Cambridge: Cambridge University Press, 2000.

Jenkinson, Clay. *A Free and Hardy Life: Theodore Roosevelt's Sojourn in the American West.* Bismarck: Dakota Institute, 2011.

Krech, Shepard III. *The Ecological Indian: Myth and History.* New York: W. W. Norton, 1999.

LaPier, Rosalyn. *Invisible Reality: Storytellers, Storytakers and the Supernatural World of the Blackfeet.* Lincoln: University of Nebraska Press, 2017.

Lee, Wayne C. *Scotty Philip: The Man Who Saved the Buffalo.* Caldwell, ID: Caxton Printers, 1975.

Linderman, Frank B. *Pretty-shield, Medicine Woman of the Crows.* Lincoln: University of Nebraska Press, 1972.

Marriott, Alice, and Carol K. Rachlin. *Plains Indian Mythology.* New York: HarperCollins, 1975.

Mayer, Frank H., and Charles B. Roth. *The Buffalo Harvest.* Union City, TN: Pioneer Press, 1958.

Mayhall, Mildred P. *The Kiowas.* Norman: University of Oklahoma Press, 1962.

McCullough, David. *Mornings on Horseback.* New York: Simon & Schuster, 1981.

McHugh, Tom. *The Time of the Buffalo.* Lincoln: University of Nebraska Press, 1972.

Miller, Char, and Clay S. Jenkinson, eds. *Theodore Roosevelt: Naturalist in the Arena.* Lincoln: University of Nebraska Press, 2020.

Momaday, N. Scott. *The Journey of Tai-me.* Albuquerque: University of New Mexico Press, 2009.

———. *The Way to Rainy Mountain.* Albuquerque: University of New Mexico Press, 1976.

Mooar, J. Wright, as told to James Winford Hunt. *Buffalo Days: Stories from J. Wright Mooar.* Ed. Robert F. Pace. Abilene, TX: State House Press, 2005.

Mooney, James. *Calendar History of the Kiowa Indians.* Washington, DC: Seventeenth Annual Report of the Bureau of Ethnology, 1898.

Morris, Edmund. *The Rise of Theodore Roosevelt.* New York: Ballantine Books, 1979.

Moulton, Gary E., ed. *The Journals of the Lewis & Clark Expedition.* Lincoln: University of Nebraska Press, 2002.

Nijhuis, Michelle. *Beloved Beasts: Fighting for Life in an Age of Extinction.* New York: W. W. Norton, 2021.

O'Brien, Dan. *Buffalo for the Broken Heart: Restoring Life to a Black Hills Ranch.* New York: Random House, 2001.

———. *Great Plains Bison.* Lincoln: Bison Books, 2017.

Parkman, Francis. *The Oregon Trail.* New York: Library of America, 1991.

Patterson, Daniel, ed. *The Missouri River Journals of John James Audubon.* Lincoln: University of Nebraska Press, 2016.

Price, B. Byron, and Wyman Meinzer. *Charles Goodnight: A Man for All Ages.* Bastrop, TX: Badlands Design and Production, 2012.

Punke, Michael. *Last Stand: George Bird Grinnell, the Battle to Save the Buffalo, and the Birth of the New West.* Lincoln: University of Nebraska Press, 2009.

Reiger, John F. *The Passing of the Great West: Selected Papers of George Bird Grinnell.* Norman: University of Oklahoma Press, 1972.

Rinella, Steven. *American Buffalo: In Search of a Lost Icon.* New York: Random House, 2009.

Roberts, Jack. *The Amazing Adventures of Lord Gore: A True Saga From the Old West.* Silverton, CO: Sundance Publications, 1977.

Roosevelt, Theodore. *Hunting Trips of a Ranchman & The Wilderness Hunter.* New York: Modern Library, 2004.

Russell, Don. *The Lives and Legends of Buffalo Bill.* Norman: University of Oklahoma Press, 1960.

Sandoz, Mari. *The Buffalo Hunters.* Lincoln: University of Nebraska Press, 1954.

Scott, Douglas D., Peter Bleed, and Stephen Damm. *Custer, Cody and Grand Duke Alexis: Historical Archaeology of the Royal Buffalo Hunt.* Norman: University of Oklahoma Press, 2013.

Siegle, Clive G. *Ciboleros! Hispanic Buffalo Hunters of the Southern Plains.* Chadron, NE: Museum of the Fur Trade, 2012.

Silvestro, Roger L. *Theodore Roosevelt in the Badlands: A Young Politician's Quest for Recovery in the American West.* New York: MJF Books, 2011.

Smith, Victor Grant. *The Champion Buffalo Hunter: The Frontier Memoirs of Yellowstone Vic Smith.* Ed. Jeanette Prodgers. Guilford, CT: Globe Pequot Press, 1997.

Smits, David D. "The Frontier Army and the Destruction of the Buffalo: 1865–1883," *The Western Historical Quarterly* 25, no. 3 (Autumn 1994).

Spiro, Jonathan Peter. *Defending the Master Race: Conservation, Eugenics, and the Legacy of Madison Grant.* Burlington: University of Vermont Press, 2008.

Stands in Timber, John, and Margot Liberty. *Cheyenne Memories.* Lincoln: University of Nebraska Press, 1967.

Taliaferro, John. *Charles M. Russell: The Life and Legend of America's Cowboy Artist.* Norman: University of Oklahoma Press, 1996.

———. *Grinnell: America's Environmental Pioneer and His Restless Drive to Save the West.* New York: Liveright Publishing, 2019.

Utley, Robert M. *The Lance and the Shield: The Life and Times of Sitting Bull.* New York: Henry Holt, 1993.

Vanderwerth, W. C. *Indian Oratory: Famous Speeches by Noted Indian Chieftains.* Norman: University of Oklahoma Press, 1971.

Wallace, Ernest, and E. Adamson Hoebel. *The Comanches: Lords of the South Plains.* Norman: University of Oklahoma Press, 1952.

Walter, Dave. "The Unsaintly Sir St. George Gore: Slob Hunter Extraordinaire." In *Speaking Ill of the Dead: Jerks in Montana History.* Helena, MT: TwoDot, 2000.

Ward, Geoffrey C. *The West: An Illustrated History.* Boston: Little, Brown and Company, 1996.

Warren, Louis S. *Buffalo Bill's America: William Cody and the Wild West Show.* New York: Random House, 2005.

West, Elliott. *Contested Plains: Indians, Goldseekers, and the Rush to Colorado.* Lawrence: University of Kansas Press, 1998.

———. *The Essential West: Collected Essays.* Norman: University of Oklahoma Press, 2014.

———. *The Way to the West: Essays on the Central Plains.* Albuquerque: University of New Mexico Press, 1995.

Whealdon, Bon I., and others. *"I Will Be Meat for My Salish": The Buffalo and the Montana Writers Project Interviews on the Flathead Indian Reservation.* Ed. Robert Bigart. Pablo, MT: Salish Kootenai College, 2001.

Wishart, David J. *An Unspeakable Sadness: The Dispossession of the Nebraska Indians.* Lincoln: University of Nebraska Press, 1994.

Zontek, Ken. *Buffalo Nation: American Indian Efforts to Restore the Bison.* Lincoln: University of Nebraska Press, 2007.

Page numbers in *italics* refer to illustrations.

ILLUSTRATION CREDITS

When there is more than one image, the credits will be listed clockwise from top left.

ABBREVIATIONS

Autry   Autry Museum of the American West

BBCW BBM   Buffalo Bill Center of the West, Cody, Wyoming; Buffalo Bill Museum

BBCW MRL   Buffalo Bill Center of the West, Cody, Wyoming; McCracken Research Library

DPL   The Denver Public Library, Western History Collection

Gilcrease   Gilcrease Museum, Tulsa, Oklahoma

Haley   Haley Memorial Library & History Center in Midland, Texas

Joslyn   Joslyn Art Museum, Omaha, Nebraska, Gift of the Enron Art Foundation

KSHS   Kansas State Historical Society, Topeka, Kansas

LOC   Library of Congress Prints and Photographs Division, Washington, DC

LOCRB   Library of Congress Rare Book and Special Collections Division, Washington, DC

Meriden   Ernest Harold Baynes' Buffalo Scrapbook, The Meriden Bird Club, Meriden, NH

MTHS   Montana Historical Society Photograph Archives, Helena, MT

NAA   National Anthropological Archives, Smithsonian Institution

NYPL Wallach   The Miriam and Ira D. Wallach Division of Art, Prints and Photographs: Photograph Collection, The New York Public Library

PHSNH   Plainfield Historical Society, Plainfield, NH

PPHM   Panhandle-Plains Historical Museum, Canyon, Texas

SAAM   Smithsonian American Art Museum

SDSHS   South Dakota State Historical Society, South Dakota Digital Archives, Pierre SD

SIA   Smithsonian Institution Archives

WCS   © WCS. Reproduced by permission of the Wildlife Conservation Society Archives

YELL   Yellowstone National Park Archives, Research Library, and Museum, Gardiner, Montana.

PART ONE

7   *Buffaloes,* George Catlin. Gift of Thomas Gilcrease Foundation, 1955. Gilcrease 01.2172

46–47   *Buffalo Bulls in a Wallow,* George Catlin. Gift of Mrs. Joseph Harrison, Jr., SAAM 1985.66.425; *Dance of the Mandan Women,* Karl Bodmer, Coll. of St. Louis Mercantile Library at UMSL; after Karl Bodmer, Alexandre Damien Manceau, engraver, *Bison-Dance of the Mandan Indians,* 1842, Joslyn, 1986.49.542.18, Photo © Bruce M. White, 2019; after Karl Bodmer, Carl Christian Vogel von Vogelstein, engraver, *Herds of Bisons and Elks on the Upper Missouri,* 1839, Joslyn, 1986.49.542.47

48–49   Painting on Muslin, detail. Attributed to Siyosapa (Hunkpapa/Yanktonai), collected at Fort Peck, MT in 1880/1881. Dept. of Anthropology, Smithsonian Institution, EL81-0; after Karl Bodmer, Carl Christian Vogel von Vogelstein, engraver, *Magic Pile Erected by the Assiniboin Indians,* 1839, Joslyn, 1986.49.542.63; Photo © Musée du quai Branly—Jacques Chirac, Dist. RMN-Grand Palais/Art Resource, NY, 71.1934.33.4 D

50–51   *Buffalo Hunt under the Wolf-skin Mask,* George Catlin. Gift of Mrs. Joseph Harrison, Jr., SAAM. 1985.66.414; *The Buffalo Caller,* © Tom Lovell, 1973, image courtesy Coeur d'Alene

Art Auction; *Driving Buffalo Over the Cliff,* Charles M. Russell, 1914. Photo © Sotheby's / Bridgeman Images, SPB7305730; *Buffalo Chase in Winter, Indians on Snowshoes,* George Catlin. Gift of Mrs. Joseph Harrison, Jr., SAAM 1985.66.416

52–53   Charles Russell, *The Silk Robe,* c.1890. Amon Carter Museum of Art, Fort Worth, TX, 1961.135; 479891, Karl Bodmer. *Mih-Tutta, a Mandan village.* Rare Books Division, The New York Public Library

54–55   *La Historia general de las Indias,* 1554. Courtesy John Carter Brown Library; *Coronado's Expedition, Crossing the Llano Estacado,* by Tom Lovell, courtesy Abell-Hanger Foundation and Permian Basin Petroleum Museum in Midland, TX, where this is on permanent display; Father Louis Hennepin, *Boeuf de la Nouvelle France,* c.1698. The Pierce Coll. from Roy Pierce and Winnifred Poland Pierce, National Museum of Wildlife Art, W2001.167.013; Unknown, engraved by Jacobus van der Schley, *Buffel,* c.1770. Amon Carter Museum of Art, Fort Worth, TX, 1964.15

56–57   *Daniel Boone escorting settlers through the Cumberland Gap,* George Caleb Bingham, 1851–1852. Washington University, St. Louis / Bridgeman Images, PHD29102; 94.0035, Buffalo Bill Museum and Grave, Golden, CO. Sarony, Major, and Knapp, after John Mix Stanley: *Herd of Bison, near Lake Jessie,* c.1860

58–59   Narbona Panel in Canyon Del Muerto, Canyon de Chelly National Monument AZ; Seth Eastman, *Skinning the Buffalo,* c.1850. Denver Art Museum: Museum Purchase, 1966.108; *Indians Traveling Near Fort Laramie,* Albert Bierstadt, 1861. Courtesy American Museum of Western Art—The Anschutz Collection. Photo by William J. O'Connor; LOCRB 02005383

60–61   Charles M. Russell, *The Medicine Man,* 1908. Amon Carter Museum of Art, Fort Worth, TX 1961.171; Charles M. Russell, *Indians Hunting Buffalo,* 1894, Sid Richardson Museum, *The Buffalo Hunt,* Charles Ferdinand Wimar, Gilcrease 01.1597

62–63   Painting on Muslin. Attributed to Siyosapa (Hunkpapa/Yanktonai), collected at Fort Peck, MT in 1880/1881. Dept. of Anthropology, Smithsonian Institution, EL81-0; Image courtesy Univ. of WY Art Museum, Shoshone Hide Painting, 1900, Cadzi (Cosiogo) Cody, 2016.3.1; National Museum of the American Indian, Smithsonian Institution (23/0246)

64–65   *Captain Clark Buffalo Gangue,* John Ford Clymer. The Eddie Basha Collection and the John Ford Clymer Family; Karl Bodmer, *Dead Bison on the Prairie,* 1833, Joslyn, 1986.49.208, Photo © Bruce M. White, 2019

66–67   *James Bordeaux: Trading with the Sioux, 1856,* John Ford Clymer. The Eddie Basha Collection and the John Ford Clymer Family; *Buffalo Crossing the Missouri River,* William de la Montagne Cary. Gilcrease, 01.1851; *Comanche Village, Women Dressing Robes and Drying Meat,* George Catlin. Gift of Mrs. Joseph Harrison, Jr., SAAM 1985.66.346; Child, Hamilton. *Gazetteer and Business Directory of Oneida County, NY* (Syracuse), 1869, p116. Yale University Library, Cj22 151

68–69   National Portrait Gallery, NPG.70.14; SAAM 1985.66.100; SAAM 1985.66.407

70–71   Pioneer caravan preparing the camp for the night, 19th century. © NPL—DeA Picture Library / Bridgeman Images, DGA5184296; John Gast, *American Progress,* 1872. Autry 92.126.1; *Covered wagons heading west,* N. C. Wyeth. Peter Newark American Pictures / Bridgeman Images, PNP246207

72–73   *The Offering to the Dead Warrior,* William de la Montagne Cary. Gilcrease 01.1846; *Funeral Scaffold,* Karl Bodmer, 1836–1841. © Newberry Library / Bridgeman Images, NBY3673609; Royal Ontario Museum 912.1.26; John Clymer, *Ciboleros,* 1979. Tacoma Art Museum, Haub Family Coll., Gift of Erivan and Helga Haub, 2014.6.26. Photo: Richard Nicol

74–75   National Gallery of Art, Washington, 2014.79.5

116–117   *Indian Viewing R R From Top Of Palisades 435 Miles From Sacramento,* Alfred A. Hart photos (PC0002). Spec Coll & University Archives, Stanford University; KSHS 207966; *Rawding family sod house, north of Sargent, Custer County, Nebraska,* 1886. RG2608 Solomon D. Butcher Coll., 10600, History Nebraska.

118–119   DeGolyer Library, SMU, U.S. West: Photographs, Manuscripts and Imprints; BBCW MRL, MS006 William F. Cody Coll. P.69.0032; *Train Passengers shooting Buffalo for sport,* c.1870. Peter Newark American Pictures / Bridgeman Images, PNP246679

120–121   *Satanta.* INV 01158300, Photo Lot 3912 NAA; Gilcrease. 4336.3863; Indian Peace Commissioners in Council with Arapahoes and Cheyennes, Ft. Laramie, Photo: Alexander Gardner, 1868. The Brinton Museum L2015.24.0573; DPL WH185; SAAM 1985.66.384,184

122–123   BBCW MRL P.69.0819; *New York Daily Herald* Jan. 16, 1872, p. 7; Gilcrease 4326.4144; George Bird Grinnell, Images of Yale Individuals (RU 684), no. 827. Manuscripts and Archives, Yale University Library; National Archives 518892; BBCW MRL MS6.0592

124–125   KSHS FK2.F2 D.5 FRO.S *1; Mayer, Col. Frank H. History Colorado-Denver Colorado, F-1974; Men in AZ carrying Winchester, Sharps and Henry rifles, William I Koch Collection; National Park Service, Gateway Arch National Park; *Putnam Machine Company's shop, interior view.* NYPL Wallach G90F232_015F

126–127   *Buffaloes for the meat market.* SDSHS 2014-12-03-309; 981-014, MTHS; 981-013, MTHS; 1/112-1, 1874 Buffalo hunt photo coll. Archives and Information Services Division, TX State Library and Archives Commission; 981-011, MTHS

128–129   1/112-6, 1874 Buffalo hunt photo coll. Archives and Information Services Division, TX State Library and Archives Commission; DPL Z-2301; *Fort Worth Star-Telegram* coll., Special Coll., University of TX at Arlington Libraries, AR406-6-968; KSHS FK2.F2 D.3 *2

130–131   *The News Journal; Harper's Weekly,* v. 18, June 6, 1874, p. 484; LOC LC-USZ62-56429; Chicago History Museum, ICHi-182861, Henry Taylor, creator; LOC LC-DIG-ds-12612

132–133   William S. Soule Indians Photo Album, Dolph Briscoe Center for American History, University of TX at Austin; Haley JEH-Y-276.2

134–135   1980-251-24 PPHM; DeGolyer Library, SMU, Lawrence T. Jones III Texas photographs; 1907 (first edition), courtesy Haley; 17/9, PPHM; Scurry County Museum, Snyder, TX; *Adobe Walls, 1874* by John Eliot Jenkins. 1069/197, PPHM

136–137   BBCW MRL P.71.969; DPL B-751

138–139   *Offering the Head.* INV 03252000, Photo Lot 59, NAA; LOC LC-USZ62-48427; DPL Z-3556

140–141   State Historical Society of ND 00739-v0001-p52b; Burton Historical Coll., Detroit Public Library, DPA4901; Heritage Auctions

PART TWO

143   KSHS QL.5 Bu.2 *38

178–179   LOC LC-USZ62-136255; John F. Reiger; Photo: G. Allen Brown, 1987, courtesy John F. Reiger; LOC LC-DIG-ppmsca-35864; Theodore Roosevelt Coll. at Houghton Library, Harvard University, Thomas Collier Platt photo album of Theodore Roosevelt (Roosevelt R500.P69a), R500.P69a-005

180–181   All SIA: MNH-6071, MNH-4077, MAH-44711, MNH-4079, 74-12338

182–183   SIA MAH-8008A; insert from *The Extermination of the American Bison,* William T. Hornaday, 1889, YELL

184–185   BBCW MRL from Inman, Henry: *Buffalo Jones' Forty Years of Adventure* (Topeka, KS: Crane & Company, 1899), p. 50, SK 45.j615; BBCW MRL from Inman p. 244; Haley JEH-I-Y-131.2; Haley JEH-I-Y-133.1; BBCW MRL from Inman p. 78

186–187   2011.0003.128, Buffalo Bill Museum and Grave, Golden, CO, Street & Smith; BBCW BBM MS006 William F. Cody Coll. 1.69.6354; 2011.0003.953, Buffalo Bill Museum and Grave, Golden, CO, postcard for Buffalo Bill's Wild West Show, 1889; BBCW MRL MS006 William F. Cody Coll., P.6.0870; DPL NS-591

188–189   State Historical Society of ND OCoLC26950174; Timber Yellow Robe (also called Chauncey Yellow Robe), Henry Standing Bear, and Wounded Yellow Robe (also called Richard Yellow Robe), soon after arrival at Carlisle school, c.1883. INV 06842700, Photo Lot 81-12, NAA; Wounded Yellow Robe (also called Richard Yellow Robe), Timber Yellow Robe (also called Chauncey Yellow Robe), and Henry Standing Bear in school uniform, c.1884. INV 06819400, Photo Lot 81-12, NAA; LOCRB LC-USZ62-11487

190–191   *Shooting steers at beef issue.* SDSHS 2008-03-31-015; Wm. Notman & Son, *Buffalo Bill and His Troup, Montreal, QC,* 1885. II-94132. McCord Stewart Museum; LOC LC-USZC4-7960; KSHS FK2.H4 .62 *1

192–193   Ghost dance painting on buckskin Look and Learn / Elgar Coll. / Bridgeman Images, LLE980561; *Ghost Dance shirt,* c.1890. Museum of the SD State Historical Society, Pierre SD, 2004.029; National Museum of the American Indian, Smithsonian Institution (N13559)

194–195   LOC LC-USZ62-46006; LOC LC-USZ62-44458

244–245   YELL 007757, no. 39; H-03274 MTHS

246–247   WCS WCS_5252_Hornaday at table_AE_BZ_00 00 10; *American Bison at the Central Park Zoo, New York.* NYPL Wallach, 101815; SIA 2003-19498

248–249   *Fred Dupree family.* SDSHS P148; *Bison with matadors in the Juarez bullring,* SDSHS H92-064; Meriden; El Paso Public Library, Border Heritage Center. Postcard Coll. pc-2024-12; Philip Family, Hays, KS

250–251   ST 001.044, MTHS; 944-242, MTHS; 940-336, MTHS

252–253   Dayton Duncan Coll.; YELL MSC 087: C.J. (Buffalo) Jones Papers, YELL 208394; YELL 118718; John F. Reiger; Courtesy National Park Service, NPS History Coll., HFCA 1607, Y-66-2000/282

254, t–b   PHSNH Box 27; Larry Cote Coll.; PHSNH Box: Buffalo-Corbinherd, Slide #258.

255   PHSNH Box: Corbin park/Deer.Elk.Moose.Coyote.Timber wolf, Slide #899; PHSNH Box 42, Slide #1482; American Museum of Natural History; PHSNH Box 27, Slide #2798; Cornish Historical Society, Cornish, NH; PHSNH Box 14, Slide #1249.

256–257   PHSNH Box: Buffalo Corbin Park, Slide #400; *The Chester Advertiser,* Sept. 30, 1905, p8; PHSNH Box: Buffalo-Corbinherd, Slide #565; Meriden; PHSNH Box: Buffalo-Corbinherd, Slide #535; PHSNH Box: Buffalo-Corbinherd, Slide #504.

258–259   Gilcrease 4336.3850a–b; 1510/200, PPHM; Bell #302, Photo Lot 80 NAA; 1977-137/34, PPHM; BAE GN 01747A, Photo Lot 176 NAA

260–261   LOC LC-USZ62-127717; LOC LC-DIG-ds-16132; LOC LC-DIG-stereo-1s02033

262–263   All WCS: WCS_3816_Hornaday Crating Bison Wichita Expedition_10 00 07; Bulletin 28 Bison Crates On Wagons At Cache USA 1907-00-00; WCS_3873_Comanche Indians with Bison Wichita Mountains Oklahoma_USA_10 00 07; WCS_5642_Bison Herd at Wichita Oklahoma_USA_02 00 13; WCS_3870_Bison train going out West_USA_10 00 07

264–265   PHSNH Box: Buffalo Corbin Park, Slide #744; Meriden; Norman A. Forsyth glass negative, c.1900, Autry, 2003.83.5.74

266–267   All: Norman A. Forsyth glass negative, c.1900, Autry, Numbers: 2003.83.5.73; 2003.83.5.41; 2003.83.5.60; 2003.83.5.26; 2003.83.5.87

268–269, collage   Charles M. Russell letters, including: *A Game Country,* 1917, Rockwell Foundation. 85.63 F; *Friend Goodwin* [To Philip R. Goodwin], January 1909, Stark Museum of Art, Orange TX, Bequest of H. J. Lutcher Stark, 1965 11.106.19.A; *Friend Young Boy,* Charles Russell, Gilcrease. 02.1584; Bruce Smith

268–269, other   Gilcrease TU2009.39.5650a; Charles M. Russell *Friend Fiddel Back* [To Bertrand W. Sinclair], Jan. 12, 1910, Stark Museum of Art, Orange TX, Bequest of H. J. Lutcher Stark, 1965, 11.106.13.A; Trails End Collection, Dr. Van Kirke and Mrs. Helen Nelson

270–271   Meriden; Meriden; WCS Bison scrapbook acknowledgement 1007-04-02-055; Meriden; Milwaukee Public Museum 41223

272–273   Haley JEH-I-H-53.10; Postcard, courtesy Wildlife Conservation Society Archives, original photo by Bates Studio of Lawton, OK, c.1900; Photo by Wright's Studio, OK Historical Society Photo Coll., No. 2847.1; 4/424h, PPHM; Molly and Charles Goodnight, 1916, Cleo Hubbard Collection

274–275   SMC 53, PPHM; Nickel courtesy Kennedy Galleries, Inc., New York; Municipal Archives, City of New York

276–277   PAc 77-64.2, MTHS; 945-864, MTHS

278–279   Photo: Sandy Sisti/Wild at Heart Images

280–281   © Buddy Squires, ASC 2021

FILM CREDITS

The American Buffalo
A Film by Ken Burns

Directed by
KEN BURNS

Written by
DAYTON DUNCAN

Produced by
JULIE DUNFEY
KEN BURNS

Edited by
CRAIG MELLISH, ACE

Co-Producer
SUSAN SHUMAKER

Associate Producer
EMILY MOSHER

Consulting Producer
JULIANNA BRANNUM

Cinematography
BUDDY SQUIRES, ASC

Narrated by
PETER COYOTE

Voices
ADAM ARKIN
TANTOO CARDINAL
TIM CLARK
TOKALA CLIFFORD
JEFF DANIELS
HOPE DAVIS
PAUL GIAMATTI

MURPHY GUYER
MICHAEL HORSE
GENE JONES
CAROLYN MCCORMICK
CRAIG MELLISH
JON PROUDSTAR
CHASKE SPENCER
RICHARD WHITMAN

Assistant Editor
J. ALEX CUCCHI

Post-Production Supervisor
DANIEL J. WHITE

Technical Director
DAVE MAST

Apprentice Editor
NORA COLGAN

Associate Producer, Research
WILL DUNCAN

Research Assistant
CHARLIE GRAHAM

Assistant to the Technical Director
LOREN HOWARD

Senior Advisor
W. RICHARD WEST JR.

Program Advisors
KEITH AUNE
JASON BALDES
GERARD BAKER
COLIN CALLOWAY
SARA DANT

DAN FLORES
ANDREW ISENBERG
ROSALYN LAPIER
DAN O'BRIEN
MICHAEL PUNKE
GEOFFREY C. WARD
ELLIOTT WEST

Additional Cinematography
BOB LANDIS
SKIP HOBBIE
BEN MASTERS
BOB POOLE
JEROD FOSTER
LINDSAY JACKSON
JUSTIN HALSTEAD
KYLE STAMBLER
DYANNA TAYLOR

Additional Drone Pilots
ISSIAH BOYLE
BLAKE KIMMEL
GUSTAVO LOZADO

Sound Recording
MARK ROY
FRANK COAKLEY
JAMES B. GALLUP
MIKE MATTHEWS
ROYCE SHARP

Assistant Camera
JARED AMES
MARK ANTHONY DELLAS

Gaffer
RYAN ALAN HALSEY

Field Producers
PAUL BARNES
CRAIG MELLISH

Line Producer
NORA COLGAN

Music consultant
PETER MILLER

Production Assistants
JULIA DANIELL
KATY HAAS
MILES T. RED CORN

Chief Financial Officer
JENNIFER FABIS

Coordinating Producer for Ken Burns
ELLE CARRIÈRE

Executive Assistant to Ken Burns
JILLIAN L. HEMPSTEAD

Assistant to Ken Burns
CHRISTOPHER DARLING

Accountant
STEPHANIE GREENE

Administrative Assistant
KATHLEEN OHLSON

The Better Angels Society
AMY MARGERUM BERG,
     President
COURTNEY CHAPIN, Executive
     Director

Digital Image Restoration / Stills Animation
BRIAN T. LEE

Design & Animation
PHLEA TV

Music Editor
CRAIG MELLISH

Dialogue Editors
MARLENA GRZASLEWICZ
MATT RIGBY

Sound Effects Editor
MARIUSZ GLABINSKI, MPSE

Assistant Sound Editor
MATT RIGBY

Transcription Services
MARY L. BAILEY

Legal Services
DREW PATRICK
MICHAEL McCORMACK
SARAH BRYNE

Original Funding Provided by
Bank of America
Corporation for Public
    Broadcasting
Public Broadcasting Service
The Better Angels Society, and its
    members
The Margaret A. Cargill Foundation
    fund at the Saint Paul and Minnesota
    Foundation
Diane and Hal Brierley

The Keith Campbell Foundation for the
    Environment, Inc.
John and Catherine Debs
Kissick Family Foundation
Fred and Donna Seigel
Jacqueline Mars
John and Leslie McQuown
Mr. and Mrs. Paul Tudor Jones
The Volgenau Foundation
Evelyn and Walter Haas, Jr. Fund
Marilynn and John Hill Foundation

Co-Produced with WETA
    WASHINGTON, D.C.

A Production of Florentine Films

Executive Producer
KEN BURNS

A NOTE ABOUT THE AUTHORS

Ken Burns, the producer and director of numerous film series, including *The Vietnam War*, *The Roosevelts: An Intimate History*, and *The War*, cofounded his documentary film company, Florentine Films, in 1976. His landmark film *The Civil War* was the highest-rated series in the history of American public television, and his work has won numerous prizes, including multiple Emmy and Peabody Awards and two Academy Award nominations. He lives in Walpole, New Hampshire.

Dayton Duncan is the author of thirteen other books, including *Out West: An American Journey Along the Lewis and Clark Trail*. He has worked with Ken Burns as a writer and producer of documentary films for more than thirty years and has won numerous awards, including two Emmy Awards for his work on *The National Parks: America's Best Idea*. He lives in Rindge, New Hampshire.

A NOTE ON THE TYPE

This book was set in Janson, a typeface long thought to have been made by the Dutchman Anton Janson, who was a practicing typefounder in Leipzig during the years 1668–1687. However, it has been conclusively demonstrated that these types are actually the work of Nicholas Kis (1650–1702), a Hungarian, who most probably learned his trade from the master Dutch typefounder Dirk Voskens. The type is an excellent example of the influential and sturdy Dutch types that prevailed in England up to the time William Caslon (1692–1766) developed his own incomparable designs from them.

Composed by North Market Street Graphics, Lancaster, Pennsylvania
Printed and bound by Mohn Media Mohndruck GmbH, Gutersloh, Germany